1105 B·7 30.0

Can Anything Beat White?

CAN ANYTHING BEAT WHITE?

A Black Family's Letters

ELISABETH PETRY

UNIVERSITY PRESS OF MISSISSIPPI • JACKSON

Margaret Walker Alexander Series in African American Studies

www.upress.state.ms.us

The University Press of Mississippi is a member of the Association of American
University Presses.

The letter from Willis H. James, writing as L. J. St. Clair, on pp. 63–64
from the Anna Louise James papers appears courtesy of the Arthur and
Elisabeth Schlesinger Library on the History of Women in America.

First edition 2005

Library of Congress Cataloging-in-Publication Data

Can anything beat white? : a Black family's letters / [edited by] Elisabeth
Petry.— 1st ed.
        p. cm.
    ISBN 1-57806-785-5 (cloth : alk. paper)
    1. Petry, Ann Lane, 1911– —Family. 2. Novelists, American—20th century—
Family relationships. 3. African American novelists—Family relationships.
4. African American families—History—Sources. 5. African Americans—
Correspondence. 6. James family—Correspondence. I. Petry, Elisabeth.

PS3531.E933Z55   2005
813'.54—dc22   2005005444

British Library Cataloging-in-Publication Data available

For Larry

CONTENTS

❧

INTRODUCTION

Farah Jasmine Griffin

Can Anything Beat White? A Black Family's Letters only offered us a glimpse into the life of a nineteenth-century African American family that would more than warrant its publication. So rare are letters from African Americans, particularly from the late nineteenth and early twentieth centuries, that their very existence signals a significant historical find. That the letters document relationships between a family that produced a critically acclaimed author, Ann Petry, warrants even more interest. That the members of the James family were in and of themselves exceptionally interesting individuals whose lives could fill the pages of a number of novels also makes their correspondence valuable. While the letters and Elisabeth Petry's compelling narrative certainly succeed in painting a portrait of a unique family and in providing a context for the emergence of its most well-known member, it also offers us a great deal more. For this book lends insight into a very important moment in the history of the United States through the eyes of ordinary people who are participating in and affected by important historical events.

The era documented by this correspondence—1891 to 1910—was a time of tremendous growth and change as the United States became an industrial nation. Cities experienced great growth and factories emerged on the landscape. Entrepreneurs and industrialists like Rockefeller, Vanderbilt, Guggenheim, and Carnegie came into power and wealth, and with the creation of Sugar, Beef, Steel, and Oil Trusts, came the birth of the labor movement. Finally, it was the age of the railroad. Americans became more mobile over vast territories, and members of the James family were no exception to this. Railroad trips took them up and down the East Coast as well as through and across the growing nation.

Significantly, this was also a period of increased nationalism. Having recently emerged from the Civil War and Reconstruction, the young nation sought unity through patriotism. The period witnessed the birth of organizations like the Sons of the American Revolution and the Daughters of the American Revolution. But this sense of national unity and patriotism came at a cost. For black Americans, the time would become known famously as "the nadir" of black history. In a book titled *The Betrayal of the Negro*, historian Rayford Logan used the term to describe the period between the end of Reconstruction (1877) and the beginning of World War I (1917). The 1890s were perhaps the lowest point of the nadir. The hope of Reconstruction with its promises of black citizenship, education, and land-ownership was replaced by despair as black people were systematically disenfranchised and dispossessed. With the demise of the Populist Movement in 1896 (which for a time had united poor white farmers with southern blacks), the South succeeded in disenfranchising blacks. Southern white elites were able to use the ideology of white supremacy and the fear of blacks to convince poor whites that their best interest lay in abandoning blacks and affiliating themselves with the program of privileged whites. Poll taxes, grandfather clauses, and a number of other inventions were used to keep black voters from the polls. By 1898 southern states amended their constitutions so that blacks were disenfranchised throughout the entire region.

Although African Americans in the North were able to exercise their right to vote, they were relegated to segregated housing and often denied access to opportunity. The James family appears to have been unique in this regard: they were neither southern nor did they find themselves stuck in racially segregated and/or impoverished communities. Nonetheless the conditions that affected the majority of African Americans still had an impact upon them. This is especially evident when we look to the extralegal means used to help ensure and maintain white rule throughout the nation, but especially in the South.

Race riots occurred throughout the South where white mobs sought to destroy black communities and instill fear and control. The two bloodiest took place in Wilmington, North Carolina, in 1898 and Atlanta, Georgia, in 1906. Both riots were connected to elections and false reporting in white newspapers. Though occurring in the South, the riots had national, even international, implications. While W. E. B. Du Bois would write and publish the poem "A Litany of Atlanta," less famous black people would describe details of the event in their correspondence to each other. Bertha James Lane received a letter from her friend, Birdie Ford, who witnessed the riots firsthand. In a letter dated October 1, 1906, she wrote:

Out in South Atlanta, the officers went out in citizen clothes; they had battle with the negroes. One officer was killed. The next day, 200 some odd negroes were arrested and all weapons taken away. In darktown another one of their quarters they broke every lamp around. They were ready to fight to a finish. The mob did not venture there. These white people saw, the negro would strike back.

Throughout her letter Ford notes the violence of the white mob, but she also stresses the courage of blacks who acted in self-defense. In her own letters Bertha would share her friend's observances with others.

The riot was indicative of the kind of violence against blacks that became more and more commonplace during this time. From 1884 to 1900 more than 2,500 lynchings occurred throughout the South. In 1900 alone more than 100 blacks were lynched. In a letter from Tallahasse, Florida, Helen James writes: "There was a man lynched here at the jail between midnight Saturday and dawn of the next day. We knew nothing of it, though many on the campus heard the firing. There may be no account of it in the papers since the South is inclined to conceal these things." Many of those who did not die at the hands of a lynch mob found themselves in servitude on chain gangs. Chain gangs were yet another means of enforcing control over black bodies in the postbellum South.

Perhaps the most significant blow to black Americans during this era was the 1896 *Plessy v. Ferguson* Supreme Court decision. *Plessy* made racial segregation, "separate but equal," the law of the land. This decision joined the Jim Crow laws, which first began to appear in the 1870s, in guaranteeing separation of the races in schools, hotels, shops, restaurants, theaters, and transportation. By 1910, white supremacy reigned supreme in the United States. It would also inform American foreign policy as well.

Prior to this time the United States had not been a dominant participant in world affairs. But with increased wealth and the drama of the Civil War and Reconstruction behind it, a newly confident nation strove to become a major player in international affairs. It also sought new markets and materials for manufacture. The opportunity to meet both of these desires arose when the United States entered the war for Cuban independence from Spain on behalf of Cuba. Even before this period Americans had shown interest in Hawaii, and Americans owned a number of plantations there. In 1898, with support from most Americans, Congress annexed Hawaii. By the end of the century the United States had begun to acquire an empire in the South Pacific: Guam and Wake Island also came under U.S. control and, with Hawaii, provided a series of "stepping-stones" to the Far East, especially China.

In January 1898 the battleship *Maine*, off the coast of Havana to protect American lives, exploded, and the United States entered war with Spain. Black Americans were reluctantly supportive of the war. A number of them, while supportive of the independence struggle of Cuba's people of color, feared the involvement of the United States because they believed their nation, unlike Spain, would export Jim Crow. At the end of the war with Spain, the United States acquired Puerto Rico and the Philippines. Cuba, Puerto Rico, Hawaii, and the Philippines all had black populations. In Hawaii and the Philippines the dominant cultures were nonwhite. Helen writes home about the black citizens of Honolulu: "[The negroes] came out with the Puerto Ricans, having first gone from the Southern States to Puerto Rico to work in the cane. They are a low ignorant class and have given up plantation work to enjoy life in the Hawaiian metropolis."

There is a particular irony to black American soldiers having been involved in wars that brought other people of color under the dominance of the United States. It is also not insignificant that the black press in the United States expressed a large anti-imperialist sentiment prevalent amongst black Americans. On the other hand, a number of black leaders adopted the language of the so-called "civilizing mission" of the United States and saw this expansion as an opportunity for African Americans to contribute to the national project. It is in this context that we must understand Willis James's time in the Philippines and his prejudicial statements about Filipinos. Willis James went to the Philippines as part of the Forty-eighth U.S. Volunteer Infantry, a black company, during the Philippine Insurrection following the Spanish-American War. It is also the context in which we must understand Helen James's time in Hawaii. Both are of the same historical moment of American imperialist expansion. In contrast to her brother, Helen writes in admiring tones about her encounters with Hawaiians. She is excited about meeting the Hawaiian queen whom she describes as "a portly brown skinned woman with a heavy head of straight black hair. . . . It was worth a great deal to me to have this opportunity. I am extremely anxious to make some good friends among the Hawaiians as I know they will be delightful and I shall learn a great deal from them." Queen Lili'uokalani was Hawaii's last queen; she devoted much of her time to unsuccessfully trying to preserve Hawaii for native inhabitants. By 1898 when Hawaii was annexed to the United States she was forced to give up her throne. Neither provincial nor ethnocentric, Helen displays the kind of cosmopolitan curiosity often only attributed to male intellectuals. Her life and experiences warrant further treatment by scholars and writers.

Although both Helen and Willis James were witnesses to these international events, their letters also lend insight into the domestic experiences of black Americans as well. Both found themselves in the South at some point, and each experienced different aspects of black life under white supremacist rule. Willis barely fled a lynch mob and seems to have spent time on a chain gang. In a letter dated November 1, 1905, he writes to Bertha:

I would not write to you but I am in a terrible fix here I got into after leaving Savannah, Ga. . . . While going through this place I shot a white man for bothering me, and tried to get away but they put the blood hounds on my track and they caught me in a swamp, and tried to lynch me. . . .

If Willis gives life to one end of the spectrum of black southern existence, Helen represents the other. She became part of the Talented Tenth engaged in the project of racial uplift. Her educational experiences brought her under the influence of the greatest black institutions and figures of the day. Helen's experiences reflect the strategy African Americans adopted during this time. They did not sit by idly as their status eroded. They met these challenges head on with organized resistance and self-help efforts. Among of the most important institutions for creating a culture of uplift and self-help were black churches and educational institutions. One of the greatest accomplishments of Reconstruction had been the establishment of schools to educate the freedmen and their children. Schools such as Howard University, Hampton Institute, Atlanta University were all part of this legacy. Samuel Chapman Armstrong founded Hampton, alma mater to three James siblings. Armstrong encouraged a foundation of land and home ownership as well as vocational training. Hampton, as with many black schools, also trained a number of teachers. It became the model for alumnus Booker T. Washington who as founder and president of Tuskegee Institute would become the leading proponent of vocational education.

Helen took this mission of uplift with her as she pursued her teaching career in Hawaii and in South Carolina at the famous Penn School where Charlotte Forten Grimké taught during the years immediately following the Civil War. History has positioned Washington's mode of vocational education as diametrically opposed to the theories of the brilliant W. E. B. Du Bois. Helen's experience demonstrates that one could actively participate in both visions. As a student of Dr. Du Bois at Atlanta University, she excelled in an environment that emphasized social science solutions to Negro problems and that hosted a number of scholarly conferences on the study of the Negro Problem. At the same time Tuskegee held Farmers' Conferences. Both were efforts to address the concerns and needs of blacks and to establish programs of self-help.

The last decade of the nineteenth and the first decade of the twentieth centuries were periods of great organizing on the part of educated blacks. In 1905, under the leadership of Du Bois, black leaders and intellectuals met at Niagra Falls, Canada, to devise an agenda for black rights. After the Springfield, Illinois, race riot of 1908 a number of liberal whites saw the need for immediate social reform. In the spirit of the abolitionists, they invited members of the Niagara Movement to a national conference. Representatives of the two groups established the National Association for the Advancement of Colored People, which became a formal organization in 1910. Black Americans would look to the new organization to help meet the challenges of living in the United States. In a letter sent to the organization's publication, the *Crisis*, Peter Lane, husband of Bertha James Lane, wrote of his family's problems with the Saybrook School system. Racist teachers refused to instruct or promote his very bright daughters, Helen Louise, and Anna Houston, (who later became Ann Petry). Lane writes:

I want my daughters to have a good education and they want to get one also. I am a laboring man and have got to have some one to help me to get my girls through this school. . . . I have been advised to write to you as you are one of the directors of the National Association for the Advancement of Colored People and that they would assist and advise me what to do.

Both daughters would go on to complete their education, receive college degrees, and have successful lives and careers. In fact Anna's first published stories would appear in the *Crisis*. In spite of the obstacles placed before them, the girls had family members who modeled success for them and who were willing to stand up and fight for them as well. The young girls also came from a line of independent, intelligent women who paved the way for them.

While the founding of the NAACP would have a profound impact on the lives of the Lane family, perhaps even more important to the James women, the era that gave rise to this most important of civil rights organizations was also "the Women's era." Black women began to raise their voices in organized protest against lynching and the sexual exploitation of black women. They founded their own organizations that sought to address the needs of the entire race. The motto of the National Association of Colored Women, founded in 1895, was "Lifting as We Climb," and it encapsulates the driving vision of black middle class women at the time. While the majority of black women worked as domestics and laundresses, a number pursued careers in teaching and nursing. Helen belonged to this group: an intellectual, well-read and widely traveled Race Woman with all of the refinement and class prejudices that accompany that status.

The period gave birth to a small number of black women entrepreneurs who created their own businesses, thus avoiding work in white people's homes and creating employment for others. It is to this latter group the eldest James sibling, Bertha, belonged. The stalwart rock of her family, Bertha started a number of successful businesses to supplement her family's income and to assist in the education of her younger siblings. A third sister, Louise, pursued the path of education by gaining a degree in pharmacy, as well as a path of entrepreneurship as she ran one of her family's drugstores. The James family women are exemplary new women: driven, ambitious, intelligent and accomplished. They were rare among American women, and their letters give us insight into their inner lives as well as their social and cultural surroundings.

Louise, Bertha, and Bertha's husband, Peter Lane, were among a number of black business people who owned grocery stores, general stores, drugstores, dressmaking establishments, and restaurants. Unlike most though, they catered to a largely white clientele. Perhaps this is the difference that makes the James clan a not so typical black family of the day. They were among a small percentage of African Americans who lived outside the South. In 1900, 90 percent of blacks were southerners and three-fourths of those lived in rural areas. In contrast the vast majority of northern blacks lived in cities.

Bertha not only sold her goods and services to white families, she also employed poor and working class white women in one of her enterprises, a linen-making business. In this way she was unique amongst black business owners and entrepreneurs, as was her sister, Louise James. Louise gained fame as the first black woman in Connecticut to acquire a pharmacy license. She attended the Brooklyn College of Pharmacy, one of the best established schools in the nation. Louise was the only member of her family to attend a white institution, and while she did not travel far from the Connecticut homestead, she ran one of the family pharmacies and contributed greatly to the family's legacy of achievement and success.

Brother Harold Edward James followed a path in agriculture, a path pursued by the majority of African Americans. But unlike the many black tenant farmers and sharecroppers in the South, Harold owned and operated his own farm in Connecticut, so he too demonstrated the spirit of independence evident in each of his siblings.

In these ways and more the James family stands out among African American, indeed, American families of the time. While their status did not entirely protect them from racial injustice, it did provide them a sense of independence and a foundation for the pursuit of their ambition. What is perhaps most inspiring about the James family is the strength of the family bond. The siblings were deeply devoted to each other, and each individual owed his or her success to the emotional, spiritual, and financial support of other family members. This bond is probably one of the factors that contributed to their success. The black family was a bulwark against the assaults of a hostile and racist society. Each member was assured of his or her self-worth through the love and devotion of other family members.

History is made and remade by the availability of new documents, sources, and interpretations. *Can Anything Beat White?* contributes a great deal to this process. The experiences of the James family as documented in their letters challenge representations of black people at the turn of the century as well as our contemporary sense of the past of black Americans. During the time that members of this family wrote to each other, the prevailing images of African Americans in public policy and media discourse were buffoons on the minstrel stage, happy go-lucky and simple-minded plantation workers from nostalgic lore, and criminally inclined vagrants. When members of the black middle class appear, they do so as pretentious and bumbling imitators of white society. While the black press and leading black writers sought to present alternative pictures, they had an uphill climb in attempting to reshape popular conceptions of black life. Many writers, particularly the emerging black novelists, had to create characters who were virtuous beyond belief so as to not play into stereotypes. Members of the James family offer a counter to both of these tendencies. They are far more complicated figures than those that appear in American popular culture and African American literature. They and their experiences bear witness to the true complexity and diversity of black life. Relatively privileged, they nonetheless are economically challenged. Well read and intelligent, they are not exempt from work as domestic servants. And one family member, Willis, proves to be a colorful character, articulate, smart, and somewhat shady and irresponsible. In other words, this multidimensional portrait of a family helps to lend a sense of humanity to portrayals of black life and bears witness to the strength of black families.

In terms of our contemporary understandings of African American history, the letters are especially relevant in helping us to have a fuller understanding of wide-ranging diversity of that history. Although the volume documents tensions between black ethnic groups, it also documents the existence of ethnic diversity long before the Great Migrations of the twentieth century. That their father's marriage to a West Indian caused such dismay amongst the James siblings is not only evidence of their hostility toward Caribbean blacks but also evidence that in the nineteenth century, U.S.-born blacks and those from the Caribbean already occupied the same neighborhoods and communities. Furthermore the letters give us encounters between northern and southern blacks as well as provide evidence of the presence of black American plantation workers in Puerto Rico and Hawaii, outside the immediate confines of the American South but under the control of white elites nonetheless.

The contemporary reader has much to learn from the James family history. The story demonstrates the participation of ordinary people in major historical events. It suggests that each life story has light to bear upon our understanding of larger issues and occurrences. Hopefully, it will encourage more families—especially families of color—to preserve their own documents and correspondences, for these are the things of which history is made. Finally this family history demonstrates the way that local histories have global implications. In a world that seems to be increasingly smaller this history serves as a reminder that we have always been connected by historical events that shape our lives in ways we might not even imagine.

ACKNOWLEDGMENTS

When I started editing these letters, I had no idea how much I would be learning about the world inhabited by my ancestors. My task became far easier because of the kindness and generosity of friends and family who answered my persistent questions and listened to me lament the slow progress of my work. So, thank you to all— especially my beloved husband Lawrence Riley, who has the patience of a saint and who has supported me with enthusiasm and with love.

My James and Houston families deserve medals, too. Ashley James and Anna Bush filled in details that I did not know about Willis, Anna Houston, and our grandparents and great aunts and uncles. In the course of my research, I found Rod Hudson, great-grandson of Uncle Charley Hudson, who supplied extensive information about Charley and his wife, Clothilda.

Here in Connecticut, I came to know descendants of the James patriarch's first and third wives—Gertrude Thompson, great-granddaughter of Anna Webb, and Beatrice Marone, granddaughter of his third wife, Anna Phillips. Gertrude's interview with Louise and with Helen's husband Frank Chisholm provided background that helped me understand more about them and the other James siblings. Likewise, Bea helped to solve the mystery of Bertha's dislike of West Indians and gave me valuable information about relatives I didn't know I had.

I am also indebted to several friends without whom this work would not exist. Writer Gina Greenlee provided much-needed editorial services that helped me shape and trim the narrative through its first and second drafts. Genealogist Judith Johnson and the staff at the library of the Connecticut Historical Society shared their vast knowledge and expertise on Connecticut's history, helping me locate information and suggesting avenues of research. Mark Wilson, a retired professor of English at the University of Hawaii and a wonderful friend to my mother and to me, directed me to information about the schools in Hawaii where Helen worked and suggested other avenues of research. My friend and fellow journalist Nick Sambides Jr. provided sources for information about the Civil War and made many perceptive suggestions to improve the narrative.

PROLOGUE

Willis H. James had seen more than his share of conflict and grief in his twenty-eight years. After leaving his hometown of Hartford, Connecticut, he survived guerrilla warfare, near starvation, and forced marches barefoot through the mountains of the Philippines as a soldier in the U.S. Army. Upon his return from Southeast Asia, he had taken jobs, often in hostile environments, as a waiter and a barber. None of his battles in or out of uniform, however, prepared him for the horror he encountered in a southern town in the fall of 1905. When he reached the limits of his endurance, he did as always, as everyone in the family did: he wrote to his older sister, Bertha James Lane.

From the jail in Jesup, Georgia, Willis told Bertha, "I would not write you but I am in a terrible fix here I got into after leaveing Savannah, Ga." He had shot a white man "for bothering him" and tried to escape by running into a swamp, but the vigilantes put bloodhounds on his trail and caught him. They put him in a cell "guarded with white men who have guns and try to get at me." He begged Bertha "for dear Mother's sake" to rush thirty-five dollars to bribe the sheriff so he wouldn't be lynched en route to his trial the following Monday morning.

That letter was one of some four hundred cards, notes, and letters written by James family members between 1891 and 1910 that Bertha saved. By accident or design, Bertha found the perfect storage space when she put the letters in an ice cream cone tin from our family's drugstore. Though Bertha saved innumerable keepsakes of her brothers and sisters, few of them preserved any of her letters. Thirty remain in the collection, mostly relating neighborhood gossip and enclosing money for her youngest sister, Anna Louise. Bertha's daughter and my mother, the author Ann Petry, acquired them when she emptied Bertha's house in the late 1980s. The letters came to me after my mother's death in 1997.

My mother set the tin by the fireplace in the dining room of her home in Old Saybrook, Connecticut. Not long after she brought it home, she told me, "Your Uncle Bill's letters from the Philippines are in there. He wrote to your grandmother, and she had to pay for the postage." Uncle Bill—Willis H. James—was one of the colorful uncles my mother mentioned when people asked her about the sources for her stories. She called these men her "foot-loose and fancy-free" uncles. Uncle Bill's feet were particularly loose and his fancy especially free. He lived all over the country but came several times a year to visit Bertha and her family when my mother was a little girl. Each time he or any of the other uncles arrived, my mother knew she would hear stories about their adventures and the people they encountered.

The tin with the letters inside soon became just another piece of furniture in my mother's home. At two feet tall with a flat top, it was a perfect spot for one of the many piles of magazines, newspapers, books, and other tools of a writer's trade that found their way onto every flat surface in the house. Most of the piles remained when my mother died—volumes of material that needed examination to separate drafts of stories and speeches from ancient shopping lists and even older notes to call her sister.

The tin and its contents had been in Saybrook's damp, salty air for about seventy years. Rust had eaten away at the edges of the container and covered the handle on top. It took considerable effort and a scraped knuckle to work the cover loose. After a final tug the lid flew off, and the aroma of sandalwood filled the room. One letter from Hawaii still contained bits of leaves and flowers. The perfume lingered a century later.

Of course the tin contained far more than letters from the Philippines. It represented twenty years' history of a family whose mother and father had begun their lives in slavery and came to settle in Hartford, Connecticut, just after the Civil War. The correspondents were Bertha, Willis, five other brothers and sisters, as well as their mother and father, and their mother's brother Charles Hudson.

As far as the family knew, the patriarch, Willis Samuel James, was born a slave in about 1847 and escaped during the Civil War from a plantation near Fredericksburg, Virginia. By 1867 he was married and living in Hartford, where he served as coachman to a governor and later became the janitor at a public school. He and his first wife, Anna Webb, had two children, one of whom survived. Willis Samuel James did not learn to read and write until adulthood, and Bertha preserved thirteen of her father's letters, most describing illness, death, and religious observance in the Hartford's Negro community. Anna Webb died in the early 1870s, and James married Anna Estelle Houston, who bore him nine children. He died in 1917, survived by his third wife, Anna Mathilda Phillips, and five of her six children, as well as the children from his first two marriages.

The earliest notes in Bertha's collection came from her mother. Anna Houston wrote in 1891 urging Bertha to come home from New York in time to start school. Anna wrote five additional letters the following year from the New Jersey shore, where she had gone to recover her health. In those brief notes, she displayed a fiercely protective love for her family. Like their father, Anna kept her past shrouded in mystery. She was probably born in Alabama between 1843 and 1846. By the late 1850s she and her mother and brother, Charles, were living in Connecticut. The mother, Mary Houston, died of phthisis in New Haven in 1857, and Anna and Charles went to live in the nearby town of Cheshire with the family of a Congregational minister. Family history indicated that Anna moved to Massachusetts and then returned to Connecticut before she married Willis Samuel James in July 1874. The couple bought a house on Winter Street in the city's North End, where Anna cared for her stepson and her own children. She died of phthisis in 1894.

After her death, Anna's brother, Charles Thomas Hudson, played a significant role in the lives of his nieces and nephews. His descendants believe he was born in Georgia and came North on the Underground Railroad, but he, too, was almost certainly born in Alabama, probably in 1847. The minister sent Charley to work as an apprentice, but he rebelled and ran away. Charley told his niece Helen how he changed his name from Houston to Hudson, added about four years to his age, passed for white, and enlisted in the cavalry. He faced the Confederate Army in Virginia's Shenandoah Valley and was wounded during the waning days of the Civil War. Charley returned briefly to Connecticut after the war, then moved to New York, where he married Clothilda Delsart in 1876. Settling in Toms River, New Jersey, he found work as a barber and as a carpenter. He returned to New York around 1900 to manage a restaurant. By 1915 Charley had moved to Massachusetts, where he became the manager of a paper mill, and he moved back to New York for good shortly before his wife's death in 1927. His experience living sometimes as a Negro, sometimes as white man, contrasts with the choices made by his sister and her children. Charles Hudson died in 1934.

Born May 26, 1875, Bertha Ernestine James had a reputation for being the consummate businesswoman, as well as an expert in homemaking skills. She dropped out of school at sixteen because she wanted to start earning her own living and became a hairdresser, chiropodist, and lace and linen maker. After her mother died, Bertha married Peter Clark Lane, whose family had moved to Hartford from Hunterdon County, New Jersey, in the early 1870s. Peter Lane became the first Negro in Connecticut to hold a pharmacy license. In 1900 he and Bertha moved to Old Saybrook, a resort town on the shoreline, where he operated Lane's Pharmacy and Bertha ran her businesses. He corresponded with his brothers- and sisters-in-law, and Bertha saved letters addressed to him as well. Three years after they moved, Bertha gave birth to her first child, Bertha Harriet, who died of peritonitis at age three. Two more daughters followed: Helen Louise Lane, born in 1906, and Anna Houston Lane, born in 1908, who became Ann Petry. My grandparents continued to live in Old Saybrook until his death in 1949 and her death in 1956.

Anna Houston James next gave birth to Helen Lou Evelyn on September 1, 1876. By far the most prolific and best-educated correspondent, Helen left behind 196 letters, the first written in 1899, at the end of her final year at Hampton Institute and Normal School in Virginia. Subsequent letters follow her through three years in Hawaii; two years at Atlanta University, where she studied with W. E. B. Du Bois; two years teaching at the Penn School on St. Helena, South Carolina; and a year at Florida State Normal and Industrial College for Colored Students. She wrote the last letters in the collection just before her marriage in 1910 to Frank Pierce Chisholm of South Carolina. Helen and Frank settled in Cambridge, Massachusetts, where he worked as the field agent for Tuskegee Institute and where she gave birth to a son, Frank Pierce Jr., who died, and a daughter, Helen Emily, who survived. The family moved to a house in Old Saybrook next door to Bertha and Peter. Helen died in 1971 at the age of ninety-four, her husband died in 1977 at ninety-eight. Many more letters and other papers belonging to Frank and Helen Chisholm are part of the archives at Emory University in Atlanta, Georgia.

Willis H. James was born December 9, 1877, a little more than a year after Helen. In the summer of 1899, after working in Old Saybrook, he enlisted in the U.S. Army and shipped off to war. He wrote twenty-five of the thirty letters that Bertha saved during his years in the military and gave a first-hand account of America's earliest experience in fighting a guerrilla war in Southeast Asia. After his discharge, Willis adopted the alias L. J. St. Clair and worked as a waiter in resort hotels and on railroad dining cars between New York and Florida and as far west as Chicago. The family believes he had had five children, but they had little contact with them. Willis lived in a boarding house in Chicago toward the end of his life and died at age sixty-two at the veteran's hospital in Hines, Illinois, in 1940.

Harriet Georgiana was born on May 10, 1879. She ran her father's household from the time Bertha married and Helen went to Hampton until he married again. She suffered bouts of illness as a teenager and had consumption when she enrolled at Hampton in 1900. Harriet's twenty-three letters offer a picture of the students, teachers, and especially the medical staff, as she spent much of her time in the infirmary. She was preparing to marry a fellow student when consumption killed her in 1902. Bertha also saved some fifteen sympathy letters that faculty, students, and staff wrote to her and Helen following Harriet's death.

Bertha saved only thirteen letters from her brother Fritz Morris, and none of them was written during the period covered by this work. Born March 23, 1882, Fritz lived with his father or with Bertha and Peter during his frequent and protracted periods of unemployment. He did not write when he traveled, possibly because he was involved in illegal activities. (My mother wrote of a colorful uncle who helped smuggle Chinese immigrants into the United States from Canada.) The tin contained a postcard from Fritz, postmarked April 24, 1915 from Montreal. He was the only family member who showed any evidence of spending time north of the border. Even when he was in the States, he was uncommunicative. He once sent his sister Anna Louise a note that ended, "Don't give any of the others my address. I never would write them and never care to see them again." Fritz returned to Connecticut in the 1920s, and Anna Louise helped him open James' Pharmacy in Old Lyme. She filled his prescriptions, and he operated the pharmacy until his death in 1957.

Where Fritz struggled, his brother Harold Edward thrived. Born February 3, 1884, Harold went to Hampton in 1899 and seemed to enjoy it all—even the hard work and inedible food. "Rama Hama James," as he called himself, wrote to Bertha, Peter, his father, and Helen, discussing his "swell" clothes and expressing his general exuberance at life. Harry dropped out of Hampton after Harriet died and returned to Connecticut, where he worked at various jobs until he married Helen Blanche Robinson, whose family came from Richmond, Virginia. The couple bought a farm in Wethersfield, a few miles south of Hartford. They had two sons: Harold E. James Jr., born in 1909, ran a highly successful funeral parlor in Hartford; Floyd James died at age five in 1920 following a collision between a trolley and a car in which he was a passenger. Harold Sr. and Blanche moved to Virginia, where he died in 1945 at age sixty-one.

Anna Louise James, named Louise Clegget at her birth on January 19, 1886, became the celebrity of the family. She left her father's house as a teenager and moved in with Bertha and Peter. After graduating from Saybrook High School, she enrolled in and graduated from the Brooklyn College of Pharmacy, the only woman and the only Negro in her class. She returned to Connecticut and is believed to be the first woman to receive a pharmacy license in that state. She took over Lane's Pharmacy from Peter in the early 1920s and ran it as James' Pharmacy until 1968. The building at 2 Pennywise Lane is on the National Register of Historic Places. She died in the living quarters behind the store at age ninety-one in 1977. Anna Louise wrote and received volumes of letters during her lifetime, but they are not included here because only two remained in the family. After her death, my mother donated all her aunt's papers to the Arthur and Elizabeth Schlesinger Library on the History of Women in America at the Radcliffe Institute for Advanced Study in Cambridge, Massachusetts.

Bertha also saved a dozen letters, postcards, and notes from friends and customers addressed to her and to Helen. One is reproduced here, a description of the white riot that drove Negroes from Atlanta in the fall of 1906. Like Willis's letter from prison, it cried out for publication.

Now I would like to explain my editing of the letters in this book. I had originally planned to reproduce the letters verbatim. I rejected this method as less effective than providing a narrative that would allow the reader to see each family member's reaction to a given event, in context with the reactions of others. For example, Helen, Harold, and Willis wrote to Bertha over a period of months in 1900 about their father's plans to marry. Their outrage has more impact when read together, rather than included with Helen's list of the books she was preparing to read, Harold's complaints about his teeth, and Willis's mention of the death of a fellow soldier. Letters from their father posed additional problems. Willis Samuel James never used paragraphs and never quite mastered rules of grammar and punctuation. His creative spelling and disjointed style made for difficult reading under the best circumstances. Selective editing allowed me to provide context for his comments. Finally, repetition is inevitable in a collection as extensive as this, and the narrative form allowed me to pare the material to a manageable length and to eliminate Helen's favorite opening—that she had been too busy, too tired, or both to write.

Though most of the letters were well preserved, portions of a few were missing or obliterated by rips and stains. One of Helen's letters from Hawaii looked as though a large dog had taken a bite out of it. Willis wrote most of his letters from the Philippines with pencil on poor quality paper, so some of the words have rubbed away or faded. Otherwise the collection was in pristine condition, better than letters from forty and fifty years later.

The grammar, spelling, and punctuation remain as they appeared in the originals. My editorial comments are in brackets. To maintain the historical context, the descendants of Africans are referred to as "Negroes" (with a capital "N," an exception to the usage of the time) or "colored people" rather than "black" or "African American." Ethnic references considered derogatory today remain. Also in keeping with the period, Anna suffered from "phthisis" and Harriet from "consumption," rather than the contemporary term, "tuberculosis."

Can Anything Beat White?

Chapter 1

SURVIVING THE PATTERROLLERS

Willis S. James's only legacy to his children and grandchildren from his years as a slave was a nursery rhyme that he sang as he bounced them on his knee, "Run, little baby, run. Or patterrollers goin' come. Run, little baby, run."

He was born into a society that did not keep many vital records, particularly of its colored citizens. According to family lore, Willis grew up in Fredericksburg, Virginia, and escaped the "patterrollers" in the early 1860s as war raged around the city. Before he made his final dash to freedom, he served as a water boy for the Union Army. His children never knew much more about his early life.

"My father was very close-mouthed," said his daughter Louise. "He never spoke of his infancy or his growing-up of childhood. I don't know whether he felt that he was so awfully poor growing up. I never knew. And we never questioned, never asked him any questions. If the boys started, my sister [Bertha] would kind of have some way of signaling us children, shaking her head so we never went any further with questions." Willis's reticence about his background began the James family tradition of keeping secrets from each other.

Family members did learn that after he left Virginia, Willis went via Buffalo to Canada. En route he met and married Hannah or Anna Webb, who came from a family of free people of color in Westchester

County, New York. By 1868 the couple had settled in Hartford, Connecticut, where Willis worked as a porter and Anna had twins on November 21, 1866, while the couple lived at the home of Governor Marshall Jewell on Farmington Avenue. One child, Charles Howard James, survived.

Willis had a powerful sponsor during his early years in Hartford, Marshall Jewell. Though described in biographies as a supporter of the abolitionist cause, Jewell left no written evidence of his work. Willis worked as coachman for the family while Jewell served as Connecticut's governor and then as President Grant's ambassador to Russia. Among Willis's prized possessions was Jewell's letter of recommendation, dated June 28, 1873: "To whom it may concern, The brave Sam James has worked for me for six years and is *as good a man as I ever saw*. Honest, reliable, faithfull, a first rate driver and groom. Always on hand when wanted & what I value about as human as any thing always good natured. Marshall Jewell." [Emphasis in the original.]

After leaving the service of the Jewell family, Willis returned to being a porter. He made a name for himself as a contractor and foreman who supplied gardeners and other laborers to Hartford's wealthy families. His services were also in demand as a caterer. Daughter Louise said that the city's white elite always asked for "Mr. James" to select the food and hire the staff for the most elegant dinner parties and other social affairs. In 1893, Willis took a position as janitor at Hartford's Second North School and supplemented his income by raising fruit and vegetables.

During his early years in the city, Willis transformed himself from Sam to W. S. to Willis Samuel James. Whatever Sam had been, Willis became a man of moderate height and erect bearing who carried himself with dignity. He had medium-brown skin, close-cropped hair, and a large walrus mustache from which a clay pipe frequently protruded.

Willis's philosophy of life was simple. "I think there is a deal of trouth in it as Fredrick Douglass says the best place for the negro is as near the white man as he can get." He followed that truth with his purchase in 1875 of a three-story house at 6 Winter Street in Hartford's North End. A newspaper account described him as one of the first

Negroes to buy property north of downtown, but histories of the city spoke of a "Nigger Lane" near Winter Street and indicated that colored families had lived in the area as early as the 1820s. With the exception of his downstairs tenants, however, Willis's immediate neighbors were all white. Negroes were a rarity in Hartford, representing less than three percent of the population at the turn of the twentieth century.

About the time Willis bought his house, his wife died, and Willis married Anna Estelle Houston (pronounced "How-ston"). Willis had remained silent about his childhood, but Anna and her younger brother Charles deliberately obscured details about themselves. When she married Willis in 1874, she said she was twenty-two and had been born in New Orleans; a note in the family Bible gave Anna's birth date as August 2, 1852. But in 1880 someone told a census taker that she was thirty-six (that is, born in 1844) and born in Alabama. Bertha made another note that her mother had been born in Virginia. When Anna died in November 1894, Willis gave her age as fifty years and three months and her place of birth as Alabama—with a question mark. Charles generally claimed he was born in Connecticut to parents from Cuba. He, too, gave various birth dates.

Anna never tried to pass except when she and Charles were living with the family of the Reverend David Root, a Congregational minister in Cheshire, Connecticut, where she worked as a servant. Root gained a reputation as an abolitionist in the 1850s, when he served as minister of a church in Guilford, Connecticut, that had formed because its members held anti-slavery views. Root was probably responsible for telling the census taker in 1860 that Anna and Charles were white and born in Connecticut, even though he undoubtedly knew otherwise.

Despite her appearance, Anna made certain that people knew she was not white and on occasion paid a price for her honesty. "As a child I heard from my mother of how she had applied for a room at the Y.W.C.A.," her daughter Helen wrote, "of how she had been welcomed by the secretary and shown over the building with all graciousness, and of how, when she gave her race as Negro, she was treated as though she had said she was a leper."

The incident shook Anna's faith in humanity, but the treatment she received from other members of the board of trustees helped to restore it. According to Helen, they "resented this attitude of the secretary of the Y.W.C.A., and were so fine and loyal in the expressions, through the press and personally, that they did much towards strengthening her faith in Christianity, at just the point where it might have weakened, it doubtless did much in giving her the broad outlook and large comprehension of life that became characteristic of her. She taught her children that God is universal; that the Church may be larger than the people who compose it, and that institutions are often more liberal than those who represent them." Her children benefited from their mother's experience. Bertha and Helen inculcated those values thoroughly; the others adopted them with varying degrees of success.

While Anna stayed on the dark side of the color line, Charles walked back and forth. He crossed a second time when he ran away from home, changed his name, lied about his age, and enlisted in an all-white unit during the Civil War. Uncle Charley explained to his niece, Helen, that he left because of the Reverend Mr. Root. "He was good to everybody but me," Charles said. "He took me in the barn, stripped me naked and whipped me with a little rattan until the blood ran in streams. I'll never forget that. He took me in the house with nothing but my little shirt on." Charles was still persecuted after Root sent him to New Haven to learn a trade. He worked for eight months as an apprentice, but his treatment was "horrid." "The boss would take a hammer or saw or anything he could get his hands on and knock me down. I told my step father and he wouldn't take any account of it."

Charley and his friend Eddie Shaw caught the boat from New Haven at eleven o'clock one night. When they arrived in New York, they went directly to the recruiting station in Brooklyn. The recruiters weren't paying attention as Charley signed his name Charles Houdson. The army clerks changed it to Hudson and accepted his affidavit that he was a nineteen-year-old farmer born in New Haven. At five feet three and a half inches, he barely met the height requirement. Charles T. Hudson volunteered for a three-year term in the Company H, First Regiment,

New York Cavalry, the illustrious Lincoln Cavalry. Private Hudson and his fellow recruits left almost immediately for Baltimore, where they picked up their horses.

Charley soon found Army living was not much of an improvement over life in New Haven. "One night in camp in Woodstock Virginia, at one o'clock at night, had 4 inches of snow. We almost froze that night. Charlie Marlow had a tent together. We got along fine. Capt. Newton said you and Marlow are pretty tough. How's that Capt? You lived thro' that snow storm." From there they "saw action in South Carolina. No real battles. All skirmishes. Looking for the enemy. When we came to the rebels we fought like the devil."

The Lincoln Cavalry needed fresh recruits when Charley enlisted. The men had gained their reputation as indefatigable fighters when they defended Washington, D.C., in 1861, then joined the fierce action for control of the hamlets of the Shenandoah Valley. As part of the Army of West Virginia, they routed Jubal Early's men in the fall of 1864 and carried out General Sheridan's campaign to destroy the rebel food supply in the fertile valley. Private Hudson was there to help finish the job in the spring of 1865 when 1500 Confederate soldiers surrendered at Waynesboro. He was also part of a small contingent that stayed to guard the prisoners and to secure the area from the renegade bands that continued to harry the Union troops. On April 3, 1865, six days before Lee surrendered, Private Hudson was on skirmish duty near Woodstock when a bullet pierced his right thigh. He never discussed the injury that kept him in Baltimore's Jarvis U.S. Army Hospital for nearly two months and qualified him for a disability discharge.

Charley was able to join in the cavalry because of equine training he received when he lived with the Root family. After the war, he traded horses with Captain Newton. "He gave me $500.00 to boot. Money was no object in those days. . . . I owned two or three hundred horses after that. Sent west for horses, truck horses and trotting horses. Sold one to Wm. L. Bradley of Boston. Horse as pretty as a picture, flowing mane and tail. Jet black with a white star in his forehead. $5000.00 cash Bradley paid for the horse."

Charley earned his living in more conventional ways as well. When he recovered from his injury he returned to New Haven and learned the art of barbering from Allen Cooper. "He was an Indian, his wife a colored woman," Charley said. "Leaving Cooper I opened a shop for myself on State & Chapel over Fitche's clothing shop." Charley sold that business and moved to Brooklyn, where he continued to work as a barber.

In 1876, two years after Anna settled down with Willis, Charley married Clothilda Françoise Delsart, whose family came from Martinique. The couple soon had their first child, Georgiana, and they moved to Toms River, New Jersey, where Charley worked as a barber and as a carpenter. "The tenants objected to my living in the house because I was colored," he said, but "in five years [I] didn't owe a penny on my property in Toms River."

While the Hudsons encountered racism, Anna and Willis made certain that one aspect of their lives remained free from bigotry. They worshiped at one of Hartford's original Negro churches, North Methodist Episcopal (now Metropolitan African Methodist Episcopal Zion). In 1889 Anna subscribed to pay twenty-five cents a month toward the $2300 fund-raising effort for salaries and church building expenses. Willis became a class leader who read and explained Bible verses. His students were the maids, butlers, and coachmen who worked in private homes and attended the classes on Thursdays, their day off.

Willis maintained a lively interest in the activities of all the city's colored churches. "The Tolcott Street are going to dedicate theire church on neaxt Sunday the union Baptist has not got in to theire new church as yet they were to of had theire annel fair in it on Thanksgiven week [1906] but it is not ready for that as yet," he wrote to Louise. During the early years of the twentieth century, the Talcott Street (now Faith Congregational United Church of Christ) and the Union Baptist churches moved to larger facilities to meet the demands of a growing Negro population.

Both Willis and Anna were anxious for all their children to receive a good education. The earliest letter in Bertha's collection was written to her in September 1891 by her mother, in Saybrook, Connecticut: "I hope you will continue to have a nice time and be ready to come on the Monday boat. . . . Be sure and get home for school. Pa will have a fit if you don't get home so as to be in time for school."

Anna stayed at a house at Saybrook Point, on the west bank of the Connecticut River at Long Island Sound, run by the Heartsease League. With a view of the North Cove and the salt marshes that form the mini-delta at the mouth of the river, the house became a fresh-air camp for poor people from Hartford, New Haven, and New York and operated for about twenty years. Bertha fell in love with the town as a result of her visits.

Anna was already fatally ill when she wrote that letter to Bertha. The following year, she spent several months at the New Jersey shore in an effort to recover her health. Her letters never mentioned a diagnosis, but her symptoms—hoarseness, cough, loss of appetite—and the treatment—beer, whiskey, glycerin—meant that she had phthisis. Besides alcohol in various forms, doctors prescribed bed rest for the illness that suffocated millions before antibiotics became available. During her "rest cure," Anna stayed with her brother in Toms River, where she was able to breathe fresh air and leave the care of a husband and seven children to others.

In her first letter from the shore, Anna asked Bertha to send her the name of "that best tonic" because "these hay seeds down here don't know what it is, and I could not tell them whose make it is." She preferred the tonic to lager beer, which didn't help her hoarseness or her cough. Within a few days she was beginning to feel stronger and her appetite improved. Still, she despaired about returning to Hartford. "I am afraid that it not going to do me any good in staying here. As long as I am in the house I am all right but my hoarseness comes on if I go out doors. The folks say that I will not know for a long time whether it is going to do me any good or not." The tonic had helped immensely, she said. "It is just what I want to keep my appitite." After the first shipment, she told Bertha not to send any more because of the cost. She planned to buy it in Trenton to save money.

Each time she wrote to Bertha, Anna was preparing her oldest daughter to assume the role of mother. For instance, she wanted to make sure that her family had enough food for the coming winter. "It is queer that they had Taylors and Plato kill their chickens and not disturb ours. such happens to our luck. What did Mrs. D. put up for us? and how many peaches did you get out of ours and did the melon rinds spoil? Make Pa get some wild grapes for her or someone to put up. . . . tell Hattie to look out for my plants take up the Lantana and the large geraniums put into large pots and stand in the cellar. let Mrs. R. have all she wants."

Uncle Charley sent a box of quinces by freight, and Anna instructed Bertha to use the skins and cores to make jelly and the flesh for preserves. She also fretted over warm clothes for the children. "Bertha don't fail to see that Louise has on her long sleeve shirt and the boys too. has she got her sack yet she must need it if it as chilly up there as it here. tell Pa not to let my plants get frosted tell Hattie not to forget to water the plants in the cemetary." The family plot in Old North Cemetery contained the remains of Fred and Fuller, Anna's children who each died at about nine months of age. She also instructed Bertha to "take good care of Pa and the children write me a grand long letter. Tell Lou that she will get a letter next time. Make Louise write me a letter also Hattie tell me all the news when you write give all a kiss from Your Loving Mother A.E.J."

Though the New Jersey climate seemed beneficial for her health, Anna found life otherwise tedious. On September 23, 1892, she answered Bertha's "welcome letter" immediately, saying that it was the first one she had received from home. "It is not very lively here and I go to bed so early it makes a long night and a still longer day. . . . I am feeling much better than when I wrote to you. I am still hoarse and sore throat all the time but doctor says I will get over that soon it is the change in the climate. I still sweat nights a little if after I have been here two weeks I am no better you may look for me at home." She closed with a promise to write, and instructions to Bertha to "Kiss all the children and tell them to be good and I will come to see them some day."

Anna's illness did not lessen her interest in her friends and neighbors in Hartford and Saybrook. "I want you to send me the papers ask Mrs Richie if she will let you send me her papers when they are through with it. give her as many of our papers as she wants, any time." In subsequent letters she told Bertha to "give my love to Mrs. O'Brien and tell her she knows what the Jersey weather or climate is. how are all the nieghbors around has old Kate returned from Brooklyn yet." As to her illness, Anna remained optimistic.

Anna also raised what became recurring theme, Willis's reluctance to provide adequate support for his family. "Tell Pa he will have to send me a little money soon for everything costs so much more here than it does home. the whiskey and glycerine costs a quarter every time I have it filled. I have only medicine to last till the first of next week." Instead of writing directly to Willis, Anna had Bertha ask her father for money for the cough syrup. That letter also represented the first of many times that Bertha acted as messenger for various family members when they needed to pry money from their father, who imposed on everyone rigorous habit of saving. Louise observed later, "My father should have died a very wealthy man, 'cause he pinched the pennies till they hollered." There is no indication that Willis sent the money.

In early October, Anna was becoming

allright again after my sick spell. I have been in the yard quite a little while today. I hope I will pick up again and feel as well as I did before my cough is not near so bad as it has been. . . . I am tired from going out this A.M. but that will be all right in a little while. . . . I will close this by sending a message to Mrs. Richie from Uncle Charlie. he says tell Mrs. R. I am still standing, and hopes to have another glass of lager with her sometime, and his regards to her. . . . Uncle Charlie says in sending a box—anything send it freight for it so much cheaper. Now I will close this with love to all from your affec. Mother

Anna replied to Bertha's next letter that she was "all Right" and had stopped taking the medicine, which was only for the severe pains "and to check the sudden coughing. . . . I am comfortable in the house and out but I shant stay all winter not by a long shot." Charley was furious because of a report in the Negro newspaper, *The Christian Banner*, that

Anna was not getting any better. "He sat down and wrote a card which you will see in that paper next. I tried to keep him from sending but he was so angry he would send it any way; now you will laugh when you read it it sound just like him." The letter concluded with a note "to my little Louise, Your little letter was just as cunning as it could be. I was delighted with it. You must be sure and when you write write a long letter you must be a good girl. I am coming home some day to see you I wish you were here with me. You would have fine times with [Charles' daughter] Bertha. Now I will say good by from your loving Mama."

Shortly after she wrote that letter, Anna returned to Hartford. Before the infection weakened her and confined her to bed, she exercised by walking down Winter Street to greet Willis as he returned from work. Soon, however, the fevers began to strike more often and last longer. Then she lost her appetite and began coughing up blood. Fatigue brought on by malnutrition and exhaustion from the bouts of coughing robbed her of the energy to get out of bed.

"I used to sit at her bedside sometimes," Louise remembered. "She'd read me funny stories, or tell me funny stories. I never remember my mother doing any housework. She was always an invalid. My sisters had to do all the housework." Bertha, Helen and Harriet took care of the cooking, cleaning, and other chores and nursed their mother. As Helen wrote later, "I shall never cease to be glad that I was able to care for dear mamma and to do my best for her. It means so much in after years."

Anna Houston James died on November 19, 1894, and life in the James household began to change. Bertha married Peter Lane in the spring of 1896. Helen went off to school at Hampton Institute and Normal School in Virginia. In 1899, brother Willis enlisted in the Army and Harold enrolled at Hampton, with Harriet enrolling the next year.

Through all of their wanderings, the children kept the memory of their mother alive. "Tomorrow Nov. 19 is the anniversary of our dear mother's death 12 years ago," Bertha wrote to Louise in 1906. She was "as usual" arranging to have chrysanthemums put on the grave. Louise was eight when her mother died. Years later she found someone whose experience resonated with her. "A little girl has come here to be my room mate," she wrote from pharmacy school, "and I am sure that I will like her. She has no mother, her aunt and grandmother have raised her." Helen offered the most poignant remembrance on the tenth anniversary of their mother's death. "One of our girls is expected to die to-night with appendicitis. They took her away to the hospital yesterday. . . . She herself must have suffered some great loss not long ago for her [clothes] are all black and she has such a sad patient face. My heart always goes out to those who have known loss. What have we not experienced through the loss of a mother?"

The children felt the loss of their mother more acutely after their father married again. The date was July 3, 1900, the day after the anniversary of his marriage to Anna Houston. Even before they met her, the James children disliked Anna Mathilda Phillips, finding the very concept of stepmother repellant.

"Is it true that Papa is going to get married?" Harold asked. "I think he must be out of his head and I bet if I come home this summer and my old stepmother tries to boss me I will settle her." Helen was more articulate and philosophical. The news reinforced her conviction that she would never again be able to rely on Willis for emotional or financial support.

Your letter arrived yesterday morning [March 1, 1900] and its contents have not been wholly out of mind one moment since. I wanted to write to you at once for I feel that at this time, a critical one to us all, we need each other more than ever. Last night I could not sleep. After I had lain abed for a long time trying to woo sleep, I had to get up, dress and go down stairs. There I plunged desperately into a book which for a time routed cares and worries. It should not be the shock that it is for we have long expected it. What I want to know is, who is the woman? Whoever she may be I hope that she is deserving of papa. He deserves a good woman, surely if he will marry. I try to think that good comes out of lots of things that we least expect it will. Let us do nothing rash or hastily, for we may repent it at our leisure. Papa is papa. He has been a good man and a good father to us all. We can not complain. All men have their weaknesses, he of course is no exception.

My only regret is that I am old enough to realize them for God knows that nothing would give me greater joy than implicit confidence in every movement that papa makes.

We as the oldest girls have a very great responsibility at this time. We must conduct ourselves in a way that will make the younger children have a respectable bearing toward papa and his movements. Louise and Harold are yet to be educated and Harriet must be given the chance that she needs to make her an independent woman. Poor Fritz! At times I almost despair of him, but pray constantly that God will strengthen him. I think that he has inherited his father's weaknesses with out his strong qualities, for papa has many. You know this all makes me think desperately for it means simply this home never will be the same to me again. From the day the deed is done I think that I shall be only a visitor at No. 6. I shall probably work both winter and summer at something if my health is spared me.

Beyond hastening her toward her goal of self-sufficiency, the marriage meant that Helen had to contribute more to the support of her brothers and sisters than she had anticipated. "I shall try hard to fit myself for a better salaried position that I may be better able to help those at home. Let me know when the event is to take place please. I shall doubtless make my arrangements accordingly." She began to contemplate leaving her student-teaching position at Whittier School in Virginia to earn more money. She rejected an offer of help from Bertha's husband, Peter. "I feel now as I felt then, since I have gotten so old it is best for me to strike out for myself and make a home for myself. Perhaps papa is right in feeling that 'he has carried the whole load long enough.' Some day I shall hope to have a home for myself when all will be O.K." "So old" was twenty-four.

The reality of their stepmother did nothing to improve the children's opinion of her. Anna Phillips was less than a year older than Bertha. With her pale skin, curly hair, and thin lips, she bore a startling resemblance to their mother. As beautiful as she was, the new Mrs. James had a disability that created problems for the entire family. Her legs were severely deformed by rickets, and she walked with difficulty. Willis doted on her and hired a servant to help with the housework, which increased as they started another family.

Harriet, who enrolled at Hampton shortly after her father's marriage, realized that the school offered a more wholesome environment. "With such an outlook as I had before me perhaps I should not have come here," she told Bertha, adding, "I am happy here and that means being well, which was an impossibility at #6, that is chiefly why I came here for I knew that every body was kind to every body else and it was best that I should come."

About a year after the wedding, Helen asked Harriet how their brother Willis "got on" with the new Mrs. James. "No one ever mentions her in any of the home letters, not even papa, and had I not been there myself at the wedding, I fear that I would doubt there having been one. I notice these people a great deal and note in them a strong resemblance to the West Indians that I have *not* known." Anna Phillips was born on St. Croix, and the James children developed a violent prejudice against "Jamaicans," as they called all West Indians.

Harold had a less subtle analysis. "Mrs. James is sick or lazy as—for she remains in her room and hasn't been downstairs for a week." A few days later he reported that "the old woman" was up and about, but they still had a maid "and we live better than usual." He told Louise that he could not wait to have a "good home" where he could have what he wanted to eat when he wanted it.

Maid service for Anna Phillips meant less money for Anna Houston's children, and a greater burden fell on Bertha and Peter. They paid bills at Hampton for Harriet and Harold and later assumed the cost of Louise's tuition and living expenses at pharmacy school. Harriet suffered the most from her father's financial neglect because of unpaid bills. In the spring of 1902 she begged Peter and Bertha for twenty dollars so she would not be forced to leave school. Two weeks later she died.

The hostility between Bertha and her father escalated over the disposal of Harriet's body. Willis wrote to Bertha in Saybrook, "Why a friend met me on main st. and ask me was it a fack that I refused to allow Hatties remains to be brought to the house now I have said let them all talk all they wish as George Carr has often said that a dog that will bring a bone will carrie one." Willis never denied the charge, but Harriet has a tombstone near those of her mother and infant brothers.

A large measure of the children's animosity toward Anna Phillips was misdirected anger at their father. He, in turn, blamed Louise for problems at home, and she became so unhappy that she ran away. "He didn't know where I was for a long time," she said. "He went almost crazy. He went to every house in the neighborhood, Mather Street, Winter Street, Brook Street, Green Street. I had kids telling me this . . . afterwards." Louise made her way to Bertha and Peter in Saybrook. When Willis found out, he wrote to Bertha on June 29, 1902:

My Dear Bertha

first I though I would go with a lot of details in riteing you but what is the use in harrowing up thing all the time there is one thing I wish to straiten out you said that I said I would shut the doors aginst Louise I said in the presents of your self and Louise that some boddy might shut the doors aginst her. I had trouble aboute that same befoure and I charged Louise befoure she left the school to besure and leave the door unlocked when she entered the house I know the disposition of every child I have and if Louise is left alone she is all right—on cose it was your place to streighten out matters and bring Louise in the family where she belongs now I want to say Dear Berth if Louise will do what is her duity in her Farther's family I can asure you that she will have a good and happy home as I can give her you know as well as I I have put up with more than most men would now nothing would please me more than to see us all come to gather as one family you know it would be the best thing for the chrilden surpose any of them should be taken sick. . . . Bertha I have nothing but the verry best of feelings as a father for his child I should like to see us all set down at one table on thanksgiven days as we have in past if they were all like your husband we would."

The duty that Willis expected of sixteen-year-old Louise included cooking and any cleaning not done by the maid. Like many troubled children, Louise stopped attending school while she lived at her father's house but returned once she moved out. She graduated from Saybrook High School, then from Brooklyn College of Pharmacy, where she was the only Negro and the only woman in her class. She was reportedly the first woman to receive a pharmacy license in the state of Connecticut.

The family believed that Louise had been neglected, too, because Willis had refused to pay for piano lessons. Helen did not address her concerns directly to Louise but confided in Bertha. "I am more sorry about Louise's music than I can say. I think it is a shame that her lessons are not continued. All I can say is, may God's greatest blessing rest on papa to the extent that his last years may be his best. No one thing, not one penny do I desire of him, if the holding of it makes him happier. I only pray that he will do what is right by those at home." Helen repeated her concerns to Peter. "I am sorry that papa does not see the necessity of keeping her music up. I refrain from any remarks. My aim is to keep 'iron' out of my heart and to be liberal."

With Louise's departure from 6 Winter Street, Willis repeated a pattern he had started in the 1870s. He sent Charles, his eight-year-old son by Anna Webb, to live with his mother's relatives in Eastchester, New York. Charles returned in 1887, and after marrying he rented Willis's first-floor apartment. Later he and his family moved around the corner. Anna Houston's children always treated their stepbrother Cholly as a full member of their family and remained close to him throughout their lives.

Willis never thought that he was depriving his family of financial or emotional support, believing he had fulfilled his obligations. But he always sought to limit his spending. He pressured Harold into skipping the church wedding desired by the bride's family because the house "would be more appropriate at this time," meaning less expensive. Worse than the financial neglect were the feelings of abandonment when he failed to acknowledge his children's accomplishments. He stayed away from Louise's pharmacy school graduation. Months later he wrote that he had told Bertha he could not attend because he did not "dare risk my self through New York at that time as I did not explain my condishion to her at that time trouble that Fritz brought on us all my mind at times were simply blank when my wife were sick in the hospital." The sum total of his woes: "I were simply breaking down under the strain."

Though Harold and Fritz lived at 6 Winter Street for extended periods after their father married Anna Phillips, Helen was true to her word and paid no more than brief visits. From Hawaii she wrote in April 1903, "I enjoy the beauties of this place, the soft warm air and my free independent life so much, that I dread the thoughts of disturbing the tranquility for even three short months, even when I want to see you so much. Since home is not home in the sense that it was it hasn't quite the same drawing powers that it had three years ago. I want to return and I dread it."

When Helen did visit, she felt compelled to clean house despite the presence of hired help. During her first stay, she sorted through the belongings of the dead and departed:

Yesterday [September 14, 1904] I cleaned out the closet in Harry's room (your old room), and cleaned out, or rather went through, those old trunks containing our possessions. . . . The remainder are in the largest of those box trunks; mammas underclothes, Harriet's clothing, and remnants of wardrobes of us four girls. . . . If you say the word I will send the trunk down to you. Then there are those pieces for bed quilts they fill another trunk. Do you want them? Hattie's type-writer, violin and music are all here, where I think they are perfectly safe. They are in Harry's room. Write me immediately what to do, that I may get it done while I am here.

In each of the next two years Helen reported on her efforts to clean out the accumulated detritus. "We relieved the beds of all occupants [bedbugs] and took up the carpets. Now we are on bare floors waiting papa's time for the mattings. To get these down will be a great gain if nothing else is accomplished." Things improved in 1907, and the house looked cleaner than Helen had ever seen it "under the new regime." She also had a rare opportunity to share a meal with her father and brother. "To-night [September 27] Mrs. James and the children were away at supper time, so I got tea, and papa, Harry and I had a cozy meal together. How glad I was of that one!"

Though she had run away from home, Louise visited her father, and they exchanged letters while she was at school. His missives largely described the illnesses and deaths of friends and family members. The following, dated October 28, 1906, with a picture of the fountain in Hartford's Bushnell Park at the top of the first page, was typical:

My Dear Louise,
Your very kind letter I received and was glad to here from you and to know
that you are getting on well and enjoying good health . . . We are having
nice mild weather here I picked a nice danderline on my way from church in
full blum I used it as a button hole boquet. They are having a national tem-
perance convention here at this time there are some . . . collard women as
delegates with them. I saw Emma Connell in church this morning so I think
she is in Hartford for the winter. I did not get to speak to her. Mrs. Bird
Mrs. Hall's sister died this morning. She will be brought to Hartford for burial
Lillian [his son Charles's wife] went down there this morning Harry has
quite a few young squabs at this time let us hope he may make well on
them. . . . Fritz went out coon hunting last night he says they cought four
they are going to have a coon supper some time this week. I must close with
love from your farther

With their mother's death and their father's remarriage, the James children drew closer to Uncle Charley. He moved from New Jersey to New York, where he managed a restaurant in White Plains. Helen frequently visited with him and Aunt Tillie on her trips to and from the South. Of one day's shopping, Helen told Bertha, "I was absolutely resigned, letting him make all plans and arrangements as though I had never travelled. I have found that men like this sort of passiveness in a woman because it allows them to exert what they suppose to be a superior executive ability. I sometimes indulge one, being only an interested and amused onlooker, expressing appreciation and approval whenever it seems desired."

Helen knew her uncle was aging and struggling financially. In 1905, she told Bertha, "To see how he has grown thin and gray, lost his teeth and really grown to be an old man would make you cry." Aunt Tillie was ill, too, "and she is not able to cheer and comfort him, looking to others as she does for help and uplift." Uncle Charley wrote his last surviving letter to Bertha on August 7, 1933:

Well how are you all I hope all are well I have been miserable since the (2) of dec. Then I had a bad fall in a store here hurting my shoulder blade, my back my knee my hand, and split my lower lip. and have been miserable ever since. I could not get out Decoration day so that was not me in the picture which is enclosed. Thank you *I wanted to come to see you once more But I can't come alone my eyes are very poor and having my doctor he says I must not travel alone . . . my health is very poor which I cant expect to be O.K at my age which on the 30 of this month I have turn 85 years old. . . .*

The Depression here is some thing awful our People have nothing to eat But sleeping in the parks on the grass so now know I must close with a sweet kiss to all the girls I would like to hear from them all I wrote Louise never heard a word from her I hope she is not sick again.

After writing this letter, Uncle Charley lived for another ten months. Bertha pasted his undated obituary in the back of the family Bible:

Mr. Charles T. Hudson, 86 years of age, died at the New York Hospital on Friday, June 1. Mr. Hudson resided with his daughter, Mrs. Georgiana Robertson of 2257 Seventh Avenue. He was a veteran of the Civil War, enlisted in Company K, 1st New York Cavalry in 1864. A military funeral was accorded him, same furnished by the 369th Infantry N.Y.N.G.

He is survived by three daughters, Mrs. Georgiana Robertson, Mrs. Jennie Gray of New Haven, Conn., and Mrs. W. Woodruff Chisum of this city; grandchildren, nieces, nephews and a host of friends. Interment was in Evergreen Cemetery.

Willis Samuel James died on May 22, 1917. It was a source of pride to the family that every one of his children had graduated from the Arsenal School, and when the youngest finished, a short newspaper article acknowledged their more than fifty years of attendance. "In speaking of the late Mr. James, teachers Wednesday afternoon spoke highly of his integrity and said that his descendents are of the same type."

Willis and Anna's children for the most part followed their father's advice about Frederick Douglass's truth and positioned themselves close to white people. When Bertha and Peter Lane moved to Saybrook in 1902, the town was home to a handful of Negroes, mostly domestic servants. Louise, then Helen and her husband, then Fritz followed Bertha to Saybrook. Harold bought a farm in Wethersfield, a town just south of Hartford that was nearly as white as Saybrook. He later rejected the truth and moved to Hanover, Virginia.

Chapter 2

THE SURROGATE MOTHER

Willis and Anna Houston James may not have been in a position to give their children riches, but they gave them a sense of self-worth and faith in their own abilities that lasted them throughout their lives. That confidence began with their oldest, Bertha Ernestine James. Anna cherished Bertha, molding her into a loving woman who nurtured her brothers and sisters and later her own children and their friends.

Bertha, "Bert" to her brothers, loved children. Her daughter Ann's childhood friends said, "I wish your mother were my mother, too." Bertha devoted her undivided attention to each person she met and it made everyone feel as if "She's been waiting all day just to see me!" She found genuine ways to praise nearly everyone she encountered. Her favorite expressions were: "If you can't find something nice to say about someone, don't say anything" and "You catch more flies with honey than with vinegar." Where her sisters excelled at seeing the negative, Bertha searched for the good.

Through the letters she received and the few of those she wrote that survived, a picture of Bertha emerges of a hard-working, creative woman with a whimsical sense of humor and strong opinions, especially in matters of style and deportment. A product of the Victorian era, Bertha adopted many of the values that she learned from the rich white people who hired her to style their hair and repair their corns and bunions. She passed the values she learned along to her younger sisters and to her daughters.

Bertha's devotion to people, ladylike demeanor, and refined looks belied the survival skills she learned in childhood. Though she preferred to run her businesses, she could as easily operate a farm. Bertha impressed her children and their friends when she caught and killed chickens. She transformed fruits and vegetables as well. Jams, jellies and pickles poured from the kitchen, as she sold the results and kept the family supplied with food year-round. Bertha annually drove her family, weeping, from the house as she prepared cauldrons of homemade horseradish.

Bertha and her sisters inherited plentiful fine strands of "good" hair from their mother. Helen told Bertha, "I should love to see the little Bertha. I know she is dear. Does her hair fly about as much this cold weather as it did in the summer?" Saybrook's humid summers added curl and body, making the hair somewhat more manageable, but winter's cold air straightened any hint of curl and separated each fine strand. As a beautician, Bertha knew how to care for her daughter's hair and used her ingenuity to make it stay in place. Bertha, Helen, and Louise tamed their own locks by knotting them in tight buns that they wore on top of the head or at the nape of the neck. By the time she reached middle age, Bertha's hair had turned a bright shade of silver that women envied, and she had added some weight to her slender figure. Days outside in the garden and the chicken yard had turned her skin a beautiful nut brown. She never believed it, but her friends and relatives considered her one of the most beautiful women ever to walk the planet.

Early in life Bertha began collecting people by collecting autographs. The first signatures were from family members, but soon she had captured Hartford's resident celebrities, beginning with the woman Lincoln said had started the Great War. She wrote, " 'Trust in the Lord and Do Good,' written by your sincere Friend, Harriet Beecher Stowe, Dec. 5, 1889." Bertha and the rest of the James family met Mrs. Stowe through her neighbor and their benefactor Mary B. Lewis, who lived on Farmington Avenue around the corner from Mrs. Stowe's home on Forest Street.

Within the week, Bertha had secured the autographs of the entire Clemens family. Susan and Jean Clemens signed their names on December 12, the same day their father wrote, "Yours truly, Mark Twain." Bertha met the Clemens family through their butler, George Griffin, whom scholars believe served as the model for Jim in *Huckleberry Finn*. Like the James family, Griffin attended North Methodist Episcopal Church.

Bertha devoted nearly all her energy to work, from necessity and from a need to feel useful. When her mother wrote to Bertha in the fall of 1891 telling her to leave New York in time to go to school, Bertha came home, but she did not return to school. She told her parents she wanted to earn money and went to work at a company that printed stamped envelopes for the federal government. By 1896 she had become shop foreman, a rare position for a young colored woman in that era. She also obtained licenses from the state of Connecticut that allowed her to practice as a barber and hairdresser and as a chiropodist.

Bertha found a haven when she joined the United Workers and Women's Exchange. Mary Lewis and the patrician women who served on the United Workers board of directors sought to improve the lives of poor girls and young women in Hartford. With a library and classes in first-aid, dressmaking, painting, drawing and elocution, the building on Main Street served as an early Girls Club. Children as young as nine found rest from the drudgery of the factory floor and the kitchens and parlors of private homes. Modeled on an organization founded in New York to help Civil War widows, the exchange allowed women to bring in handiwork to sell on consignment. Among its most successful activities, the board raised money among Hartford's wealthy residents to send girls as young as eight and young women to go to the country for summer vacations of a week or two. It was through the United Workers that the James family first went to Saybrook.

Because she wanted to help to support the family, Bertha continued to work when her mother fell ill. Peter Clark Lane began courting her and, after a suitable period of mourning after her mother's death, they married in June 1896. Bertha and Peter rented the first-floor apartment of her father's house after they married. She continued to work, opening a linen- and lace-making concern that she called Parlours, one of many businesses that she would own.

Peter and his family had moved to Connecticut from New Jersey when he was a little boy. His father, Theodore Lane, worked for fifty years at a pharmacy in Hartford, first as a porter and then as manager of the supply department, where he compounded salves and other medicines. In the early 1920s, Theodore Lane was one of the few Negroes to receive coverage in the *Hartford Courant*, the city's white newspaper. The story commemorated "Major" Lane's fiftieth anniversary with the firm and praised his work making the topical ointment Griswold's Salve, other medicines, and vanilla extract. Peter, oldest child of Theodore and Jennie Cooper Lane, followed his father to work at Sisson's, where he learned the art and science of compounding. He is believed to be the first Negro to receive a pharmacy license in Connecticut.

Peter and Bertha Lane were living on Winter Street when her father married in 1900. After her father's marriage, West Indians in general and Anna Phillips in particular became the exception to Bertha's generosity of spirit, though in keeping with her personal philosophy, she rarely said so. "I do not know whether George [their cousin Georgiana Hudson] will marry a West Indian or not. I hope not," she wrote to Louise. "Peter says Pap did himself brown when he married her. I should say so. As Harry says, the best of the Indians are on the island."

That same year Peter went to stay in Saybrook for the summer, where he opened Lane's Pharmacy in a historic building. Located just off lower Main Street across the green from the Congregational Church, the pharmacy served as a convenient stop for the wealthy families who summered at Saybrook Point. Many of Peter's customers relied on the pharmacy for prescriptions and patent medicine, but residents and visitors alike looked forward to the treats served in the ice cream parlor. Lane's Pharmacy became a popular gathering place. His homemade fudge sauce remained famous years after his death, as visitors to the shoreline returned summer after summer to feast on sundaes, banana splits, egg creams, and ice cream sodas.

Saybrook had established itself as a thriving summer colony beginning in the 1870s, as it attracted the families of Hartford insurance executives, particularly to the borough of Fenwick, a spit of land on the edge of Long Island Sound at the mouth of the Connecticut River. The area became known as "Hartford on the Rocks" both for the geological formations and the way the vacationers preferred their beverages. The farmers, fishermen, and other year-round residents of Saybrook earned much of their annual income between Decoration Day and Labor Day by providing services and goods to the vacationers in their twenty-plus-room cottages.

Peter and Bertha decided they could run a successful business year-round and moved to Saybrook permanently in the spring of 1902, setting up housekeeping above the store. They were glad to have a home and a business of their own, but they made the move from Hartford with mixed feelings. Helen reflected the feelings of family, "It seems sad to think of your leaving No. 6 for as Mrs. Saunders said in her last letter, it means the breaking up of home. . . . I feel at a loss wholly."

With the upheaval of their father's marriage, Helen's departure for Hawaii, Harriet's death, and the Lanes' move to Saybrook, Bertha and Helen felt they were aging prematurely. "You mustn't expect me to remember how old I am," Helen wrote. "The years pass too rapidly and are growing so many that I do not pretend to know without going back to Sept. 1, 1876. It is well I do not keep the numbers before me—they would discourage me surely." Bertha concurred, and Helen reflected in her next letter, "When you talk of being old, it makes me tremble for I am a close second, you know." These thoughts of advancing years occurred when Bertha was twenty-nine and Helen twenty-six years old.

During the first year in Saybrook, Bertha told Helen she was having a "quiet restful summer." Helen replied, "I am delighted that Peter's business does so well. What will you do this winter, sit down and count your earnings of the summer?" She was being facetious, as Bertha was never idle, and when the drugstore began to prosper, Peter paid the young men who worked for him to do the housekeeping so Bertha could devote her full energies to her businesses.

With an artistic sense inherited from their mother, the James women all had exquisite taste in clothing and furnishings. They seemed to know instinctively what accessories should adorn a particular outfit and where to hang a picture for the best effect. Bertha used her talents in her business, while Helen took pleasure in decorating her person when she had the means. Louise shared their sensibilities, but she gave up the fine work once she finished school, as she preferred to concentrate her energies on running her pharmacy.

Bertha continued her linen-making business under the name Beautiful Linens for Beautiful Homes, employing at least one of her sisters. From Hawaii, Helen sent an account of the merchandise she was making that would supply the trade at Christmas. She decorated a hat with puggree, a scarf wrapped around the crown. The style would appeal to customers in Saybrook, she said, and could earn a profit of three dollars per hat. In case Bertha had not seen the fashion, Helen instructed, "The front must always be bent down toward the eyes, while the back rolls up." She had also made some pillow shams but could not decide how much to charge. Helen told Bertha to set the price at not less than two dollars. She had left the basting stitches in one and spilled blood on a corner because she had cut her finger in her haste to mail them. "Please wash out the blood and pull bastings," she instructed.

Louise contributed her share of needlework while she was at pharmacy school. Bertha was full of advice about it, wisdom that she did not follow herself. "Be so careful of your eyes my dear do not use them more than you have to. I should wait until next winter for embroidery. Mine are giving me fits, and I owe it to handkerchief making. I have just finished two trimmed with real val[enciennes]." Bertha recognized that Louise had a rare chance to excel. "What an opportunity you are having of coming in contact with nice people," she said in the same letter. "What I have always wished for you, dear child. What a lot you will have to tell us when you come home, Thanksgiving."

Even though Bertha never finished high school, she had a lively mind and read extensively. She reported, "I am finishing a library book, 'The Long Day,['] a working girl's experience in N.Y. City, perfectly splendid.

Makes me feel doubly glad you are in a sheltered place." Bertha even taught herself Spanish with the help of a dictionary that Louise gave her. Through the store she had access to a number of newspapers and over the years kept voluminous clipping files on subjects that included "Negro Affairs," gardening, and local news and gossip of Saybrook and Hartford.

When Helen was teaching in Florida, she helped Bertha sell the produce from her garden. "Whatever you get for canning, preserving and pickling get 2 or 3 jars of the same for me. Make out the bill as you go along & I will pay it. I have done up 1/2 doz. pts. of pine apple and will do up some of figs. These will be the only things that I will do up here as they are about the only things not easily obtained in Connecticut. I want very much some currant jelly if it is not too late."

Between them, Bertha and Peter earned enough money to help support Helen and the others when they were not working. Bertha's brothers and sisters rarely told her how much they appreciated her generosity, but in 1901 Helen wrote to Peter, "You and Bertha will surely receive your reward for all that you are doing for the family. I do hope that some day we can all be brought to gether and share the benefits of some of these efforts that we are making." Four years passed before Helen again said how she felt about Bertha's compassion and generosity: "Your letters have always stood to me as an illustration of true deep love, so steady and unswerving they are. Quite in contrast to my own spasmodic efforts at correspondence, which I trust, though, convey no less to you my love and appreciation of all that you and Peter have done for us. Your home may be the means of keeping the boys steady and I am sure, is a haven of rest for the poor pigeons who were pushed out."

In the fall of 1902 Bertha was about to add to her responsibilities, as she was expecting her first child. Helen wrote from Kona Orphanage, "I think of you every day in your present delicate condition and pray that it will mean a blessing to you and Peter. You are entering into a hard cold winter so take every care of yourself." Helen seemed to think that her job teaching many children demanded more effort. "If you had come out here and helped to mother these 'mitherless bairns,' perhaps you never would have married, so would not now be making wee articles of clothing over which you doubtless linger so fondly. Here I have them from fifteen months to fifteen years to love or carress, to approve or reprove at will."

Bertha Harriet Lane arrived January 12, 1903, and their father, Willis, wrote from Hartford the same day. "I received the good news and was glad to know that you are getting on so nicely Peter wrote me a few weeks ago what he expected but I had no idea that the time was so near I wish you much success in your beginning of family. I will half to come down to see the new commer you must be very careful not to take any cold I am glad you have a good nurse. that will take the best of care you and baby." Helen wrote to Peter two weeks later, saying she hoped that the baby "may be imbued with the good qualities of both of my sisters for whom she is named, having the talents of the one and the love and charitableness of the other."

After her daughter arrived, Bertha had help around the house and grounds from Louise and brothers Harold and Fritz, who visited frequently and stayed for long periods. Among them, they tended the gardens, harvested clams and mussels from the tidal flats of Long Island Sound, and did the heavy cleaning. Bertha was also blessed with a husband who contributed to the household upkeep. "I washed today, or rather bossed it as P.C. always does his share, and mine." Nevertheless, a large portion of the work fell on the new mother. Louise made a list in her diary of the Thanksgiving dinner Bertha prepared in 1904: tomato soup, crackers, turkey, cranberry sauce, sweet potatoes, onions, white potatoes, turnips, currant jelly, bread and butter, celery, gravy, squash, apple and mince pies, ice cream, cake, fruit, nuts, figs, and dates.

Little Bertha Harriet thrived until the summer of 1905. Helen wrote on August 23 from her job in western Massachusetts.

I am exceeding anxious to hear from you concerning baby Bertha. The disease, Peritonitis (?) is rather a stranger to me, so the word tells me little of its workings or whether it is serious. I shall pray for the little dear each night and expect that she will recover for your and Peter's sake at least, to say nothing of her many relations into whose affections she has worked herself so strongly. I don't know of a sweeter, dearer little girl, nor one with a lovlier disposition. As I write I can see her walking around the dining room asking Aunt Louise if she can "help," or smiling up so roguishly when her finger has slipped into the butter.

If she has to stay in bed, I know that you miss her much; she is as a light in your lives there and one that is greatly needed.

Early twentieth-century medicine was helpless against peritonitis, which inflamed the membrane that lined the child's abdominal cavity. With her illness untreated, little Bertha cried without rest for three days, as the infection distended her stomach and she grew more dehydrated. By September 1, little Bertha's condition had worsened but the family still held out hope: "Words can not convey to you my grief at being separated from you at this time when you need so much support and comfort. My heart is with you, Peter and Louise and I only wish that with you I might have the blessed comfort of ministering to the wants of the dear little one. . . . I shall pray for you and even yet trust that it is in God's providence to spare Bertha to us for many years." Bertha Harriet died on September 3, 1905. Hers was the first grave in the family plot in Cypress Cemetery by the river in Saybrook.

Helen had concluded one of her letters, "How sad it is that into her dear little system should circulate disease which knows no cure, and she so young. Perhaps it is best so. God alone knows. It would be much harder to lose her after she became grown than now, though it is hard to think of." She was wrong, of course. Bertha suffered dreadfully throughout her daughter's illness and after her death. The weeping upset her so, she said, that for the rest of her life she could never bear to hear a child cry.

Bertha went to Hartford a month later, but her father had little time to see his bereaved daughter. He wrote after she returned to Saybrook, "I muched expect to of seaned you a gain befour you left I went to the depo thinking that your train left at 4-40 but to my surprise at 2:21. I hope you arrived home safe and found them all well I should of seaned you but

Saturday is a busy day with me but I maid up my mind to see you at the train."

Willis's attitude toward infant mortality had been shaped by the loss of four of his own children: one by Anna Webb, two by Anna Houston, and one by Anna Phillips just the year before. His reaction to that death: "Well, our heavenly Farther knows what is best. So we must submit to his will." No one in the family recognized the sad irony that while Bertha had lost her only child, her father continued to produce another family, even though he was approaching sixty and had allowed his teen-age daughter to be raised elsewhere.

Bertha, too, suffered bouts of illness, starting with an attack of malaria in the spring of 1905. Helen advised her not to worry: "'Trust God, see all, nor be afraid.' Above all things cultivate calmness and patience: patience to wait, to be idle and not to accomplish all that you would. Life has been the process of evolution: so it continues to be. We can not hurry up things and the sooner we learn it the better." Not long after her daughter died, Bertha came down with a severe earache and sinus infection. Helen prescribed plenty of ginger to draw out the cold.

The fall of 1906 brought another bout of malaria, which she treated with Marburg's tincture tablets. These, she told Louise, made her sleepy and lifeless. Part of Bertha's problem may have been the late stages of pregnancy, for in November she gave birth to another daughter. "Helen Louise is asleep and I am comfortable," she wrote to Louise. "She is just like Bertha, Peter says, homely nose, dear mouth, but we can pinch the nose, hardly any hair but is so little and cute I can hardly wait for Xmas for you to come home to see her."

With the arrival of the baby, Bertha found inspiration for the verses that she wrote to amuse herself and her family:

Helen Louise is asleep, dear child.
I told her to night,
"Little bird in your nest
Mother knows what's best."
Isn't that a rhyme if you take it in time?

While she was running her businesses and caring for her family, Bertha maintained an avid interest in gardening, with flowers as her special passion. The Lane and James families worked for the Cromwells at "the Point." As the family was preparing to return to New York one fall, Mrs. Cromwell gave Bertha most of the contents of their garden—ferns, canna bulbs, dahlias, and all of the geraniums. Even Bertha thought those additions would be enough to fill her garden.

Bertha and Peter were never wealthy. Bertha practiced strict frugality even during financially comfortable times, but gave generously of whatever small amounts of money came her way to help everyone else in the family. Her artistic sense and creativity allowed her to decorate with exquisite taste even when money was lacking. "Helen sleeps in a basket all pink & white. And when brought to light it's a dream," she told Louise. "I took that bright pink skirt that was Hattie's in the trunk here back of the dining table. It had a blouse. I took that right off and put around the basket and draped white muslin (figured) over it."

Bertha's letters always contained local gossip, a recitation of her daily activities, and news of the family and of the services she attended at the First Congregational Church. She told Louise that a neighbor had sent baby Helen "the dearest little blue & white kimona" and that Uncle Charley had mailed ten pretty souvenir cards from Toms River.

Helen's friend Birdie Ford had written Bertha about the "dreadful" riot in Atlanta. Bertha saved that letter and sent an account of it to Helen in South Carolina. The riot started after racist politicians who wanted to disenfranchise Negro voters stirred up the white population. Newspapers added to the frenzy by falsely reporting twelve alleged rapes of white women by colored men. Whites launched brutal attacks on Negroes and their property that the police ignored. Birdie Ford and her family were living at 140 Howell Street in Atlanta when she wrote to Bertha on October 1, 1906.

My dear Mrs. Lane,

 I cannot say how much I enjoyed hearing from you. Your letter was the same as a ray of sunshine on a cloudy day. I can assure you we had several of those cloudy days. Well, I cannot tell you all about the riot, I guess I would be writing a journal instead of a letter.

The majority of the people knew nothing of the affair until Sunday a.m. when the loud cry of the paper boy was heard to say, "extra journal all about the riot, 20 negroes dead." Every one rushed for a paper and then the news & gossip began. Church was held in the a.m. More news was learned about 4 o'clock Sunday evening. All colored drug stores restaurants were ordered closed and the people made for home. It was said the mob was still on the go. Soldiers were stationed all around, and the people were not allowed to wander around.

It keep up until Wednesday. A white fellow passed our street Tuesday evening and some colored boy rocked him. He threatened to burn a store, Mr. Foster's. Helen will know and the mob which had formed not far off said the whole street of this high tone negroes. We telephoned the affair down to the police headquarters, and the officers came and later on the soldiers were around and we heard no more. Wednesday a.m. around the corner, near Mrs. Huntons, two colored boys were shot to death. I do not know whether the officers or the mob did it. They were all mixed in.

I send you a copy of Saturday night affair. I am told that more whites were killed than anyone has the least idea. The authorities would not allow it to be published. The negroes fought them to a finish. The authorities came to the conclusion, the negroes must be unarmed, they were afraid of them. Every negro man was searched, and pistols taken away. Certain negro quarters were ready for them, sent for the mob to come.

Out in South Atlanta, the officers went out in citizen clothes, they had a battle with the negroes. One officer was killed. The next day, 200 some odd negroes were arrested and all weapons taken away. In darktown another one of their quarters they broke every lamp around. They were ready to fight to a finish. The mob did not venture there. These white people saw, the negro would strike back.

It went so far until the martial law was threatened, and both white and black were disarmed and they began to treat both alike.

Several of the whites are serving out the time, for 3 days and are to be punished again.

*The better class of whites are meeting the negro men, and urging that
they stay and swore they would fight themselves before such happen again.
They rushed every where negroes were Saturday night. Post office barber
shops, hotels and streets. The town was completely torn up, commerce was
prevented, the stores were nearly closed for the week and the town is in a bad
fix. Some of our friends, not particular, were killed.*

    *Dr. Penn's auto is safe. His house was searched, and I do not know
whether he is in town or not. His family had to leave home and were not far
from here at Bishop Gains.*

    *Some of the best negroes were arrested on little charges, Because they
told the negroes what to do. Max Barber, editor of the Voice of the Negro
had to skip town Saturday on account of a piece he sent to the N.Y. World.*

    *We are just breathing a little fresh air. I went to school during the whole,
attendance was down.*

    *I do not suppose you do care to walk on this soil of Ga. the odessa of the
south. This thing has been in existence for quite a while. The lower class
were angry about the League. They asked for the police to be made larger
the week before.*

    *One thing, the white man has been damaged. They say a million dollar
fine would have been better than what happened. My brother in law left the
terminal stations only 10 or fifteen minutes before the mob reached there, or
our home would have been saddened.*

    *I wish that it was possible for us to move to Connecticut. I like that part
ever so much.*

Contemporary accounts reduced the number of Negro dead to ten
and asserted that two whites died during the four days of rioting, while
injuries stood in the hundreds. Modern historians dispute the figures
and set the number of Negro casualties far higher. In the weeks following the riot, more than one thousand Negroes acted on Birdie's desire
and left the city forever.

After the Reconstruction the South had become more vengeful. The
U.S. Supreme Court's 1896 decision in *Plessy v. Ferguson* put the federal
government's imprimatur on separate but equal public accommodations.

By 1906, white supremacists had solidified their positions. The number of lynchings increased, and the colored man lost his ability to seek redress through the franchise. Negroes in the North, though able to vote, found themselves displaced from jobs by waves of European immigrants and the inexorable shift from farm to factory.

Bertha protected her extended family by keeping track of everyone's whereabouts and offering a home to them and their belongings. As she and Peter were preparing to move to Saybrook, Helen wrote from Hawaii, "Please take an invantory of my things. As far as I remember, the only things of any value that I have, are the trunk with mamma's clothes in it and my books. Have Louise make a careful list of those, please." Peter was constantly mailing books, clothing and personal items, as Helen "forgot" important possessions each time she visited. Bertha frequently included gifts of food, and Peter contributed items from the pharmacy.

Bertha also had the responsibility for disseminating Helen's 1906 Christmas wish-list: the poems of John Greenleaf Whittier, Walt Whitman, or Christina Rossetti; kid gloves size six and one-quarter; and a blueprint album. Bertha dutifully passed these requests on to Louise and added that she thought it was "A good scheme because Papa generally sends her a 25 cent collar, he may as well put .50 more and send a book."

Another daughter, Anna Houston Lane, was born October 12, 1908, so that by the following summer, Bertha was caring for two children, a house, and three businesses. For all her benevolence toward her brothers and sisters, Bertha did not appreciate it when friends and relatives arrived on her doorstep unannounced. Every summer uninvited guests dropped in to enjoy Hotel Lane: "It seems a blessing to live where people can not descend on you unannounced. I am enjoying it to the full," was Helen's unsympathetic response from landlocked Beckley, Connecticut.

Over the years, Bertha benefited from the generosity of several wealthy and powerful women, the most prominent among them the philanthropist Emily Malbone Morgan of Hartford. Miss Morgan devoted most of her life to helping the poor under the auspices of the Episcopal Church, through the United Workers, and through a series of rest homes in Connecticut and Massachusetts. A deeply religious woman, Emily Morgan at one time estimated that she had provided summer respite for more than 11,000 wage-earning women and girls. The first rest home was Saybrook's Heartsease, which opened in the 1880s.

Miss Morgan relieved Peter and Bertha of some of the burden of supporting Helen and Harriet by sending them money while they were at Hampton. Helen was the first beneficiary. "The letter came from Miss Morgan yesterday [July 12, 1899] with the order for fifteen dollars, so my account is all square. It was a great relief to me, for I could not help feeling a little uneasy about leaving it open for so long a time. . . . Miss Morgan asked me in her letter if I would go up to Beulahland [in Blandford, Massachusetts] during the conference as I did last year. It will be from Aug. 4 to the 13th inclusive. I shall probably wait for a letter from you or papa on the subject before I answer her letter, so do not delay."

Helen and Harriet worked in Miss Morgan's summer homes to repay some of the money. "The work in her houses is usually light enough to afford the assistant considerable rest besides giving the advantage of good climate, milk and eggs, etc. and the opportunity of making valuable friends. In my case this is an especially strong point," Helen noted. Harriet rested and worked at Beulahland, located in the Berkshires in Blandford, Massachusetts, during the summer before she died. In 1906 Bertha wrote to Louise in New York, "You are now enjoying what Lou and I used to at the United Workers. is there anything that can beat *white*."

Miss Morgan supplemented the money with gifts of clothing to all of the James women. In December 1908 she sent Helen "a most elegant brown silk suit, a pongee [silk with a knotty weave] and lace shirt waist, belts, collars and three pairs of gloves, all almost new. As I handled them, I could have cried; I know how she loves pretty things and what pleasure she takes in color. To think again that she must go into black, which saddens her, is very hard."

Helen spent almost six months at Miss Morgan's Putnam Elms in Brooklyn, Connecticut, recovering from surgery in 1909. "Miss Morgan wrote me a bit of the history of this house. Her great-grand father, Godfrey Malbone was the largest slave holder in the state. In this house are spinning wheels on which the slaves spun flax for their own garments, and in the church belonging to the estate, a gallery where they sat. In this family, states Miss Morgan, they were well treated, finally freed and are buried in the family plot with a stone to mark the spot."

Despite its horrific past, the house was for Helen a "wonderfully beautiful old house; this house which is a genuine colonial built in 1783 and smacks of large hospitality in its every corner and cupboard." And of cupboards there were many, "under the stairs, beside the fireplace, in the hallways, behind doors, just everywhere. And rooms without end," which took her several days to learn to navigate without getting lost. The grounds, too, occasioned comment:

This morning I walked cautiously into a field for a nearer view of my returned friends—the red-winged blackbirds, who were holding a conference in near by trees, where lo, before I was anywhere near them, one gave the alarm and they were off to the margin of a pond below. Their cheerful call, the running of the streams, buzzing of the occasional flies and the sight of a brave butterfly give warning that winter must be over. . . . Sunday we had a long long drive through the country which is redolent with the breath of Spring. We gather pussy willows. . . . Our center piece on the dining table is most attractive; the little soft warm pussys are so friendly.

Miss Morgan's guests included Negroes and women who wanted to help them. The "housemother" at the Elms was a Miss Graham who had taught at a school for colored students in Beaufort, South Carolina. The daughter of the Hatches, a wealthy local family who visited the Elms, "is a charming women who goes to Virginia winters to a School for Negroes in which she is interested." A Dr. Rice from "New port" came to care for Miss Morgan at another of her summer homes: "Last night she gave Miss Morgan hot compresses and took care of her. Miss Morgan is not incapacitated from work, but does need rest and care. She gives up so little that one hardly knows she is not well." The doctor was a graduate of "Ann Harber" University, Helen said. "I should like to know her, but probably shall not as she is most reticent and retiring.

I have made several 'bolts' at her, but with little success. Each time I have rebounded like a rubber ball thrown against a hard surface. She is not at all attractive in appearance nor dress. She does not seem to know how to make the best of such blessings as she is endowed with. Withal, a good physician."

Holyrood, the home just south of the New Hampshire border in South Byfield, Massachusetts, became a permanent religious retreat. Helen stayed there for the first time in 1906, and her first task was to cook and serve dinner to Miss Morgan, her brother, and his family. The menu consisted of soup "in tins," baked potatoes, chops and ice cream. "This entire trip as been one of the most delightful surprises of my life. Miss Morgan is playing *Lady Bountiful* to perfection, and it is most soothing to weary me." She and her "delightful companion" had lunch at the train station in Boston and took the trolley for a brief tour that included a stop at the library, "where rather carefully we studied the mural decorations," John Singer Sargent's frieze of "The Prophets" and "Sir Galahad." After a two-hour trip, they arrived to stay in "one of the dearest little cottages you can imagine. Furnished fresh and new throughout it is a phantom of delight."

Miss Morgan impressed Helen with her generosity throughout their stay. "Best of all we take our meals in the dining hall where I sit at Miss Morgan's left and am her friend *Miss James*. Think what a delightful surprise to be so free, practically her guest. She gives me the money and sends me sight seeing. Friday I went to Newburyport, and yesterday to Haverhill, Whittier's old home, lying among the hills which over look the beautiful Merimack River. This was a long long trip costing 40c. This A.M. I went to the old church in Newburyport with Miss Morgan where we heard a most excellent sermon by Bishop Drent (I think)."

Louise also became the beneficiary of Miss Morgan's generosity. A letter arrived from the family's other major benefactor, Mary B. Lewis, as Louise was about to graduate from pharmacy school in March 1908:

This morning when I went down to breakfast I met Miss Morgan at the door! at 7.30 a.m.! With a big box. She had just learned through Miss Pratt, to whom I had written that you needed a white dress & immediately she produced it. I am sending it this morning by Express.

It may need some alterations, but I think probably little change will be necessary, & if you iron it out, it will look quite fresh & pretty. I have put in a few other things, just to fill up the box. I also enclose check for $70.00 which will carry you through the year.

Miss Morgan hopes you can come to her country house to work out the $25.00 you owe her & I think you had better do so unless a better position is offered at once. The air up there will do you good. You can pay back my 25.00 as you are able to earn it, but don't let Bertha do any more for you. She has done enough. I know you argue with her about that.

Please let me know if you receive the check & the box promptly & write Miss Morgan before too long what she is to expect.

Bertha's subsequent letter instructed Louise in two precepts: the need to acknowledge gifts with detailed thank-you letters and the importance of absolute discretion in dealing with family members:

How are you. happier in mind I know. Miss Lewis is sending you a graduating outfit. The gown will fitting to you. . . . And she says it was a very expensive ready made. Miss Emily Morgan sent that, each she Miss Morgan loan you $25. apiece the club gave you $20.

Now money with Peter and I is scarce as hens teeth, and with every one else. so be so careful with every penny. Pay Mr. Harloe $25, and pay your back board and some board ahead, so you will have some on hand. but be careful with every dollar. Miss Morgan wants you to go to one of her houses, and pay her $25. that way. Miss Lewis will wait later for hers.

But as it is some time off until July, Miss Morgan's houses do not open until then. Be sure and write both ladies when you get to it describe the box Miss Lewis sent you for I know it is O.K. Lucky girl you. Lucky people we. What a relief off my mind, you do not know.

Keep ac. of every dollar paid out. it is some time to May 30, and it will mean more than that $70 to carry you back to Say Brook. take good care of your self, dear child. . . .

Don't write a word to Papa or any one about the $70. it is none of their
business. It makes me sick to think of their negligence.

Louise might have needed a reminder to write thank-you notes, but
Bertha was convinced that her youngest sister was otherwise in excellent
company in New York. "What a fine social to meet all of those people,"
she wrote. "Peter says you won't know how to act if you return to
Hartford society, after what you get now."

Louise graduated that spring and lived briefly in Hartford, where she
opened the first drugstore owned by a Negro. She then returned to Saybrook, where she stayed with the Lanes until 1920, when Peter turned the
business over to her. The Lane family moved to a house about a mile from
the store, and Peter returned to work at Sisson's Pharmacy in Hartford.
Bertha continued to operate her businesses. Beautiful Linens for Beautiful
Homes was so successful that she hired several women. She received letters from the wives and widows of miners in Appalachia saying that
but for the work that Bertha sent during the Depression, their families
would have starved. After she retired, Bertha lived in Saybrook until
her death in 1956. Peter lived long enough to see his daughter Ann Petry
become a best selling novelist and to greet his granddaughters, Helen's
daughter, Anna Houston Bush, and Ann's daughter, Elisabeth Ann Petry.

Chapter 3

THE WANDERER

Willis H. James changed names, addresses, and jobs so often his family frequently lost track of him. He carried his father's first name, but he was not a junior, nor was he the oldest son. Charles Howard James, son of Anna Webb, was thirteen years old when Willis was born. Based on the letters he left behind and his frequent disappearances, Willis chose to be elusive—a ladies man and a con man, one not predisposed to hard work if he could avoid it. In short, Willis was the black sheep in the James family. Photographs taken in his later years show a serious individual with light skin and a long face—traits he inherited from his mother.

Though Willis disappeared for long periods, the bare outline of his life is not difficult to trace. He attended school in Hartford and in the fall of 1899 enlisted in the U.S. Army. Within three months he had shipped out for the Philippines, where he spent a year and half fighting his way through the jungles. Willis lived briefly in New York after his discharge, but he soon changed his name to Leon (L. J.) St. Clair and began to wander. He traveled up and down the East Coast, working as a waiter in hotel dining rooms and in railroad dining cars. His wanderings took him west to Chicago and south to Florida, with stops in between. Summer often found him working at resort hotels in New York State. In the winter he went south, including the trip to Georgia where he was attacked by bloodhounds, jailed, and threatened with lynching. The one consistency in Willis's otherwise unstable life was his continued devotion to Bertha and his little sister Louise.

Before he enlisted in the Army, Willis worked briefly for Uncle Charley Hudson. The James children generally loved their uncle, but Willis did not appreciate Uncle Charley's efforts at discipline: "I received a letter from Mr. Charles T. Hudson of #128 W. 53 St New York City," Willis wrote from the Philippines, "asking me to write to him and also telling me of his troubles, well you know how much trouble I will take to write to him, for I am gifted with a terrible memory and it does not recall the most pleasant of things when I was his cheep helper in New Jersey." Despite this rejection, Uncle Charley kept reaching out to Willis. "The attitude of the Hudson family is beautiful toward Willis," Helen wrote. "It is something that we should be grateful for. He is always welcome in their home and they are glad to see him. While they laugh and joke with him and make him happy they are trying to impress on him the necessity of his doing his duty."

Willis had a caring side, especially when it came to Bertha. Ann Petry wrote in her journal, "He was genuinely fond of her, I think because the other two sisters Lou [Helen] (especially) and Louise tended to look down on him. They went to college, he didn't, he was a wanderer, had lived and worked all over the world." Ann described Willis in a letter: "He was nicknamed Bill. He was a veteran of the Spanish-American War, supposed to have gone up San Juan Hill with Teddy Roosevelt. . . . Became a sergeant, most unusual because black soldiers rarely ever achieved the rank of sergeant in those days. He was a sergeant of Company E, Forty-eighth regiment U.S. Volunteer Infantry who was enlisted on Sept. 26, 1899, . . . to serve for the period ending June 30, 1901, was honorably discharged June 30, 1901. He was made a sergeant March 4, 1900, at La Loma, Manila, Philippine Islands."

In fact, by the time Willis enlisted the Spanish-American War was over. The United States and Spain had signed the Treaty of Paris, and as part of the settlement Spain sold the Philippines to the United States for twenty million dollars, with Guam and Puerto Rico thrown in. U.S. troops spent several years convincing the Filipinos to accept foreign control, which they thought they had escaped with the end of Spanish rule. At first the Filipinos sent regular armed forces against the Americans but soon changed tactics as they shed their uniforms, broke into smaller bands, and waged guerrilla warfare in the mountains and jungles of the central province of Luzon and the outer islands. Historians have called the war in the Philippines "America's first Vietnam," and Willis's accounts of his skirmishes resemble the descriptions of firefights sixty years later, with mules and horses in place of tanks and jeeps. He wrote to his sister from Fort Thomas, Kentucky:

We have got our Regemient full so its full strength 12 Companies and 100 men to the Company, so you can just imagane the crowd of men there is here. We expect to start away for the Phillipines in about a months time. We are all outfited now. We have got the [Krag-Jorgensen repeating] Rifles. It shutes 6 times.

They are drilling the men terrible here 5 drills a day besides a dress parade at night. . . .

We still sleep in tents out doors with small stoves in them to heat them.

Well I will have to bring this to a close as it is near time for guard mount at 4.45. I went on at 4.45 last night and stay till 4.45 to-night the 18th.

Above the salutation of these letters, Willis always included the name of the town where he was stationed, and at the end he was meticulous about writing his entire address. "I remain Your Brother. Will. Address. Corporel W.H. James Co. A Ft. Thomas Ky, 48th Reg." He wrote to his father from aboard ship, "I hope when you get this you will be able to read it as I have hard work to write at all, for the roll of the boat makes it hard. . . . when you write to me address Corp. W.H. James Co. E. 48th U.S.V. Inf. Manilla Phillipine Islands, and be sure to have it very plain and I think I will get it all right."

The Army called up the Forty-eighth Infantry Regiment of U.S. Volunteers, one of two colored regiments, in late 1899 to supplement the

Regular Army. With their white counterparts in the Thirty-eighth through Forty-seventh regiments, the men in the Forty-eighth and Forty-ninth received the best training from top-flight officers. Willis wrote of the constant drills before and after they left Fort Thomas. In *The Philippine War, 1899–1902*, Brian Linn McAllister called the Volunteers among the best troops "man-for-man the United States has ever fielded." A number of the colored troops became officers and non-commissioned officers, though the senior officers were always white. Many Negroes lost their commissions after the war.

Willis was preparing to ship out from Fort Thomas on November 7, 1899, and sent Bertha a brief note from Cincinnati. He asked her to save his letters so he could read them when he got home. "I am sitting on a pile of lumber now writeing this. We are all packed up ready to leave here. We go to Cincicinatta to give a parade and then go aboard the train for San Francisco. I will drop you a postal from large cities on our way there to keep you posted on our route. . . . Friday morning there was four inches of snow here. We liked to froze in our tents." Willis sent two postcards en route to California. One went to his father from Kansas City, Missouri; the other, to Bertha, bore an obscured postmark, "Inroute to coast all well in mountains watching them ship cattle. Bill"

From Utah he wrote that they expected to cover the last seven hundred miles to San Francisco in a day. "This is the wildest country I ever saw. While I am writeing this I can look out at the mountains and see them covered with snow and houses built under the ground where the people get when they have cyclones. We have left the prairie and now we are in the mountains and valleys. You can see tons of snow on the mountains and dead grass in the valleys and thousands of head of cattle grazeing and cow-boys rounding them up. We have two engines on each train to pull us over the mountains." Willis fell in love with his surroundings on the trip west:

We left there on the 7th of the month for here and arrived on the 14th after the finest trip of my life, the finest scenery you [Helen] ever saw something fine. We had to go through 43 miles of snow sheds, over the mountains, where the snow was 2 feet deep and then down in the grand valleys.

We stopped at Kansas City and Denver, Wells Nevada and several western cities and paraded.

The west is simply grand, we saw several wild wolves, cow-boys, Indians.

It seemed like passing from death to life, that is from the cold climate of the north to the sunny paradice of here.

The grass is nice and green, flowers in bloom just like summer of home every thing is nice and well as good as anybody could wish for.

We are in sight of Golden Gate, we can see it from where we camp.

Once settled in San Francisco, Willis started practicing to become a sharpshooter. The Forty-ninth shipped out for Manila on December 2, but the Forty-eighth was delayed because of twenty cases of smallpox. Willis "forgot" to tell Bertha until the crisis had ended. It was his only mention of the illness that had closed the camp. Willis may have treated the illness casually because he was immune, probably from contracting the less severe cowpox as a child.

When Willis wrote again just before Christmas, he demonstrated a flair for the dramatic. It became a skill that he had perfected by the time he wrote his letter from prison. "This is your last letter from me for a long time, as I am laying in my bunk on board the transport Grant now, while writeing this note. We will be to *sea* at midnight on our way to fight. . . . Kiss them all for me. . . . I will have to stop as I am in a hurry and not feeling well. . . . I will tell you where to write in my next, which will be at Honolulu."

The troopship *Grant* sailed on the morning of December 21, 1899, and Willis could not mail another letter until the ship docked in Japan in mid-January. He started to write when they sighted Honolulu, "and I was in hopes that I could mail it there, but they were affected with what they call the black plague and were not allowed to land, and there was no mail taken from the ship." The *Grant* anchored long enough to receive mail and then sailed for Japan to refuel for the final leg of the journey to the Philippines. The trip to the battlefield took nearly as much valor and far more patience than the actual fighting, as Willis told his father in his letter of January 12, 1900:

After a long voyage we ar. here [Japan] safely, only to stay long enough to get coal and water and then we continue on to Mannila. it takes 11 days to go from here to Manilla, our voyage has been something grand.

We were taken from Angel Island in boats over to San Francisco and then marched aboard the transport Grand [Grant], . . . While passing through the Golden Gate we had a grand chance to see the grand scenery on each side, and on each side of the Golden Gate there are large parrot guns commanding the entrance of the bay. After getting out of sight of land it was the same thing over gain every day the sea the blue sea to be seen every- where, now and then a vessel passing by. And Christmas was just the same as the rest of the days and spent in the same manner as all the rest . . . .

The way we go through our routine might interest you and the rest of the family, as follows:

Reveilie, is when we get up in the morning, our bunks are like steamer bunks one over the other, but they are made out of Iron with canvass bottoms. Well after we get up we go and wash and get ready for mess, we eat between decks at tables, after we get seated, the men wait on us. after mess we wash our tins in tanks of hot water and cold water, and then go and get our blankets and hang upon deck so they can air, and while we are doing this there are others cleaning up our sleeping quarters, and then after inspection we can go where ever we want to on deck. I pass all my time reading books and novels. . . . We have been fourteen days now to Japan, and have got 2 more days yet.

The port we are going to is called Yokohoma, tell Louise to look on the map and find out where it is. Then after we leave there we have 9 days sailing before we get to Mannila.

For the past two days we have been in a storm, and tons of water has broken over the deck, and every thing had to be lashed on deck to be kept from getting washed overboard.

About every few hours you can see a whale near the ship, and see whalers out in long boats after them. The weather here is real cold and we wear overcoats, but as soon as we leave here and start south again they say it gets to hot for you.

I am going to mail this at Japan where we are to stay for a week to get coal and to exercise, and I only wish you were here to see the sights. . . .

After you get this tell all that ask about me that I am well, and did not have time to write to them. . . .

Kiss Louise for me and tell her I will bring something home with me from here. If I ever do come for her. As now I am going in all kinds of danger the Lord only knows who returns and who don't. . . .

P.S. getting ready to go ashore, where I am going to visit tea farms and silk mills. We have commenced to [take on] coal and women carry it all in baskets, well this is all Will

Willis always remembered his little sister Louise in his letters. He concluded many "Kiss Louise for me and tell her to be good." He was especially proud of her academic brilliance and of her musical abilities. He grew concerned when he learned that Bertha had to leave Hampton, where she was nursing Harriet, to care for Louise. "I was surprised and sorry that you were called home on account of Louise sickness. and I hope you will give her the best of care that she can get and I hope for a speedy return of good health to her. Kiss her for me and tell her that she must get well." He cherished her letters, too.

Well when you get this kiss dear "Louise," for me and tell her that she has began to forget me, but that will not do. She must write to me once a year at least, she can not expect me to write to every member of the family seperate, as I am willing but do not have the time to do so, as it is hard for me to find time to write once a month to anybody.

How is Louise progressing in her studies, and the most important her music. I am in hopes that she has improved in health by this time. You must look out for her through the winter, and see that she goes properly dressed.

The *Grant* docked in the Philippines on January 25, 1900, and the men went ashore on January 28. They "formed in close order on the main st. of Manila, and then marched ten miles in the interior, where rested and then we were split up by companies. Each camped one mile apart, on the north fireing line." Willis toured the area a few days later: "it is a grand old city and by going down to the bay you can see the holes in the walls of the fort of the city and the recks of the ships that Dewey destroyed."

The regiment established headquarters near the battlefield at La Loma, "in a great large church which the soldiers had a hard fight in takeing it lasting seven days. It is all walled in, and in the wall are large vaults where they bury their dead, and also in the yard they are buried, and you can look in the vaults and see the skeletons and bodies all decayed in them for the U.S. Artilery tore the walls terrible leaveing large holes in them." A few weeks later he sent photographs and told Bertha to be sure to notice the black spots on La Loma Church, holes left by the Sixth Artillery when they shelled in November 1899. He also sent a picture of "a group of us boys taken on top of rifle pit that head is one he just picked up as there is plenty of them laying around and all kinds of bones of the enemy where the native dogs have dug them out of the trenches and cleaned the bones of all the flesh and left them on the surface to bleach." Less gruesome photos included the blockhouse where American troops had taken up a defensive position, a native hut with two women in the window, and a group of officers and men on the march.

The company had little time to adjust to its new surroundings, and Willis was preparing for his first battle when he wrote on February 3, 1900. "Well when you [Bertha] get this I guess we will be through our worst fight, as the enemy are being drove from the south line over to us, and we are getting ready for them. We have two hundred rounds of ball cartridge to the man and each man has a red cross package attached to his belt consisting of bandges and different things for the first aid for the wounded."

Willis's description of the fight did not survive, but he had enough of a taste of battle to write with some anxiety before the next encounter. His company was headed for the trenches seventy miles north of Manila.

He borrowed and modified the lyrics to the Civil War song "Just Before the Battle, Mother" by George Root (the original lyrics are in brackets):

Just before the battle sister [Mother], I am thinking most of you.
While upon the field were watching with the enemy in view
Comrades brave are 'round me waiting [lying]
Filled with thoughts of home and you [God].
For well they know that on the morrow
Some may sleep beneath the sod.
Farewell sister [Mother], you may never;
Look into my face again, [Press me to your breast again]
But [oh,] you'll not forget me sister [Mother].
If I am numbered with the slain
[Oh,] How I long to see you sister [Mother]
And the rest of all [the loving ones] at home
But I'll never leave our flag [banner]
Till in honor I can come
[Tell the traitors all around you
That their cruel words we know,
In very battle kill our soldiers
By the help they give the foe.]
[Hark!] Yes I hear the trumpet [bugles] sounding
Tis the signal of a [the] fight
Now may the Lord [God] protect us, sister [Mother]
As he ever does the right.

Willis and his company survived, and Willis received a battlefield promotion. His first advance in rank had come while the company was still in Kentucky, when he became "corporel of the guard." He told Bertha, "I am bluffing by and I hope I will be able to hold it." Of his second promotion he wrote, "It has been a long time since I wrote to you [brother Charles]. But I have been very busy, and I got promoted to sergeant on March the 5th [1900] and in fact ever since then we have been on the go scouting through the mountains."

Sergeant James and his company received orders to move out two weeks later. Willis was on guard duty when the regimental adjutant rode into camp with an order for the captain, "who sent for me and told me to take five men and report to Lt. Jefferies at the landing at the Pasig River to take charge of the freight, and when I got there there was twenty-five men there waiting orders." In the harbor was the troop ship that was to carry them into battle. Willis supervised the loading of the freight for the battalion, including the officers' luggage: "I had to have it loaded on large cascos what you would call bardges," he told Charles, "and after I got loaded which took all day I had to go over to the Q.M. Dept. and get a Gov. tug to tow us out to the transport Brutus in the bay, where everything had to be hoisted by derrecks and swung in the hole." Company E came aboard on March 23, "last of all came the officers horses and the mules and wagons and it took all day to swing them aboard, we were all ready by night." Boats were not allowed to move about in the harbor after dark, so they did not weigh anchor until daylight the next morning.

Their voyage took them out of Manila Bay, south and east around the Bataan Peninsula, then north into the South China Sea and east again into the Lingayen Gulf to San Fernando de La Union:

We had the worst trip we ever had, for there were no bunks, all we had was the natural iron deck to lay on, and we were crowded and down in the hole was something terrible, but the men kept up noble for the two days and nights sail, for on the morning of the 26th we landed at a small but important town with a beach to it, marked San Fernando De Union, where we landed under great difficulty for we anchored a mile from shore, well the natives came out to the ship on bamboo rafts, and we had to go ashore on them, about 20 men at a time on each till the five hundred were ashore, and then came the worst, that was the horses and freight to get ashore.

We tried all kind of ways but had to give them all up, and go at it right, that was to let them down in the water and then cut them lose and let them go for themselves, well all landed safe but one mule he got drowned about 200 yds from the ship, everything in time landed.

The men received orders to garrison San Gabriel. "It was a hard 20 miles up hill and down and wadeing in rivers and over rice fields, but we got there just the same. Well we took the town and we are stationed there yet," Willis told Charles.

The company remained in San Gabriel and nearby Balaoan for the balance of its tour of duty. Boredom set in almost immediately, but Willis preferred the monotony to the hard march between the towns. He told Bertha that he was assigned to guard duty and he was grateful to miss the march to Balaoan to get paid and inspected.

Willis wrote to Helen while she was at Hampton, but the letter took so long to arrive it had to be forwarded to Hartford, where she had returned for their father's wedding.

The people here do not know the value of our money in fact none at all as they do not need any as they grow their own rice, which is their main diet and raise cotton and make their own clothes, and build their houses without the use of a nail. They use a great deal of fruit such as bananas oranges pineapples coconuts which you can get any place you go. Then there is another race called Nigerotes which wear no clothes at all but a gee string around them, and they live mostley on dogs which they will run down and kill and cook and eat, and we use them for our pack trains, as they can carry 300 lbs on their backs, and that is the only way to move things through the mountains.

What Willis called "Nigerotes" or "Igarotes" were properly the Igarot (or Igorrote) people, who inhabited the mountains of northern Luzon. They became allies of the United States during the war and served as spies and porters in skirmishes with Emilio Aguinaldo's guerrillas. Willis used the term "Igarotes" interchangeably with "Negritos," literally "little black men," also a term for the people who lived along Luzon's east coast.

Though the weapons became more sophisticated and the transport motorized, guerrilla warfare changed little in the sixty years between the skirmishes in the Philippines and the firefights in the mountains and jungles of Vietnam. "The enemy moves in small squads and swoops down on small numbers and captures them, and then run and hide and they are very treacherous you have to watch them very close, and you can not leave camp without carrying your gun with you. We are going father on into the interior in a few days." Willis learned to trust the local residents at his peril and displayed a total lack of sympathy for the Filipinos when he first arrived. "There are 63 thousand of U.S. soldiers here on the Islands. they are about all you see except a few of the native pedlers and chinamen, and they do all of our carteing and heavy work and the Government pays them one dollar per day and they are lazy dogs. You have to guard them to keep them from running away to town. The way they get them is, when ever they want them they go to town and get as many as they want and drive them as they do so many cattle and when they get through with them give them an order on the government for their money."

In the Philippines, Willis adopted the convictions of a growing segment of the American population who believed the nonwhite peoples of the world incapable of self-government. He differed in this regard from others in the colored regiments, more than a few of whom remained in the islands after their discharge. His opinions began to change, however, when he befriended a local boy, and he sent Bertha a snapshot to frame. "The picture of the boy I think a great deal of, for he was a scout of the Ladrones whom we captured one day while out on a scout in the bamboo. that is the way their scouts go through the country they can go through the grass like a snake, and when they locate one of our outposts they will report the strength of it back to their command, and then when they march against these scouts start out ahead and kill of the outposts with their arrows, for they don't make any noise and you don't know where the arrow comes from. Now we have the boy with us and he is very smart."

During his stay in the war zone, Willis made only three brief references to individual deaths among the American troops. Soon after his company arrived in Manila, he participated in a scouting party that went "into the enemys lines 30 priv and 6 non commishon officers and one Lieut." His letter to Bertha was dated February 3, 1900:

We started out before sunrise in the morning and march 7 miles and halted and marched as skirmishers slowly through the bamboo and at 8:30 a.m. was fired on from the tree tops, and we opened fire and it lasted 20 minutes

and then all was still. The enemy retreating into the wood under cover after
they had gone we found that 3 of our men were wound. slightly and 9 of the
enemy was left on the field 5 dead and 4 wounded. Then we continued our
scout and happened till 5:30 p.m. when we were nearing camp there were a
few of the enemy in sight that fled when they saw us advanceing. We ar. in
camp at 8:30 p.m. and just laid our arms down when we heard fireing south
of us, and the General [quarters] was sounded calling us to arms again, and
we staid in line ready to move if we neaded for two hours when they let uss
fall out and go to bed. in the morning we learned that the enemy had
captured a cororpel and four men while out on a patrol along the railroad
and another co. was sent out to recapture them our men and was fired on
and one man was killed.

Two days later a member of company drowned while swimming in
the Pasig River. Willis and a group of men were detailed to dive for his
body. They spent half a day looking but could not recover it. The third
death occurred after the men had moved into the mountains of northern
Luzon Province. Willis began his letter of May 24, 1900, to Bertha,
"I write to you once more from this no man's Country. . . . We have been
suffering terrible here for the want of something to eat, for the rainy season has been and it is hard to get rations out to where we are. On the
morn of the 15th [of May] we had a hard fight in the mountains near a
town called Mantauck where we lost one of our best men Corp.
Washington shot through the stomach and we had a litter made for him
out of bamboo and had four igarotes and carry him to camp 18 miles
over the most rugged mountains, and in a terrible rain, and on our way
to camp we came near loseing our Capt. by getting drowned in one of
the innumberal river we had to swim."

Willis generally protected his sisters from the worst of his suffering
and saved the more gruesome details for letters to the men, though he
had to know the entire family read every letter. He treated Charles to
one of his more graphic descriptions of survival in the mountains:

On the 2nd of April the Col. send a native guide to camp for 40 men, and
they were to follow him so Capt. sent five sets of fours under me to report to

Lt. Johnson Troop M 3rd Cal. I followed the guide to another town in the mountains in which the troop was waiting for me. After getting my instructions I moved my men in a column of files around the left of the base of the mt. the insurgents had taken to the mts when the calvery entered the town, for the dogs alarmed them. . . .

We had poor success killing only two and capturing four, with guns, . . . the Lt. told me that it was always hard to enter a town and surprise the enemy for the dogs were as good as a sentinel on post . . . so before I left him he told me he would send some men out some day to kill off the dogs.

On the 5th of Ap. Serg. Warwick senior to me and myself took 24 men and went out on our own hook to scout a little . . . after dinner while I burnt several shacks, . . . I got word that something was wrong so I moved out with one synad of men under a Corp to the left and Sergt Warwick takes the right, and makes our way slowley up the river bed till we came to the place where we had to ford it to get to the town so we united forces and were crossing together always keeping in a column of files, when about half way across we were fired on from the mountains. We took shelter and returned the fire to good affect and had some fun for a while, but we never had any loss. . . . One afternoon a detachment of Calvery rode into camp on their way . . . to kill off the dogs, so Capt. sent me and five privates. . . . We going over a trail and entering the town at its rear and then we had a dog killing contest. Each man seeing who could make the best shot, when we got through we counted up and found 86 dogs shot all kind of ways. So now the town is about free from them.

Burning of shacks—people's homes—represented a change in the official policy of "benevolent pacification" applied at the start of the war. The U.S. military leadership issued orders to punish civilians who supported Aguinaldo and his men, although "dog killing contests" were not standard operating procedure. Constant privation pursued Willis and his company in the mountains. Hunger, illness, and lack of proper clothing and shelter did far more damage than the elusive enemy. "The heat here is something terrible from 5:00 A.M. till 6:00 P.M.," he wrote from San Gabriel in April, "but still we have to tramp through the mountains hunting the insurgents, and getting something to eat where ever we can get it." Compounding their suffering from the brutal heat, he and forty-two others in the company had mountain fever. They had been left behind while the rest went out on a ten-day scouting mission. Nearby the Fifteenth Regiment and a troop of the Third Cavalry "had a three days fight with the insurgents kill three hundred and odd and captureing a quantity of ammunition and rifles."

Willis recovered from the fever, but just as the rainy season began in earnest the company made a torturous march from San Gabriel to Balaoan. "We left camp and came here 38 miles on [May] 21st and the heat and the long march told terrible on the men. . . . Oh, if you only knew the hard time we have of it here you would be surprized but we have to stand it like a man and say nothing. I am about sick now while writeing this and have just got here from the hills with 30 men." Willis recovered again, and the company saw "plenty of fight and scouts and hard work" over the next month. When he wrote on July 4 from San Francisco de la Union, about twenty-two miles from San Fernando, he told Charles not to be angry about the delay between letters:

I have not had the time for they have been marching us all but to death. We have been in the mts. for days in and days out without proper food or clothes, when we left camp all was well, but in five days our shoes commenced to give out, and the rations also was running short.

Well in two weeks time we were barefooted and was living on the country getting whatever we could to eat.

We have everything packed by a tribe called Nigarotes. They don't wear clothes at all only a small piece of cloth around their loins.

Well if you could have seen us at the time you would have laughed for you could not have told us from the natives, for our clothes was all torn and some with one shoe on and some with know shoes at all, and in some cases the men had a cloth on like the natives. This is the way we went through the mts., and when we would sight a barrio or a small village, we would form a skirmish line and advance on it, often times we would be able to get up to the houses before being discovered but in most cases the dogs would warn the people before we could enter it.

In one town we entered we got one brass cannon and a large quantity of
ammunition and about two hundred bolos [machetes], and about 40 of the
enemy.

Then after sending them in with the scouts, we push on just the same
looking for more game. Now and then we would come across a native cow
and that was a glad moment for we knew that it was ours for there would be
know way for its escape. And our packers would kill a native poney, and kill
it the same way we would a beef and cook and eat it, they think it a great
treet.

Despite the lack of proper food and equipment, the men were expected
to maintain military discipline. "There is nothing new for four months,
and the men are a sight to behold in their rags, but we are soldiers from
our hearts," he told his father. Willis was tired and sore from a hard five-
day march earlier in September as the American troops pursued insurgents who were headed toward Manila, "and my God they marched us
nearly to death." By the third day, half the men were barefoot and had to
be carried by their fellows. On the fourth day they began their return to
camp. They halted for the night "and the men dropped down where they
were and was glad to have a chance to lay down. We had a cup of strong
coffee and some rice which we got from the natives and after eating there
was an outpost put out and the boys laid down in the trail and went to
sleep and at 3.00 in the morning the Sergt of the guard called us to get our
coffee, and at 3.45 a.m. we were on the march again making the last 29
miles that day before going into our own camp, where we are now and the
men are all played out and getting their feet bandged up by the Hospital
man. My feet are sore but still I have to go on guard tonight just the same."

Willis bore his sore feet and poor rations with stalwart resignation, for
hunger and rags were "a soldier's lot." What he found unbearable was the
isolation from the outside world. He had been in the Philippines for about
six weeks when he told Bertha that the last letter he had received from her
was December 8, 1899, "and I have not heard yet if you rec my warrant
yet or any money for me. I want you to have that warrant put in a nice
frame and hung it in the parlor where I can see it if I came back to the

States." He did not receive his first letters from the family until he had been in the Philippines for almost nine months. Bertha complained, but by the time the captain replied, Willis had started receiving his mail.

He nevertheless continued to feel that his family was neglecting him. As a letter to Bertha indicated, army life had convinced Willis that friendships were stronger than family ties. His father's impending wedding added to the pain, as he told Bertha, "I just got through reading your letter and was not surprised in hearing that pa was going to get married again, as I heard so before. There is not much news here everything is about the same here plenty of fight and scouts and hard work. . . . I got a letter from G. Grant and Mr. Bray and Alvord and was glad to hear from them all and to know the news in general. I get more news from strangers than I do from home all I get from home don't amount to much."

The difficulty in writing letters compounded his frustration. Pens and paper were scarce even in Manila. He wrote his March 15 letter on newsprint-quality graph paper embossed with the word "Amistad" in the upper left corner. The June 1 letter was on letterhead from the General Assembly of Ohio, Senate Chamber, Columbus. In September, he used poor-quality lined paper that he told his father cost twenty-five cents. He said he would write to Peter when paper and stamps became available again.

Stamps disappeared altogether once the company left Manila. He told Charles and Helen, "I have got to send this without a stamp for there is know place you can buy them for love nor money." Willis wrote "A Soldier's Letter" in the upper left corner of the envelope of his May 24 letter to Bertha. It was postmarked in San Fernando on May 26 and arrived in Hartford on July 5 with two cents postage due. The recipients had to pay for most of his letters from then on, though Bertha did send him stamps. "I just got your letter with the stamps, and they were all right, I was glad to receive them as they are the only stamps in camp and now I will write more than I ever did." The letter arrived with postage due.

Willis craved news of the world, as well as of his family, and soon after he arrived in La Union, he begged for reading material. He asked Charles for "an old paper now and then or a clipping of anything doing." He acknowledged that Bertha "did send me one paper and I wish you would send me one every week. I send you the money to get them with if it ain't to much work for you I wish you would send me a [Hartford] Times and [Boston] Globe every week." His friend G. Grant sent two copies of the Philadelphia "Colored Tribune and I found several articles of good news in them and he also sent me a copy of the Post with that letter of mine in it." Otherwise, all he had to read were a guard manual and drill regulations. His letter of July 4 to Bertha included a substantial reading list: the *Police Gazette Sporting Annual*; Jesse James stories; *the Yankee Doodle Literary Sampler of Prose, Poetry, and Pictures; Nick Carter Weekly; Diamond Dick Library Weekly; the Standard*; and *the Army & Navy Journal.* "Now have Pete get them and have them mailed the same day you get this letter, as I am dyeing for something to read. and a copy of the times. Now Bertha please send them at once, and you will be doing your brother a great favor. . . . P.S. Wrap them well and also $2.00 worth of stamps." She could either pay for them out of his savings, he said, or he would mail her the money in his next letter.

Willis's desire to leave the war zone and return to the States escalated in the fall of 1900. In mid-September he told Bertha that he wished they were leaving tomorrow, "for all of the men are run down from service and the lack of good food, but I realey ought not to complain for it is what a soldier is expected to go through while he is over on this Island." He anticipated a discharge before July 1901.

A few days later he told his father, "Well by the time you get this election will be getting warm, and I wish I was there to let my first vote for President go." William McKinley was campaigning for his second term as president with Theodore Roosevelt as his running mate against challenger William Jennings Bryan. McKinley swept to victory, despite loss of the southern vote and a small but vocal opposition to his administration's imperialist moves in the Philippines. His assassination in September 1901 brought the Roosevelt to the White House. At age twenty-three, Willis was eligible to vote for the first time but could not because absentee ballots did not become available for military personnel for nearly seventy-five years.

Willis grew increasingly bored and was disappointed not to be part of the first group of soldiers returning home in November, "but we will soon follow some old time," he promised. Amazingly, however, he was able to visit with a friend from home. He told Bertha that he was "never so much surprised in my life as to see" Morris Holden of Hartford, a member of the Forty-ninth Volunteers, who walked into camp in Kentucky. They encountered each other again in Manila and met in La Union Province, where Holden told Willis he had been in several "hard fights." Willis gave Holden the Hartford papers and "every time he comes over we have to talk over old times together and the time passes away very quickly. He is looking well, and getting along all right I guess, he is detailed with a mounted detachment here." The two met nearly every day.

Another acquaintance contacted Willis around the same time. "I was surprised the other day to get a letter from Dick Wilson, you remember him. I am sure you do, well he is in Co. 'G.' 25th US Inf. [another colored unit sent to the Philippines] and stationed about eighty miles south of us, and he says that things are quiet there, and that he is doing nicely and he wished to be rememberd to all of his friends when I wrote home."

The last of Willis's letters from the Philippines to Bertha was dated February 12, 1901. Guerrilla activity was beginning to wind down, and U.S. troops captured Aguinaldo about a month after Willis wrote.

At this writeing we are still stationed right here in the same place, and there are know signs of us moving, although the Col. has told the Capt to be ready to pack up at any time to move, but we do not know where we will go to when we do move, but we are in hopes that it will be Manila, the way things look now It don't seem possible that we can get home by June 30th this year, for they are moveing the troops very slow. I would not be surprised if they mustered this Regiment out over here, but It will not affect me any as I intend to stay over here as it is, for I have put in for my discharge two months ago and expect to be able to get it. I have not decided yet as to what course I will pursue, there is such a thing as joining a division of civilian scouts or I might take an notion and go to Cape-Town, South Africa and see what I can get a hold of through that country, but never the less, keep on writeing to me and I will let you know as to all of my movements no matter where I go to.

Willis's motives for enlisting in the Army had not been entirely patriotic. Before he left Hartford, he had been courting a young woman named Mamie Boatwright, who became pregnant in the spring of 1899. By the time Howard James was born on February 14, 1900, Willis was half a world away, hunkered down near a bullet-ridden church outside Manila. (Howard grew up in Westchester County, New York, and lived in and worked in Mamaroneck. He was killed by a bus in Pelham on December 24, 1944.)

Willis enlisted on September 26, 1899, probably after he learned that Mamie was pregnant. Once in the Army, he did not waste time seeking new female companionship. He wrote his first surviving letter to Bertha, postmarked October 20, 1899, from Newport, Kentucky:

I got your letter and was glad to hear from you, but you know that it is hard for me to write to any body. And besides I am getting ready to get married. I will send you a photo of her as soon as she has some taken.

I wish I was not so far from home and I would try and have some of you here at the wedding. Harry Plato thinks he has got the leading Belle of Hartford, but she will have to stay indoors when my wife gets there. . . .

Now when I marrie I am going to let her stay here in Cinn. Ohio with her folks till I come out of the Army. Then I am going to stay here or Chicago.

Willis never left evidence that he actually married. In a letter to Bertha from the Philippines, he referred to his "lady friend" and said, "The picture of the young lady was fine and was just what I wanted." He told his brother Charles, "I send you a small photo of the *fairy* to see if you can get it put on a button pin and send it to me. Bertha will give you money to pay for it. When you write tell me what you think of her."

After his discharge the family occasionally mentioned "Willie's wife and children." At one point, his father seemed encouraged: "I received a letter from him yesterday [January 11, 1902] his wife has been quite sick ever sense her child was born I was delighted to know that he has turned over a new leaf he has become a good christian man and has joined the church and I thank God for that. and will do what I can to encourage him in it. I shall comply with his request answer his letter tomarrow." No one ever referred to her or the children by name except for two brief references in Bertha's letters to Louise: "Leon is seriously ill. How sorry I am for Mamie. she is alone with him, quarantined." And, "A letter from Mamie this A.M. Leon is sick abed with the measles. She is home taking care of him."

Willis and Mamie lived together in New Rochelle, New York. Willis wrote Bertha a brief note in May 1902 reporting that their cousin Lottie Hudson was ill and that he was considering taking a job in Englewood, New Jersey. He abandoned his family three months later:

My Dear Sister—
You must excuse such a bolde letter from a rank stranger, but I am yours brothers wife of corse he have writen & toll you all a bout me and my condition if we are strangers now I hope we wont always be I hope when these few lines reaches you thay will finde you and all quite well as thay leave me not fealing so well at present for I am real misebal to day for I am looking most any time to be sick. have you heard from or sean any thing of Will he went of Tuesday after noon & said he was going up there & up to Hartford he did not tell me he was going up there he toled the ladie where he was working & I haven't heard a word from him since he left here in the after noon & he said he would be back to diner a bout half past seven oclock & that is all I knew of him. have you writen to him since he was up there & if you did where was his letters address to so if you know or here any thing a bout him will you please let me know for I am just heartbroken over the way he have treated me here just at the needed time all be four he have ben just as good to me as he could be I thought may be he went up there be cause he have lost his job. You must excuse poor riting and over look all mistakes for I am all most woried to death a bout him I doant know what have happen him my two rings that he left up there when he was there will you please

take care of them untill I am all right a gan he said he left them up there on
the comode when he washed his hands when he was up there last month so
will you please let me here from you & will you pleas tell me some kinde of
advice so I will know just what to doo I must close as I am all tired & worn
out Good by with love to yo all from your sister in law Mamie James

Bertha destroyed the remaining letters about Mamie and the children, leaving only hints. "I am sorry for Willis in his affliction," Helen wrote in early 1905. "I trust that in his sympathy for his wife his heart may be touched. God often turns many a man to the right by laying his hand heavily upon him in sorrow. Often I think if many had to suffer and battle more they would come in nearer to appreciating their blessings. We who have stood the storm know what it means." Willis had domestic problems again in 1907. "I am verry sorry for Willie's wife that it is tow bad that he is not more of a man than he is," their father wrote to Louise. "I was in hopes that his experance in the South would of changed him."

Willis had other personal reasons for not wanting to return home after the war. He wanted to see his family, but his father's marriage made him reluctant to return to Winter Street. "Allow me to congratulate you on the swell wedding you had," he told his father. "I had a letter from Bertha and she said it was a very swell afair, and I am glad that kept the James name up by giving a grand spread." But it was to Bertha that he expressed his true feelings:

This pay day I will send twenty dollars home the same as before to help
me when I get back, for Mrs. James I do not know so I might have to
paddle my own canoe, so I thought I might as well have a dollar enough
to keep me for a while, for I might not be able to stay home and might
not be welcome when I get there, and I know when I do get there that
I will not stand to sleep on the floor as I used to do before I left home, and
I want you to tell me in your next letter your view of the matter whether I
will have a room at home or not, and if I will not I will not come home
at all, but go to Chicago and stay, and only come home to get my money
and to see you and not to stay, but to go away again, for I would not like to

come home after going through what I have and have to get the
cold shoulder again and have things unplesant. You can find out from
Papa by talking how I stand at home and let me know in your next letter.

A discontented Willis returned to Hartford during the summer. He told his family that he planned to re-enlist, and Harriet told Bertha, "I am rather sorry because I had hoped after so long a period of hardships that he would settle down and get some real happiness out of life." Instead Willis moved to New Rochelle. He continued to visit and write to Bertha, but he lost track of Helen, who had been in Hawaii for more than four months before he realized it.

Not long after she arrived in Hawaii, Helen asked him to send Harriet ten dollars to help with her school expenses, but he never did. Later he offered to help pay Helen's college tuition. "What a lovely encouraging letter from Willis! I shall write him soon, thanking him for his encouragement," Helen wrote to Peter as she was planning to enroll in college. "My prayer is that I may succeed, for then can I through deeds express my gratitude to relatives and friends for all of their good thoughts towards me." There is no indication that Willis ever gave Helen anything but good thoughts.

"Nothing has pleased me more than Willie's offer of aid," Helen wrote to Bertha. "Tell him I am going to try it, and am glad to know that he is willing to help me. It will only be in case of need that I should send to him or any one of you for money. Even then I intend to pay it all back." A few weeks later, she told him that a loan of five dollars a month would be a great help. "Probably by the time he needs it, I will be able to return [it]. Then it would be much appreciated by him."

After his family bailed him out of the Georgia prison, he wrote his first letter to Louise on February 12, 1906, from Waycross, Georgia:

It is a pleasure of life to write you again that I am a free man at last, but
sorry to say a sick man. But it is a great thing to have your liberty no matter
what your condition is. I've been free a week last Saturday. Doctor here which
is treating me and giving me a place to eat and sleep. I have to work in his

offiece and do handy things when I am able to pay him for my treatment.
It cost me just $51.20 for my release, and father sent me $17.00 of it which
I was very thankfull for but Louise as sure as God is my Judge I never
received a dollar in my life I cherrished so much as I did the $2.00 you sent
me just to think of you who has to look sharp for a five cent piece sending
me $2.00. I am more than thankfull to you for it but this will be one time
that you will not lose anything by it as no matter where I am I will have
you in mind and do something for you that is after I am so as to get about
the Doctor says I will be able to start to New York by the 1st of April and
I hope that I am. Give Bertha and Pete my fond regards, and tell Pete he
is selfish in not writeing to me he can write now as I am a free man at last.

Tell Bert and Pete I was very greatful for their kind intentions toward me
I will close with lots of true love towards all from your Wild Brother Bill

Willis wrote next to Peter on letterhead of the Beach Investment
Company, "Authorized Capital, $300,000 Home Offices Waycross, Ga.,
Dealing in Real Estate, Timbered Lands, Naval Stores, Stocks, Bonds,
Etc." Willis reported that his health was "improveing very rapid." The
doctor had advanced the departure date to mid-March, "He wants me to
stay here with him but with God's help I will leave the south if I have to
walk from here. I sit down here nights and ponder of the past, and I have
made up my mind that my roaming days are over and I must lay them on
the shelf." With that pledge to change his ways, Willis was preparing the
family for another request for money. It came two weeks later in a letter
to Bertha:

I write this time to you as usual to beg you to send me something to get
away from here with, as the $14.00 I paid the Dr. to treat me till April was
all I had.

And he has hinted several times to me that it was getting near the 1st.
now to be plain so as you can understand me, I am going to leave here on
Sunday April 1st 1906 money or no money. . . .

Now I know well I have not done what was right towards any of my
people in the past, but they forget that I am of the same flesh and blood and

that I have been in a very bad fix and also broke intirely down and unable to help myself. and then they refuse to help me mend my health. But thank God I am a great deal stronger than what I was. Now Bertha I was aware of your expence and did not look for any help from you when I was in trouble but now I want to get enough to get away with from you. I told you what the fare to N.Y. was I can get from here there for $18.00 now if you cant spare that amount do what you can just so I get out of this country. I will pay interest on your money for this summer I work and not travel.

Now Bertha do not read this and lay it down and forget about it and me, but answer at once and let me know what you can do, for leave the 1st I will just as I say, but I am afraid of the country to rough through it.

Willis left Waycross soon after. For the James family the town came to symbolize all the fear, hatred, and evil that the South had imposed on slaves and their descendants from before the Civil War. The story evolved that Willis had been arrested because Waycross was a "sundown town," where Negroes could not legally be present after the sun set. In other words, the family believed he had been arrested for a curfew violation. From that time forward, when family members had to go to the South, they avoided white people whenever possible. Ann Petry, who traveled all over the country to teach and lecture, refused all invitations to venture farther south than Hampton, Virginia.

Though he said he wanted to head North, Willis lacked money to return to Connecticut. Instead he went to Jacksonville, Florida, and wrote that he had received two dollars from Louise and had "borrowed $1.00 from a colored mail carrier to help me to get here where I arrived this a.m. in a bad fix." He wanted to buy one of the inexpensive fares offered to the waiters headed north for the summer, either a $12.50 steerage ticket on the Clyde Line to New York or the Merchants and Miners Transportation Company "by the way of Savannar by rail V.S. boat from there to Phila V.S. rail from there to N.Y. for $15.00 2nd class. Now Bertha please send me a ticket or the money so as I can get back north again." And he asked Peter for a loan that he would try to repay within sixty days. "Sure you know you have never lent me since I have been a man so give me a chance to get back north again. I intend to make a good summer and your money is sure. Now I asked you to answer last letter but you never done so." Willis added that he had been denied a waiter's job at the Windsor Hotel because he was not strong enough, but the head waiter had paid a week's rent on a room for him. He concluded, "Now Bertha please do not forget that I am your brother and help me to go home. Send me a ticket or money and I will leave at once for home. . . . Please try and get my ticket here by the 12th before my room rent is up and I have to leave here." Willis never repaid any of the money, and Bertha and Louise considered their contributions gifts, not loans.

Though he had promised to stop roaming, Willis seemed incapable of staying in one place. The poor relationship with his father meant he could not live at 6 Winter Street. His work dictated an itinerant life, as he waited on tables in fancy resort hotels from New York State to Georgia, including the Hotel Oglethorpe in Brunswick, and in railroad dining cars between the East Coast and Chicago. To save on travel expenses, he hopped freights when he was able. As he told Bertha, "Now if I was as strong as of old and had one dollar in my pocket I would jump out here and ride a train on top or on the front of it and feel at home but as it is I have nothing to make a start with."

Over the years, Willis made a point of returning from his wanderings to visit Bertha and her family in Saybrook. He told my mother, Ann Petry, the story of Ma Jones, which she used in *The Narrows*. She was "an old black woman who ran a rooming house in Chicago. During the 1919 race riots a mob of white men broke down the door of her house. Ma Jones stood at the top of the stairs with a shotgun in her hand pointing it down at them and saying quietly, not shouting, 'I'm goin' to kill the first one of you who puts his white feet on my stairs!'" According to my mother, "Uncle Bill said nobody moved. Nobody."

Willis entertained the family in this fashion until his death in 1940 in the veterans' hospital in Hines, Illinois. He is buried in Cypress Cemetery in Old Saybrook, Connecticut.

Chapter 4

CONSUMED BY LIFE

Harriet Georgiana James's brief life was a study in youthful energy, joie de vivre, and pathos. Consumption took her before she turned twenty-three, but while she lived, lack of faith in herself caused her greater anguish. Not long before she died, she wrote to Bertha from school, "I wonder and wonder why it is these people are so kind and good to me?" The answers came in letters of condolence from the faculty, staff, and students, who adored her.

When Harriet enrolled at Hampton Institute and Normal School, it had been open for thirty-two years, training freed slaves and their descendants as teachers and offering education in practical skills. Brigadier General Samuel Chapman Armstrong, a commander of colored troops during the Civil War, ran the Freedmen's Bureau on a spit of land at the confluence of Chesapeake Bay, Hampton Creek, and James River in southeastern Virginia. Here he secured 159 acres to establish what became Hampton Institute. Armstrong and his most famous pupil, Booker T. Washington, soon became the targets of independent Negro thinkers who called the school "a slave pen and literary penitentiary." They believed that emphasizing manual labor and morality over intellectual pursuits hindered the improvement of the race.

The climate of the school, however, allowed a modest young woman like Harriet to blossom. She and her beau led the grand march at the

New Year's social in 1902. "(I hate this part of it) I heard that I was the belle of the occasion—unusual among so many pretty girls," she wrote. Except for the group photograph, no pictures of Harriet survive. Panic about her finances frequently overwhelmed Harriet, but her despair never stopped her from making friends or becoming a favorite of the staff. Her sister Helen shared the opinion of others at Hampton when she wrote, "The school is in love with her and teachers and students alike agree that she is a very prepossessing young woman and are anxious to keep her among them." They succeeded only briefly, as illness forced Harriet to leave school in January 1901. She returned in the fall of 1901 to a warm welcome that she said "made me believe that here I was quite at home."

Harriet James, born May 10, 1879, became the housekeeper for the family after Bertha married and Helen went to Hampton. Harriet followed Helen shortly after her father remarried and quickly made a favorable impression. After her death, their friend Helen Virginia wrote, "Sometimes I would find her in her room working on beautiful baskets or taking a siesta preparatory to going out in the evening, or in the classroom, where I would sit and watch her go ahead of the others in reasoning and expression, then receive a solemn wink and the assurance (written on a slip of paper) that she had not opened her book to study for two days. All her teachers were proud of her and showed her off on every possible occasion."

Harriet's playful, rebellious side manifested itself in various ways, though she was more likely to confide in Helen Virginia than in her sisters: "Tonight . . . I left D. Science building at 7.45 AFTER DARK and came home ALL ALONE the size of letters can assure you what an enormous thing that was to do at Hampton. Miss Young was entering the library building when I passed (question) 'Well what are you doing out ALONE at this time of night?' (answer) 'I believe any woman can safely cross the grounds at night alone'—Entrance Va. Hall—Miss Barclay 'Well what is this girl going out at this time?' 'Not out, I'm in now Miss B.' I fully believe that they will learn that I am a woman some time before I leave here."

Harriet never became a good correspondent. More than once she apologized to Bertha after a long silence, and Harriet described one letter as "quite unsatisfactory to me but it is a letter & perhaps a poor one is better than none at all." She preferred working and playing when she was not confined to bed with recurrent bouts of illness or fatigue.

When she was well enough, Harriet wove baskets to pay school expenses. She sent Bertha a note, "Here are your baskets which I hope will be satisfactory as I have worked very hard to make them so I have been so awfully busy of late that I became very tired the last of the week." During her second semester at Hampton, Harriet began learning a new technique for weaving palmetto leaves. "This new basketry is very hard & it does require a great deal of time patience and attention," she told Bertha. Some months later, she wrote that her projects were progressing slowly, and she had an expert instructor in Robert Evans, who taught manual training and basketry in Newport News and in Norfolk. Harriet also became a proficient typist and could have earned a substantial income if she had survived. Helen told Louise that a good "type writer" could earn between $75 and $150 a month in Honolulu.

Consumption had begun to ravage Harriet's lungs before she arrived at Hampton. Most of the family and many of their friends believed that living at 6 Winter Street hastened her death. At school she was "always cheerful, hopeful and ambitious, she did not seem to see the dark side of her illness at all," her friend Helen Virginia reported. "So often she said to me, 'If I stopped to mope and think of my feelings, Helen, I should be in bed half the time. But I live in an atmosphere above them.'" Harriet was "again in bed but looks well," in October 1900, Helen told Bertha. "Strange though it is she does not cough any. I do not worry because of her being sick for I know that she is much better off here than she would be anywhere else." Even with improved care and surroundings, Harriet did not recover.

Dr. Martha Waldron was regarded as an expert in the treatment of consumption, though a number of public health professionals challenged her credentials. She arrived at Hampton in 1872 as a teacher and became the school physician after an investigation revealed that an alarming number of Indian students had died on campus or shortly after they returned home. The cause of death in many cases was consumption. As part of her work Dr. Waldron had written controversial papers defending the school against accusations that living conditions at Hampton had caused or contributed to the deaths. Dr. Waldron told Helen that if Harriet had stayed home, "she probably would not have lived until spring. Her nervous system has received some great shock and was completely shattered. Even now she says that it will mean slow patient work to get her built up," Helen wrote, admonishing Bertha, "do not mention this to her as the doctor says her knowledge of it might prove disastrous." The family tradition of keeping secrets, which started with their father's family history, continued.

Harriet understood the connection between her illness and her environment, as she told Helen and Bertha. "I wonder and wonder why I came back, but here I like it, every body is so kind and good. Every day and almost every hour I pray that I may be able to stay here until Bertha gets moved to Saybrook, for to go back to Hartford to No. 6 to live would kill me. I would rather be stoned to death or undergo any terrible torture than that." Helen concluded, "Here lies the secret of her whole trouble. Worry over her finances and the return home. [House matron Mary] Galpin said there was evidently no special reason for the attack, but she doesn't know as I do." The attack had followed a notice that Harriet would have to leave school if she did not pay her bills. "Poor girl! How sad her life has been. Such a long, patient sufferer and so unsympathised with. . . . If it had not been for Hampton what would her last months have been?" Helen asked.

Dr. Waldron's "slow, patient work" continued, but Harriet grew weaker. Peter and Bertha came to Hampton to nurse her in December 1900, but she continued to decline until just before Christmas. She expected to celebrate with Helen and Harold. "Ten o'clock came, eleven, twelve and then one and neither Hattie nor Harold had put an appearance and I had spent my whole morning watching the cars for Hattie," Helen wrote. Their hostess was expecting them at two. "I hurried and went to the school, finding as I then expected her in bed with a fever and feeling pretty gloomy. My own spirits had fled by this time, making, as you can imagine, a gloomy day. I 'picked' Harold up (he had forgotten the invitation)," and the two arrived a half-hour late for dinner. Helen wrote for help the next day. If Harriet "can get where she has absolutely nothing to do she may be able to build up." The doctor said that she "really should be able to lie abed until twelve, have her meals served her and have no care or strain on her, and feels that she can not keep up her studies much longer. In her present condition she thinks that if she goes home to her step-mother that it would mean but a short time for her to live. . . . I am in a perfect dilemma myself and almost crazed with anxiety" about Harriet's care. She could live with a friend of their mother's in Hartford, Helen suggested. "Write just as soon as you can formulate any ideas for the doctor and I are anxious to know what is best to do for Hattie." Dr. Waldron told Helen "if there is a possibility of her standing it she will keep her," though she was becoming more discouraged about Harriet's condition.

Harriet could not stand it, and Helen made travel plans for both of them as she began the first leg of her journey to Honolulu. Before they left, they invited Harold to a farewell dinner "and I killed that chicken you bet," he told Bertha. "Just before we started to Old Point Lou's friend Mr. Deveaux and Hattie's friend Mr. Blunt came to the house and we all went to the boat. You ask Hattie about Blunt for she has his picture and he has hers." Mr. Deveaux was Helen's classmate John Deveaux of Savannah, Georgia; Mr. "Blunt," Harriet's classmate, George Blunt of Henderson, North Carolina. A few days later, Harold could not resist more gossip. "I went down to Lou's that night and Blunt and Deveau & Hattie were there and Hattie & I ate supper alone. . . . I think Blunt kissed Hattie on the boat that night for when all of us went on the deck of the boat Blunt & Hattie lingered a minute when the rest of us went inside."

From Philadelphia, Helen sent Bertha an account of their journey:

Hattie and I are here and safely protected from the rain which is steadily falling. We left Old Point at eight oclock last evening amidst the good byes

and good wishes of many friends. Our trip was via. of boat to Baltimore . . .
one of the finest that it has been my privledge to travel on. . . .
*   We arrived in Baltimore at an early hour and were transfered by bus to*
the station of the B. and O.R.R. [Baltimore and Ohio Railroad] . . . Miss
Galpin had provided us with a beautiful lunch of which we partook heartily
aboard the train, being ravenously hungry. After a ride of about two and one
half hours we reached this city and the house [on Stiles Street] shortly after.

After a short delay because of bad weather, Harriet arrived in
Hartford, where she stayed until summer. She escaped the oppressive
heat and humidity with a visit to Emily Morgan's house in the
Berkshires, where she rested, then went to work at Holyrood. Harriet
returned to Hampton in the fall and took her time about letting her
family know how she was. "Possibly you have been wondering whatever has become of me; as I have not written much arriving here at
Hampton," she wrote on October 26, 1901. "We are having delightful
weather yesterday and the day before it was 90° but today is a trifle
cooler. I have not missed one day at school & enjoy taking up studying
again." She waited to write, she said, to see the effect of the climate,
which was hot and humid in the summer and cold and damp in the winter. Nevertheless Hampton had advantages over Hartford. "Although it
is low here the air is very good for it is not as though it were a thickly
settled place and bad drainage here."
   In other respects, Harriet regarded the situation as ideal. Her first
semester had brought her "many pleasures and perhaps a few pains.
There is a difference between my whole self then and now." Upon her
return, she spent less time in bed, rarely took a nap, and frequently
stayed out until eight o'clock because she was busy supervising the
"middlers" and taking lessons in basket weaving. She maintained her
health with only occasional relapses through the winter. On February 8,
1902, she attended the Indian Citizenship Day commemorating the fifteenth anniversary of the signing of the Dawes Bill, "which gave the
Indian the right to land in severalty and American Citizenship." Harriet
saved the program, which she folded into a small square and wrote on

the top, "The folding of the paper is due to being tired and served as a relaxation of nerves while the program was being rendered." As part of the celebration the students sang "My Country 'Tis of Thee," with the verses sung alternately by the colored students and the Indians.

Indian students had been attending Hampton for more than twenty years when Harriet arrived. The controversial program continued until 1923, but the numbers remained small, representing less than twenty percent of the school population at the turn of the century. The profile of Hampton's Indian students started to change in the early 1890s, when the school began rejecting those who could not meet the academic requirements. As a result, the enrollment of mixed-race (white or black) Indians increased while the number of "full-blooded" Indians declined. About the time the James children attended, the government began enrolling Indian students who were equipped to take advantage of Hampton's specialties in manual training, which led to the admission of fewer members of western tribes. Harriet befriended these girls as well: "Last night [October 25, 1901] I had considerable company two of them full blooded Indians (which are some what rare these days), one of the girls who is a great friend of mine is a descendent of the original Sioux indians & her father is a great chief."

Helen Virginia described Harriet's extended acquaintances. "She was at once the envy and wonder of all the other postgraduates and a dear, true friend to so many obscure little juniors and middlers, girls who were in the background and needed the sunshine of a friendly smile. She smiled, and they turned to her like flowers to the sun. She made them realize that she wanted to help them and they sought her for advice and sympathy. It did me so much good everytime I went to see her, to see how many friends she had."

Despite the special place she occupied at Hampton, Harriet suffered from culture shock. Because of their mother's death and the family's poverty, the James girls were not sheltered, but their upbringing was as close to genteel (white) society as their mother and Bertha could make it. Harriet was thus unprepared for the rough speech and behavior she encountered at Hampton. She complained to Bertha, "It seems to me that I can never adapt myself to the slang that so many of these girls use. I often tell them of it & how it sounds but my breath is wasted." Physical confrontations caused greater anxiety. "A queer thing happened the other night, the girls here thought nothing about it but I should have been scared," she told Peter. One of the girls accused another of scorching her shirtwaist in the laundry. The girl denied the charge "and then made herself sick by crying about it." The other girls rallied to the victim's defense and followed the accuser from classroom to dorm, pulling her hair and sticking their fingers in her face. They threatened but did not seriously hurt her, Harriet said. "This was to me a good illustration of the mobs which these hot-headed southerners can form almost instantaneously and just now treacherous they are at times." Harriet also confided her fear of the hot-headed southerners to Helen Virginia, who shared her feelings. "She is often afraid of them & always has to bridle her tongue in conversing with them," Harriet told Bertha.

Harriet's popularity also occasioned a jealous outburst from a fellow Hartford resident. Anna Cross asked to be introduced to Harriet's friend George Blount. "Then first thing she said was, 'Miss James has been sick ever since she came down from the Mountains.' You see she even wanted her story to *go* every where," Harriet wrote. Harriet watched as Anna Cross created more problems. She was "making quite a fizzle out of being here. She made a very low class and this A.M. she told me that in three weeks she expected to be home." By Thanksgiving, Miss Cross had behaved so that "everybody became quite disgusted with her. I never believed she was half as crazy acting as when down here. To have seen her one would think she was just from a lunatic asylum." She left shortly thereafter.

Harsher realities soon overshadowed the hazing, gossip, and Anna Cross's real or feigned insanity. A girl in the hospital wing where Harriet lived died of typhoid fever, and a measles quarantine forced her out of her room. Despite the illness around her, Harriet suffered only occasional bouts of weakness. She maintained an active social schedule, and Harold believed "Hattie has better health this term and I hope she may continue so." At Christmas, Helen sent Harriet a large selection of items from Hawaii to distribute: a pair of "sleeve buttons" for Harold that bore a Chinese inscription for long life; for herself and Helen Virginia "things produced from the soil" made from the lauhala tree. "I sent you the fan because I thought it would strike your fancy. You can use it a life time and still have a curiosity. The word 'Aloha' is the word which means all the blessings one can wish thee." Also included were a tortoise-shell card case, a sandalwood paper cutter for Dr. Waldron, and two little Japanese trays. Harriet catalogued her own gifts in her thank-you letter to Bertha: books, a silver thimble, a pair of Japanese slippers, and money. Her happy conclusion, "This has been the pleasantest Xmas season I've spent for two or three years." In a rare reference to her schoolwork, Harriet decided she had to stop writing to study physiology and chemistry, even though it was Saturday.

Harriet continued to maintain her schedule after the holidays but added an afternoon nap. She joined the Congregational Church at the beginning of 1902. "I am trying to make myself the highest type of woman and thought that this would aid me for the year's beginning." Her aim in attending Hampton was to be educated among "my own people that I may be better fitted for work among them." Hampton emphasized the need for its graduates to uplift the race, and Harriet made that doctrine part of her personal philosophy.

A two-week stay by *Man Without a Country* author Edward Everett Hale became a highlight of the lecture series during the spring. Harriet raved about his talk on "Poor English": "It was good!—to me a treat, to have heard such a man as he," she told Bertha. An abolitionist before the Civil War, Hale gained fame as a minister and author. He returned year after year and drew respectful reviews from all three James siblings. Hampton brought in other men, and a few women, who helped to shape Reconstruction and who exerted a positive influence on the lives of Negroes all over the country. After Hale spoke, Harriet went to listen to the "Hon. Mr. [Robert Lloyd] Smith, a one armed colored man from Texas," who was "Such a bright & witty man, smart as a whip." Hampton looked north for much of its religious instruction. "Every day sometimes twice a day my ears have been stretched wide to catch the words of Prof. [Frank K.] Sanders of Yale who every year gives a course of lectures on the Bible. We have one today [March 30] instead of Sunday school. Oh! they are good. There have been speakers & such good ones every night for the past week that you wonder how your head can hold it all."

Harriet was otherwise improving her mind with *The Right of Way* by the Canadian novelist Gilbert Parker. Her commentary: "It is a good story but I am dissapointed in its ending." Bertha found all this activity far too erudite and replied, "What a very refined atmosphere you live in at Hampton so very intellectual—I do not know how anything ordinary will satisfy you."

Harriet believed she had recovered her health when she returned to the campus in the fall of 1901, refusing to acknowledge that she remained in the grip of consumption. She told Bertha that she had "one of those fine colds of mine. I think that it is much better than yesterday. I don't know how it came unless it is that I did not have any flannel waists to wear during the severe winds of last week. I really feel the need of a couple of good warm waists for these winds are some times so penetrating." She was planning to spend the beautiful fall day indoors trying to "subdue" her illness. Otherwise she "kept very well," and had only missed one afternoon of school during the first six weeks of the term.

Harriet had acquired a powerful protector and defender in Martha Waldron, who recognized Harriet's virtues and made her a favorite. "Dr. Waldron is so kind and good to me that I sometimes wonder what I would do with out her goodness to me. The many privileges which I have would quite make the girls turn green with envy if they knew." According to Helen Virginia, "I think Dr. Waldron never fell so completely in love with a student before. She even neglected Miss [Helen] Ludlow to attend her. She used to call me into her office or her room, and tell me how strong, brave and ambitious Harriet was. 'She is one in a thousand girls, Helen,' said Dr. Miss Thomas, the nurse, was devoted to her, and Harriet returned her affection with interest. . . . She was very happy at Hampton, she did as she chose." Harriet returned to Hampton not knowing how her bills would be paid. By the end of October 1901 she owed $7.23, and Helen wrote that she might be able to help "a little" after the first of February but that she had other financial obligations until then. Helen and Bertha concluded that Harriet would not be able to "push herself through" as Helen put it. A number of Hampton students whose families could not pay the full cost of their education received help from wealthy white people, Harriet among them. She also practiced the strictest frugality. "I wish instead of your putting away your black jacket you would send it to me as my is wearing like the mischief and your would just be convenient for me if you would send it."

Bertha and Peter gave her money when they could, but they were saving for their move to Saybrook. Harriet asked Fritz to pay $10.00 for her board, plus $3.40 for books at the end of October. While she waited for a response, she made another basket that she planned to sell in Florida. She closed her letter asking Bertha, "Has the M.O. for the 75c from Winsted arrived yet? When Miss Lewis returns will you ask her if she will intercede for me toward getting the money from the poor box of Dr. Twichell's church." Mary Lewis raised money and collected clothing among the parishioners of Asylum Hill Congregational Church, which served the families of insurance executives. (Mark Twain called it "The Church of the Holy Speculators.") As colored people, the James family could not attend.

The money from Fritz did not arrive, but Harriet managed to earn $1.26 during November 1901 by working in the school's office, where she pasted newspaper clippings into the permanent records. No one made payments on her bill, and she incurred a charge of $0.50 for medicine. By early December she owed $28.06 and was in utter despair.

"Peter wonders about my finances!" she wrote. "I do not have one cent and as to my account there is nothing towards it. Day in and day out I looked forward to rec. a money order for the ten dollars which Fritz promised me, that would at least make the people here believe that I did have some sort of relation. I have been dissapointed and I believe they have. I suppose I must tell them that my brother has forgotten his promise and is after all 'his father's son.'" She added, "I try to look forward to some help but at times become utterly discouraged." She could not do any "laborious" work but did expect to send some baskets to Springfield, and "after rec. that palfrey sum my bills will amount to about twelve dollars." She was impatient to recover her health so she could earn more money working in the office. In the meantime, she asked Bertha to "beg" a couple of nightgowns because the school nurse said she really needed them. Harriet soon became desperate, writing on January 9, 1902, "Saturday night I cried & cried for [I] tell you I wished I was in the bottom of the sea or some where else for it does seem as though I were nothing but a trial & trouble to this world. I hope that some good Samaritan may appear but as yet my eyes are dim as to coming. . . . I have so little money that postage for your letters is 'scarcer than hen's teeth.'"

Harriet earned $2.10 for office work in January, and her benefactor, Mrs. Evan Randolph, paid $16.00, leaving a balance of $20.96. Even Miss Lewis "was at a loss as to what means she could secure for me and I have had no other help—my finances are in a deplorable condition." Anticipating the January bill, Harriet told Bertha, "think of it about thirty-two dollars staring you in the face & only about one half of it accounted for."

Harriet rarely asked their father for money but occasionally requested clothing—without much hope of actually receiving anything. "As yet I have seen no rubbers from papa," she wrote in February. "I shan't in the least expect them for I know about things from that source." A week later, she told Bertha that she had to stay inside because she had no suitable footgear.

She still had not given up on Fritz, though four months had elapsed since he made his offer. Harriet asked Bertha to have Peter "get five dollars out of Fritz to send me." By this time her bill was the equivalent of $820, and she despaired of ever paying it. "I think about it & pray more impatient. Since writing to you the last time I think I have had two letters from you, both of which I enjoyed, the basket from Miss Lewis has not arrived yet. Oh! how I long for it. She sent me one dollar to pay the freight. Isn't an angel. I hardly know how to write & thank her for the kindness she has shown me." Harriet asked Bertha to look elsewhere: "If Miss Post of WesBrook [Westbrook, Connecticut] is liberal I wish you could strike her about my board money. The corridor on which I live is hospital indeed. I have moved at least four or five times now & am packed up in case I should be asked to move." Hampton officials did give Harriet special treatment because of her health, however, and she knew it.

Dr. Waldron imposed a quarantine because of a case of scarlet fever and several cases of measles. "My room is right opposite the stairs, & I am not the prying inquisitive kind which they are trying to guard against." The lack of visitors made her lonesome and gave her more time to worry about her finances. Harriet recognized that she was engaging in an exercise in futility but felt compelled to turn to her father for help again: "I am going to write to papa to give you the money to buy me goods for the regulation gingham dress for Anniversary," she told Bertha at the end of March 1902. "I would almost rather eat dirt than ask him for it but who can I ask? This thing is compulsory." Among Hampton's many traditions, each girl was required to sew her own dress for the celebration. Harriet had definite ideas about how she wanted to look. She asked for twelve yards of "a pretty delicate light blue and white check" about one-eighth inch and three yards of embroidery "a narrow & *cheap* one," along with five yards of trim.

Her letter to her father was abrupt. "The first of April is Anniversary when every girl is obliged to have a gingham dress & she has to make it herself. Will you please give Bertha the money to get the material for a dress for me. This is something which every girl is compelled to have and most of them have theirs nearly made." A week later, she renewed her plea to Bertha: "Oh! by the way what about the dress I wrote to papa for. I wish he would give you the money for it right away as most of the girls have theirs almost complete. Must I stay in bed, when on the grounds that day every girl is supposed to have a dress and will have? . . . I wish you could get it & send it this week sure." Bertha interceded, but the results were less than satisfactory. Willis would not let her buy the fabric, "guess he thought I would be too extravagant, so he bought it

and expressed it himself," Bertha wrote. Willis engineered it so that neither Bertha nor Louise saw the material before he sent it. Harriet mailed
her response the day the goods arrived. "I depended upon my dress
even, for anniversary. Tonight I rec. a package of coarse blue & white
apron gingham. I know full well who bought it. This I don't care a rap
about but my account." A few days later, she displayed a rare note of
sarcasm, "I must send you a bit of the beautiful dress goods our dear
papa sent me. Fortunately sort of through another girl my dress is to
come from Wanamakers. It has not come yet & I will have to hustle
when it does."

The reality of her financial situation intruded before the big day
came. Harriet mailed this plea to Peter in care of his employer and
addressed Peter and Bertha:

*Please, please, for goodness sake cant you someway or somehow come to my
rescue. Tonight I have had the second official announcement that I must
leave school before April 22nd if my bill is not immediately straightened out
somewhat.*

*Oh if you could just "beg borrow or steal" twenty dollars at least & send
it to me before the last of the week it would save me. My account is today,
April 1st, $34.00 in debt to the school. Can't you go to Miss Morgan,
Mrs. Rexford, Miss Hansel and tell them about it and ask them please,
please to help me. I tell you this is one of the times when you almost wish
you'd never been born. . . .*

*If you would only tell the people just how much I owe perhaps they might
help me more.*

Even before Harriet's letter arrived, Bertha was rallying the benefac-
tors. Miss Morgan and Miss Lewis joined Peter and Bertha in coming to
the rescue. School officials sent Miss Lewis a copy of the bill, and she
immediately paid ten dollars. She told Bertha that Willis ought to pay
the balance, "but probably he won't." Bertha and Peter contributed
about fifteen dollars. Harriet wrote, "I have no words to express to you
my thanks, and to Peter Oh! You don't know what this means to me.

Your letter just came this noon [April 5] and when I opened it I knew not what to do. I could not weep for joy for my tears have all been spent in worry and anxiety. . . . I am going to start early to school this noon to get the order cached that it may go immediately on my bill." Harriet realized that Bertha and Peter had taken funds from their savings for the move to Saybrook and earnestly hoped she would be able to repay them. "Your harvest will certainly be tenfold," she concluded. She planned to write "begging letters" throughout the month to raise more money.

Despite seemingly insurmountable difficulties, Harriet never let her problems completely overwhelm her and remained active and optimistic until the last month of her life, relying on friends to sustain her through the difficult times. Among the closest was Helen's classmate and friend Helen Virginia. The two Helens had begun their student-teaching careers together, and Helen Virginia went to teach in Newport News after Helen James left for Hawaii. Harriet wrote in December 1901, "Life here at school this year seems so positively pokey without you or Lou to bring some pleasures for me that I just made up my mind to make the most of things and enjoy what little there is here to enjoy." The friendship between Harriet and Helen Virginia blossomed, and the latter cherished the relationship, writing to Helen after Harriet died, "I told all my little grievances to her and together we would discuss, laugh and joke about all those things and people who couldn't be discussed to anyone else. . . . She was fearless as you know, and could put things in such a convincing way that Hyde [Elizabeth Hyde, the school's principal of women] unconsciously deferred to her opinion with regard to the course in cooking and other things."

The two had spent Thanksgiving 1901 together. The weather was cold enough to keep Harriet indoors, but she still enjoyed the festivities: "Helen Virginia came over from Newport News spending the morning and staying to dinner with me. I enjoy her coming to see me so much. She is thoroughly delighted with her present situation and says there is so much more freedom in her school work." In the evening Harriet did "duty on the committee to receive" and spent the rest of the time with Mr. Blount. Helen Virginia extended an invitation for Harriet to spend

Christmas in Newport News—at Harriet's request, "Mr. Blount wants me to come over to see you on Christmas day, and as there has been written on the board a notice to the effect that 'girls wishing to go away any time during the Xmas holidays must have a written invitation to that effect from the party they wish to visit—' Therefore please write me an invitation if you wish to have me come & I will hand it in in due season." Harriet received the necessary permission and told Helen Virginia how pleased she was. She included a description of the Christmas-night "social" in her letter: "I wore an organdie with a green ground, over yellow. It is a dress I've had for a number of years. Capt. [Allen] Washington insisted that *we* lead the march which we did and ah! me, tomorrow night *we* will be called up in chapel to be presented with a cake. Rest assured that yesterday found me very tired. I went to sleep at three (bed at one) & slept until 5:45 today. I feel fine." Bertha received a more truncated version of a second event held a week later. "Our cake is all gone & it was shared with about thirty or forty. It was very large & handsomely decorated in pink & white. We had a most enjoyable time New Years night when . . . all my *older* friends gathered in chapel to see me presented with it."

As the new year began, Harriet was optimistic about her health. "Every one here seems to think that it is remarkable how I keep up—to me it is no problem for I knew it would be quite possible if I once got away from the associations" that plagued her living situation in Hartford. "I believe my heart shall leap with joy when I learn you have moved to Saybrook." Harriet knew she could find a loving home with Bertha and Peter.

Soon she began to contemplate marriage and again confided more about her "friend" to Helen Virginia than to her sisters. "Don't you think things are coming to a pretty pass when I allow myself to be governed or rather guided by a young man. Think of it! Me?" Bertha received only snippets of information: "In the evening I went to the social and spent the time with Mr. Blount." For Christmas, he gave her a copy of Paul Laurence Dunbar's *Candle-Lightin' Time* illustrated by the Hampton Camera Club. Even Helen approved of him: "Mr. Blount made me his welcome debtor by sending me a note last month telling me that you were well and doing well likewise Harold. Kindly thank him for me and tell him that I hope the time is not far distant when I will write him my appreciation of his thoughtfulness . . . what a splendid young man he is . . . Talking with him was really a pleasure."

Everyone knew that Harriet and Blount were a couple, but the staff and some of the students seemed determined to keep them apart. Nevertheless, they found ways to spend time alone. Blount had been invited to "come down & spend a long evening" on the occasion of a birthday tea. "When they gave it out to find the seats Mr. B. went to look for ours as each boy sat with the girl he went with. Well, let me tell you about our seats, every one else's seats were all right but ours they had put us up at the same table not even opposite each other, he with a girl who he actually hates and I *fortunately* with his roommate. Every body noticed it too & they were hardly out of the dining room when remarks were flying around about it." Harriet and Blount had to sneak visits because the school practiced strict segregation of the sexes. "Mr. Blount sat down at my table (against the rules) and ate breakfast with me," she told Peter. She was planning to visit a friend off campus, "and I think Mr. Blount will come too if I let him he wants to come very much."

Harriet acted coy when she wrote to Bertha. "He seems to be looking forward to June so much as he wants to come as far as New York with me when I go North. I don't care if he does. Should you ever see the young man I hope you won't be disappointed in the make up." Bertha knew better than to believe Harriet's pretended nonchalance, and Harold had already provided a photograph of the gentleman. "What do you think of Mr. Blount's picture. He is a good looking dued isn't he. Well, he is a pretty good feller anyway and I guess Hattie thinks so to." Harriet pretended to be critical of Blount's appearance. "He hasn't really the nicest hair, has rather slanting eyes they are like Carolyn's [their brother Charles's daughter] and a complexion like no one I know at home but the girls here say 'Miss James, Blount has the prettiest complexion, and is the dearest looking man on the grounds.' These things

have I told perhaps for future use. I am always getting mad at him.
Really I think he'll do until I see someone else I like better."

She soon decided not to look further, but Bertha disapproved of her
plans and let her know it. "What do you mean what are your intentions?
Shall you marry? What are Mr. B's prospects. I have asked you many
times and you never told me." Harriet's reply was less than informative:
"You asked me lots of questions about him which I can't answer for we
have so little time to talk & it is so dangerous to write *locals* these days
that we don't. When ever we eat supper together either the capt. [Allen
Washington] or major [Robert R. Moton] come & spend the whole
evening telling stories to keep us from talking to each other. They just
follow us all over the dining room. The other day we were talking on
Va. Hall veranda. Capt. came along took the adjutant with him and told
me it was time for me to go."

Diet remained an important component of Harriet's treatment
through the last months of her life. She had as much as she wanted to eat
and drink. "It is now noon time & the students are at dinner. I eat at
D.K. [dietary kitchen] and am through before their dinner commences—
I only go in the big dining room about three times a week," she wrote
after Christmas 1901. Harriet felt especially healthy during January
1902. She reported that her face was "really getting plump," and she
shared a laugh with Dr. Waldron about how easy it was to gain weight
and attend school at the same time, as she had been unable to do in
Hartford: "You dont know how much pleasure I get out of cooking
school. . . . I am always able to give Miss Thomas & the hospital girls
something nice to eat at noon. I don't care about eating only the things
which I have at meal times & the milk & eggs which I have for lunches
which occur at 10 A.M. if I am home, and always at 3.30 and 9 P.M."
Some days she said she drank as much as three quarts of milk but then
grew tired of it and cut back to one or two glasses.

The doctor and Harriet's friends saw to it she had other good food
and enough rest. "I do not believe I have been what you call homesick
for it is quite impossible for me to reach that state here," she told Bertha.
Her friends kept her supplied with a "saucer with bread & jam, baked

sweet potato and s. potato pie," all of which she enjoyed. She speculated, "I must be acquiring some sort of a natural feeling for I am beginning to be hungry," and had felt that way for two or three days. Her appetite remained a significant barometer of her health. "Invalid's fare" became too light, but the regular meals were too heavy. She had tried a Sunday morning breakfast of beans and had "the jim-jaws" for a week. "Dr. got after me and almost forbad my going into the dining room," she told Peter.

Even with her improved appetite, she still needed extra rest. "I am awfully far behind in a number of things owing to being sick," she ended a letter to her father in March. "I must go to bed now as I am still under hospital orders." By the end of the month, Harriet was worrying about the summer and had developed a greater understanding of how her feelings affected her health:

You [Bertha] see it is of a necessity that I must forget and keep far in the back ground many, many things & I allow my thoughts to dwell upon but very few things other than my lessons, and seeing Mr. Blount two or three times a day.

Here is one thing which I try very hard not to think about and yet Dr. told me to tell you now that it may not surprise you when the time comes which I hope is a very great ways off or at least until you are settled in Saybrook. As soon as the very strong heat comes I must fly Northward, for Dr. does not want me to stay here in it as it would be injurious to me.

"For a day or two I have had a little fever," she told Bertha. "I am trying to subdue it before the Dr. gets hold of it. I took some of that '9999' [quinine] medicine & it made me sick all day. I could not do a thing in class & could not eat anything so now I only take about 1/2 teaspoon instead of a spoonful as directed." The overdose of quinine also made her dizzy and gave her tinnitus and a headache. The doctor did finally "get hold of it" and diagnosed malaria.

Helen, half a world away, complained that Harriet had only written once between Christmas and mid-April. When she did not hear from

Harriet, Helen became impatient. "Your long silence has really brought me to the point of writing on a week day night, and that one when I am completely exhausted after a trying day. . . . Now reward this goodness (?) of mine by sending me soon a long long letter telling me all about yourself." Helen wanted to know when Harriet expected to graduate. "I shall be happy to think of her nicely located in an independent position," she told Bertha.

Helen soon learned of Harriet's failing health. "Needless for me to say my heart is almost broken thinking of poor Hattie—it is hard to isn't it? Miss Galpin wrote me as the doctor wanted me to know her condition. How I wish I might be with her, poor, poor girl! Her last letter was so despondent—it was really a harbinger of the news I have received to-night."

Her friends refused to believe Harriet was dying, and many of them continued to bring large quantities of food. "All the housewives on the grounds thot of her. I [Helen Virginia] used to find a small table in the hall covered with dainties—a bit of broiled steak from Mrs. Jenks, a cup of custard sent with Miss Galpin's love, a saucer of pudding from Mrs. Purves, a broiler from Mrs. Evans. Indeed, she was constantly reminded that her friends remembered her." Dr. Waldron wrote to Bertha, "Her friends are all very kind. Today [April 27] she had some beautiful broiled steak sent in, yesterday broiled chicken. She enjoys all these things very much. Today she took the juice of an orange, the first time I have thought it safe to give her fruit."

Harriet's health had deteriorated so by the beginning of March that Dr. Waldron was willing to abandon standard treatments and begin experimenting. She had been dosing Harriet with creosote and hypophosphites, prescribed to stimulate her nervous system and relieve lung congestion. To that regimen the doctor added something Harriet called "Perles of Palmiadol," which cost a dollar for forty-five doses. About the time the experiments began, Harriet became bedridden. Fevers racked her body, and her appetite came and went. When she tried to eat, violent attacks of diarrhea robbed her of nutrition and further debilitated her. Shortness of breath and bouts of coughing further depleted her energy so that she could not talk or raise her head off the pillow. A few days before she died, she stopped coughing up blood but lapsed into unconsciousness for longer periods.

Helen Virginia went to visit and wrote to Helen:

On April first I went down and learned that she had had a bad attack of stomach trouble and was very weak. I did not want to tire her, so went again next day, when she was better. I wrote two or three letters for her, one to Mrs. Lane, one to a lady who had done her some service.

After that day I used to go down two or three times a week and always found her room a perfect garden. Miss Galpin, Miss Briggs, Mrs. Purves, Jenks, Misses Batchelor, Wire, Andris, all of them, in fact, kept her supplied with tulips, pansies, daffodils, roses, lilies, Jacks-in-the-pulpit, and other flowers. Her room was a bower of beauty.

Bertha wanted to come nurse her sister, but Harriet refused. She told Dr. Waldron, "that is just like her, but I need nothing more than I get, I would not want her to make a great sacrifice to come." Harriet did not want Bertha and Peter diverting their time and money from their move. Dr. Waldron knew there were problems at home but did not understand why Harriet did not want to go to Hartford.

By mid-April Harriet was near death, and on April 15 Dr. Waldron told Willis that Harriet's pulmonary consumption had "taken the form of the most violent disorder which threatens to be the direct cause of death." The doctor wanted Harriet to go home, but she asked to stay until after May 1, and Dr. Waldron acquiesced. "Everything has been done for her, and everything possible is being done for her now."

A few days later, Dr. Waldron sent Bertha a more complete description: "She has these sinking turns, when it seems as if she would die, & then she will rally, & seem quite like herself. Of course you know that with her lungs in the condition they are in the prospect is very poor. She has no diarrhea now, but a good deal of fever, pulse & respiration are very weak." Dr. Waldron had consulted with a local doctor whom she described as "one of the best men in the region," but they both recognized that no doctor could revive Harriet.

Dr. Waldron continued to prescribe herbs and other palliatives for temporary relief, among them Linden leaf, "not swallowing any of the fibre, and she enjoyed it very much." Harriet was also taking "mellon's food," albuminized water with whiskey, and "other mild but nourishing food." A private-duty nurse from nearby Dixie Hospital, which trained Negro nurses, gave daily baths and frequent alcohol rubs.

Harriet faded in and out of consciousness for a week and on April 27 she rallied slightly. On May 2, Helen Ludlow, English teacher and managing editor of the *Southern Workman*, wrote to Bertha:

Dr. Waldron asks me to write for her, to say that dear Harriet seems now failing so fast that she thinks it hardly possible to live through another twenty-four hours. She will of course keep you informed. . . .

The dear girl, as you know, wants for nothing that our loving care can give her, physically she suffers only from extreme weakness, mentally she is content and peaceful, resting in the love of her friends and her Savior, for her "there is no death, what seems so is transition." The entrance into the fullness of life and pleasures forever more.

For you and all the rest who love her our hearts are full of sympathy.

Harold comes daily to see her. He is well.

Harriet died that afternoon, eight days shy of her twenty-third birthday. The house matron, Mary Galpin, wrote to Helen. "Last night at prayers it was told to the students. Dr. Frissell just home from a Southern trip lead prayers himself and he read from the 14th Chapter of John 'in my father's house are many mansions['] and his prayer was beautiful, and he spoke of Harriett's loyalty to school and her love for this place. . . . This afternoon at four o'clock we are to have the funeral service in the chapel and the casket will be covered with snow balls which just now are in great beauty."

Helen received the news of Harriet's death when she arrived at Kailua-Kona, following a rough eighteen-hour boat ride and a harrowing climb on horseback and on foot up the lava flow to Kona Orphanage. She found a pile of letters waiting for her. "With hesitating hands I took and opened them and had read but a few words when I knew all. Can it be possible that Harriet is dead? Died away from home and with none of her own to even close her eyes? Poor Harriet, poor me! My heart almost breaks when I think of it and I wonder shall I ever forgive myself for leaving her? How little did I realize that when I said good bye to her in Phila. that it was for ever! . . . It has almost undone me, and oh! how I wish I was at home. I am sure that if I ever get there again, I shall always stay near. . . . God be with you all at home. May this affliction but bring us nearer the One who saw fit thus to make his presence known to us."

Living among strangers, Helen felt the "sad blow. You do not know what it means to bear a thing of this sort away from home and friends. Hattie's death has made me feel more than ever that companionship is one of the things we owe each other." She began making plans to return to the States. Weeks later she still could not "convince my self that Hattie really has left us. How suddenly the end came. It seems pretty hard that one so lovely, so talented, so artistic, one with such a bright future might not have known its realization."

Helen Virginia tried to reassure Helen about Harriet's last days. "I never saw her uncomfortable but once—the day before she died I went but did not stay except to give her an affectionate word and a smile. I always told her about my children and the people in the house; she met them Christmas Day, and their little idiosyncrasies afforded us many a hearty laugh."

Bertha and Helen saved the condolence letters they received. Helen sent hers home "to be kept as family heirlooms. They speak so beautifully of Hattie that I want you all to have the benefit of them."

Miss Galpin wrote, "I have the sad news to write to you that your sister Harriett passed away about 5:30 p.m. You will be expecting to hear it I presume. I saw her on Sunday last and she seemed very weak, but still she was cheerful and thought she would be better, but she couldn't turn herself in bed. It is so sad to see one so bright patient and industrious pass away. . . . I feel very sorry for you my dear child so far away at this time from your family friends but cast your burden on the dear Lord and he will sustain you."

Helen's admirer John Deveaux was among the more eloquent writers:

Ere this letter reach you you will have heard of the death of your dear sister. It seems so hard that we must have those who are so near and dear to us taken away. We are apt to grow discouraged and think that life is not worth living, but when we think of the noble life spent here, we can but thank God for the example of such lives. As Dr. Frissell said, your sister's life was a pure and Christ life. He thanked God that such lives are lived here at Hampton and that they might be permitted to die here. He said through her death there comes a sense of sorrow, but yet we can't help but rejoice and thank God for such a noble life spent here with us. Miss Harriet had been sick about a month. Some days it was reported that she was better would soon be out, and again word would come from the bed side that she was worse. The truth is that her great ambition and determination kept her alive as long as it could.

Her funeral services were very beautiful. School and all the departments were stopped for a half day and she was given the regular military honors that the school always gives on such occasions. Dr. Frissell and Mr. Turner spoke very highly of her. Trusting that you are well and God grant you peace and comfort in your sorrow.

The proceedings made a profound impression on Helen Virginia as well:

Beautiful flowers were sent. The tribute of the postgraduates was a pillow of white carnations and ferns on a standard of ivy leaves. Mrs. Lewis sent a bunch of [yellow] Marcheil Neil roses and ferns. Large bunches of roses, lilies, and other flowers were carried behind the casket by two boys. Dr. Frissell and Mr. Turner carried on the service which was a very touching one. I wish you could have heard Dr. Frissell. He made it so plain that what looks to us like a life cut off, has in fact accomplished a great deal. He said that Harriet was an example to the whole school, of pluck, earnestness, an inspiration to those who knew how she strove to overcome all obstacles inter-posing between her and her ideal of true womanhood. He spoke in such a

beautiful, comforting way that I cried, but felt better. The band played
Nearer My God to Thee and Asleep in Jesus. Then, just as the service was
over, and the casket borne out, Major Moton sang Nearer My God to Thee.
Everyone cried.

Dr. Waldron wrote to Bertha a week later:

In regard to any expression about being at home, which you ask about. I
cannot remember a single expression which would lead me to think that she
desired in the least to be at home, nor did she speak of any of her home peo-
ple. She said she knew that it was impossible for you to come to her, & in
that idea she rested. If it had been possible no doubt she would have liked it,
but she said nothing about it.

Her mind was clear up to very near the end, although she suffered much
for want of breath that at times she would not try to talk. She often
expressed a great deal of pleasure at having got back to what she called her
'dear home.' It was a beautiful corner room, in the girls' hospital. . . . I had
boys & the nurses do everything for her, as it was soon after her other sick-
ness, & she rejoiced continually at getting back to her room, which she
seemed much attracted to.

I do not know positively but I think that if Harriet could have seen all,
from the time I began urging her to go home, she would have done exactly
as she did do. She preferred to have the end come here.

George Blount disagreed. "She wished very much to see you before
the end came." Blount sent Bertha flowers and a condolence letter, "It is
useless for me to attempt to say how I regret the loss of Miss James," he
wrote in response to Bertha's thank-you note for the flowers. "Yet it is
the Lord's will and not ours be done. Mrs. Lane your letter was indeed
very consoling. The following part of your letter expresses my feeling
exactly, when you said 'Poor Harriet, how happy she is now, free from
care and pain, and will have perfect peace forever.'" He found the sentiment "very true indeed," though it was impossible not to wish her by his
side again.

Of all Harriet's acquaintance, Blanche Johnson seemed to understand the family's pain the best:

I sympathyʒe with you very much in the loss of your sister. She was a favorite among us at Hampton and I have faith to believe she was looked upon in the same manner home. Every body loved her and I myself was a devoted friend of her's in every respect. She was as kind and as patient as she could be through all of her afflictions. Miss James had been sick so much I had gotten the impression that she would be spared many years longer. But after all medical aid and attention she closed her eyes and left me in grief at her absence.

She use to say to me so many times B. Johnson I dont mind asking you to do things for me, but I can't bother many of them because I am afraid they will think that I want them to wait upon me. Three days before she died I took two books to the library for her and took a girl a book that she borrowed from her. She gave me a lovely piece of red ribbon before she died which I am going to keep in memory of her. She still hoped to get well until the last days of her illness . . . she use to tell me what she was going to send me if she ever got well.

You must not worry about her as the Lord knows best. I can sympathyʒe with you in the same bereavement for I had a sister to die from home. I wish I could give you comfort but that must come for a higher power than I can give.

As they had done with their mother, the family kept Harriet's memory alive throughout the years. As the fifth anniversary of her death approached, Helen wrote from St. Helena, South Carolina, "Just a hasty line to convey to you a recent inspiration. I wondered if we couldn't all contribute toward having the graves in the cemetery put in order before Decoration Day. Will you canvass the family to get the consensus of opinion. I will contribute my part the first of April or May as you desire it. Before many years I hope to be in a position where I can aid in erecting a monument to the family, or at least putting a stone to each grave." Harriet has a headstone in Old North Cemetery in the family plot with her mother and infant brothers.

Chapter 5

GETTING ALONG SWIMMINGLY

Harold Edward James, born February 3, 1884, enrolled at Hampton Institute as an energetic boy of fifteen. He found his life's vocation working on the school's eight-hundred-acre farm at Shellbanks, where students earned money to pay their tuition and produced food that the school sold to supplement its income. Shortly after he left Hampton, Harold bought and operated a farm in Wethersfield, Connecticut. Later he became the manager of a school in Hanover, Virginia.

After Helen went to Hawaii, Harold and Harriet grew closer at school, and he was deeply affected by her death. Dr. Waldron worried about him. "I feel very anxious that Harold should get a good place—and the sooner the better for him, for he will not do well, while he is idle & grieving. It would be far better for him to be busy with his hands. It is the best cure for sorrow. I thought it was a mistake for him to go north, as he was well, & doing well at Shellbanks, & could have continued there. He is becoming more manly every day. Do not let him idle long."

He had a loving, generous nature but was far more blunt than his sisters concerning his feelings about the family. Harold also displayed a lively sense of humor, as he signed his letters with variations of "Rama Hama" James, including one that he sent to Louise as "Ramastein James." He ended another letter to Bertha, "I suppose you are tired

93

reading such a trashy old letter so good bye." He used slang expressions: "swell," "out of sight," and "you bet."

He wrote his first letter home to his father on October 5, 1899. Just to make sure "Pappa" knew how to reach him, Harold put his return address at the beginning and again at the end of the letter. He and Helen had traveled together as far as New York, where he caught a boat for Old Point Comfort. "I had a lovely sail on the steamer getting supper and breakfast there also having a stateroom to myself. Lou [Helen] arrived Saturday night and I saw her Sunday. I am having a fine time, seeing Lou most every day for the school she teaches is near the institute. All the matter with this place is the food and beds. The beds and pillows are made of cornstalks. The food is on the hog, bread and mollasses for supper. Tell them all I will write to them soon and give them my love."

Harold was homesick when he first arrived. He wrote, "Tell Bert I got the picture that she sent Lou of her and Wese [Louise] and Hattie and I keep in our bureau and every time I look at it I think she is smiling at me. All the fellows are stuck on it." He missed Bertha and Peter, to whom he confided more about the daily routine and his feelings about the school than he did to his father:

This is going to be a long letter for I know you want to know all about it. . . .

There are about five hundred colored boys here and about 100 Indians. The Indians room in a large brick building called the Wigwam. The colored boys room in about 8 different buildings. One large stone building is where most of them room. I room in one of the cottages and have a fine room with two other fellows. Our room has three windows while the other rooms have only two. . . . The furniture of our room consists of three iron beds, 3 chairs and bureau, 2 bookcases and a table. We have lace curtains to all of our windows which we bought ourselves.

I am going to get my uniform Saturday and it is going to be a fine one. Here we have a fire department on the grounds. It consists of a huge engine drawn by about 100 boys, two hose carts and one hook and ladder.

We have a fire drill about once a month. There is a large sawmill here on the grounds which takes great big logs and saws them into all kinds of

lumber. Thousands of logs are towed to Hampton from N. and S. Carolina
by tugboats for this mill. There is a trade school where the boys take their
trades, shoemaking, machanical woodturning, brickmason and all kind of
trades. There is a large barn here where they keep about 25 horses and 15
cows. We get up about half past five to go to breakfast at 6 oclock. The food
they give here is bad. The dining room is a big one seating about 800.
When we come from the dining room we go to our rooms, make our beds and
sweep the floor. At seven oclock those boys that are taking a trade have to
get to work and those boys that are going to school have to go to a large hall
and study from seven to eight. From eight to nine we do what we please. At
nine we form the battalion and march to school. The school is different here
than it is home. We go to a different room for each study. In the morning we
generally have bible history arithm. and geography. In the afternoon which
is from 1.30 to 3.30 we have English and manual training or agriculture.
Dinner is at 12.15 and at twelve we have to form on the green and march
there. . . .

There is a fine church here where we hold services on Sunday. There is
also a chapel where we hold prayers every night after supper. After prayers
we have to study two hours until nine oclock at half past nine the taps blow
and everybody goes to bed. On the place here there is cotton and sweat
potatoes growing. There are loads of fine persimmons here. Up home I
never saw any buzzards, but here there are hundreds of them.

He ended the letter, "Tell the folks not to forget my box
Thanksgiving." When he wrote to Bertha he upheld the family tradition
of asking her to send him belongings he had forgotten: a comb, a tooth-
brush, "and if you could get the family to pick up a small collection for
me it would make my stay much pleasanter, for it takes money to stay
here. . . . If you have a spare bag of candy laying around the pantry I
wish you would send it for I have only had two pieces of candy since I
have been here. . . . Brother Ram. . . .

"Tell Pete dont forget to come down Christmas. Don't wait till next
week before you write me. And send me some envelopes. make them all
chip in, Fritz to."

Harold began to enjoy his studies, despite repeated and prolonged complaints about his diet. "The food they give us at the school is very bad. Sometimes I cannot eat it. We have old meat chopped up with bread and vegeatables making a kind of hash for breakfast and a little better dinner and bread and mollasses for supper." An investigation in the late 1880s by the U.S. Department of the Interior, prompted in part by the high mortality rate among the Indian students, concluded that the Hampton Institute fed the students an inferior diet while it sold the produce and milk from the farm and gave the best of both to the teachers. Subsequent inspections indicated that the quality of the fare had improved, though Harold undoubtedly would have disagreed.

When daily hunger pangs overwhelmed him, though, Harold had permission to forego the dining hall and invite himself to the house where Helen was boarding with Captain and "the very kind" Mrs. Evans, who gave him "such dainties as a half of squash pie. it is fine." Bertha obliged by sending more candy, and Harold wrote to Peter, "tell to Bert that candy was fine and a box wouldn't go bad about Thanksgiving." Two postscripts instructed Bertha to tell everyone to send "goodies Thanksgiving. I am not situated as Lou was when she was here. She did not eat student fare But I do." He had learned that for the holiday the students were to eat roast goose and pie "and all we want of it," so he was expecting a happy day.

Harold had another dining option, as well. Helen's friend and classmate John Deveaux took him to breakfast at "Ye Holly Tree Inn," built by students for use as a gathering place and temperance society. As a student Booker T. Washington had cleaned rooms there to earn money for his school expenses. The staff believed the inn kept the students away from the saloons and pool halls in town. Deveaux, according to Harold, was "dead stuck on" Helen. "He is a fine looking fellow living in Savannah, Ga. his father is a collector of taxes at Savannah and has plenty of money."

Beginning with strawberry season, Harold ate better. "The quarters you [Bertha] send me are very helpful to me. Watermelons and cantaloupes are in abundance here. Great big schooners of melons come up our creek loaded with them and we row or swim out for them at night. We can get five melons for 5 and 8 cents. . . . You know you have heard of the school farm (Shellbanks) well I want to go out there for a month to work if I can get off from the office there they have all kinds of fruits and cows mules pigs ducks geese turkeys and everything that a farm should have. It is situated right on Chesapeake bay with a better water front than we have."

Like many homesick students, Harold began making plans to return home for the summer almost as soon as he arrived. He wrote to his father in late October, "I am having a good time here. I am going to day school with the intention of taking a trade. Down here I take agriculture and manual training along with the other regular studies. Beginging next month I will have work between times which will bring me six dollars a month which will help a good deal in my board. . . . Next summer school lets out about June 15th and I would like to come home. I think I could earn enough to pay my passage both way and a little more."

Hampton operated under a strict regimen and imposed extra requirements on the boys. In addition to academic and manual-labor classes and any work performed to pay their expenses, they lived under military discipline. The boys wore uniforms, held drills, and were expected to march in formation to and from the dining hall and other group activities. They formed six companies, with upperclassmen and faculty as their commanding officers. As commandant, Robert Russa Moton, who later became president of Tuskegee Institute, oversaw military training while Harold attended. Harold had become acclimated to the routine by the end of November: "I am in middle class and am the smallest feller there," he told Bertha. "I am getting along good in school and am having a pleasant time all around." His academic record improved in successive years, and he had few behavior problems.

Like Harriet, Harold had money woes, as his father intended him to work his way through school. He managed with help from a number of sources. A sponsor paid his tuition, and Bertha and Peter supplied him small amounts of cash—ten cents here, a quarter there: "I got the quarter all right and it was just in time for I owed a boy ten cents for fixing my pants and I had to get ten cents worth of stamps," he told Bertha. Louise occasionally contributed small change, too. Harold particularly appreciated these gestures, as she was only thirteen when he went off to school. Helen paid half his room and board, and he earned the other half by working two days a week in the greenhouse, the carpentry shop, at Shellbanks and in the office of the *Southern Workman.*

Because he was still growing, however, his clothing expenses were substantial. Bertha and Peter contributed there, as well. "I received the ten cents from you [Bertha] and also the rubber collar which just fits me and is a beauty. As papa is not going to send any money for my board this month I have work that brings me $5 a month. . . . My books cost $6 but we will get straightened out after a while." Even though he knew his father was not going to contribute, Harold asked anyway. "I am getting along very well here at the school and my shoes are very much worn out. As I always have a deal of trouble fitting shoes to me, I think it would be a good plan to send Lou or me the money and I could purchase them in Hampton at $3. . . . Please send money order for we can get it cashed easy."

He had planned to stay in Virginia to work after his first year but returned to Hartford to peddle milk. That decision infuriated his brother Willis, who let their father know it. "How is it that you let Harry go out to Pease again after spending money on him to improve his character and then turn and send him to a place where he will learn more evil in one day than he can replace with good in years, and my advice would be to keep him at Hampton, or else send out to his *ranch* and let him go to pieces and not bother about him again." Harold did not go to pieces, and his summer work inspired him to write light verse:

I suppose Pease still plods wearily the streets,
His wagon a landmark for all who he meets,
You can hear some boy screeching his lungs
While Pease is around some beer barrel bung
And oft as he travels from east out to west,
He thinks of the boy he always liked best,

Peter Clark Lane

Fritz Morris James

Anna Louise James, left, with her
niece Bertha Harriet Lane

THE JAMES CHILDREN
Top row from left: Helen, Fritz, Willis, Bertha
Front row: Harry and Harriet

Anna Houston James

Bertha James Lane

Clothilda Delsart Hudson and Charles Thomas Hudson

Helen James Chisholm

Frank Pierce Chisholm

Willis H. James

Willis Samuel James

Harold Edward James and Blanche R. James with son Harold

The boy that would lead,
All the strikes of the place,
But was forever treated with the best of his grace.

Harold returned to school with enough money to pay part of his board and again managed with help from Helen, Bertha, and Peter. In December 1900, Helen asked Bertha to pay his board and suggested mailing the payments to Harriet. Helen was preparing to go to Hawaii and was concerned about how Harold would react. "Harold was lovely about it. He said, Well next year I will be able to pay my own way in school and perhaps I can help Hattie too. Then you may like it in Honolulu and when I finish my trade I can come to you. Wasn't that noble of him?" Helen promised to send as much money as she could but said it would be in the form of "*change* only" because she was paying part of Harriet's expenses.

Bertha and Peter sent Harold ten dollars at Christmas, and he "made good use of it, you can bet." He included his measurements for a new pair of pants with his thank-you letter. Peter and Bertha obliged, and he sent a thank-you note to Peter:

I received the pants and shoes the other day & they are hot stuff. The pants are just right and the shoes are out of sight. I also received the dollar & a half. I haven't a cent of that left. For I had a pair of shoes repaired and I had to settle with my tailor for little jobs he had done for me. But never mind. I guess with a little aid I can pull through the remaining months. My bill is rather large now but I guess Bert and papa will send me a few dollars to pay up now.

I hope you will thank papa & Mrs. James & Louise for the money. . . .

I have not written before for I did not have the money to buy stamps. I don't think I can ever repay you for the things you have given to me. . . .

P.S. Tell Bert to go begging among her white friends for they will be getting after me soon about money.

Bertha made another contribution before the school year ended. "I received the suit of clothes and they were just right. The pants fit just fine. That is the kind of a summer suit I wanted." He assured her that at the end of the following school year he would be a "full blooded carpenter," able to pay his own room and board.

Harold spent his second summer and the first part of his third year at the school farm at Shellbanks. "I am earning my way now and have twenty dollars to my credit," he told Bertha. "I was very glad to get that quarter as I needed a hair cut very bad. Tell Papa that I am in need of more clothes, a suit especially. I have no good Sunday clothes at all, and if pa could send me a little money, I could get fitted here. I got a pair of overalls the other day, and the length of the leg (inside seam) was 33 1/2 inches, and found them about an inch to short." This time Willis bought a suit. "I am so glad that papa sent Harold a suit for now perhaps I shall see him more often having seen him only once since being here," Harriet told Bertha. "I write to him very often & last week he told me he would come in & take dinner with me when he had a new suit." In April 1902 Harold decided to see how far he could push his father. "I am going to write to papa for a dollar or two just for fun to see if he will send it. I got a letter from him a few days ago and he always writes as if he would do anything for me."

Despite his money woes, Harold remained an active and cheerful boy. Even a serious accident occasioned not complaints but robust assertions that he was fine. He tried to keep it secret, but once the news reached Connecticut, he confided the whole story to Peter:

I suppose you heard about my being cut. Well I did get cut. I lost part of my thumb, my left one just below the nail. I cut it off on a chain saw. It did not hurt at all. They put me to sleep in the hospital with ether and sewed it up. I couldn't work for two weeks but it is nearly all well now and I have been in the shop for over a week.

I don't miss it at all so you needn't worry about it. I did not intend telling you about it at all, but seeing some fresh coon tried to tell you I thought I would tell you right. . . .

Tell Louise to write and tell me who told them about my cutting my finger. For I told every body not to say anything about it. It does not hinder me

in my work at all. I don't suppose I will be home again for 2 or 3 years.
Hoping hear from you soon.
I am loving yours, H.E. Rama James

Missing part of a digit did not affect Harold's manual dexterity. He taught himself to play the mandolin and told Bertha, "and I can play any old thing on it. You don't know who easy it is to play one." He bought one that he sold for three dollars, then bought a second one for a quarter more. He was planning to learn to play the guitar as well.

Not long after his accident, the term ended in tragedy. Harold again addressed the gruesome news to Peter:

One of the Indian boys died in the hospital last week [week of May 24, 1901]. His death was brought on by an accident he had last fall. He was riding a wheel down towards Whittier [Hampton's primary school], when he ran into a cart. The shaft of the cart hit him in the stomach and he stayed in the hospital about a week. They thought he had gotten all right. But last month we had to go to 3 large fires in Hampton. This Indian boy helped pull the hose reel. That night he was taken ill and died Saturday. His body was sent to Cherokee N. Carolina for burial. For he belonged to the Cherokee indian tribe. After he died some doctors cut him open and found that his stomach had grown up into his lungs. This was caused by the wagon hitting him.

The death of a classmate could not keep Harold from contemplating his summer. He planned to spend his free time swimming and teaching his friend Beale to swim. He went rowing and swimming every evening, attended dances, and enjoyed the amusements at nearby Buckroe Beach. The climate was his major source of complaint during the summer months. "Oh! it has been hot here. And you never saw mosquitoes. Last week at night the boys could not sleep in their beds. We would have to get up and walk around at night to keep from getting eaten up."

Tragedy visited the school again at the beginning of September 1901. "I suppose you [Bertha] have heard about that dreadful accident we had here, that indian boy getting drowned. The swimming season has about closed now so you see there is no danger of me getting drowned. I think I have had a better time this summer than ever before. I hope you and the rest can say the same."

Harold had a responsible job during August and September in the office of the *Southern Workman*. Hampton's founder, Samuel Chapman Armstrong, had started the magazine as a public-relations organ to spread the word about Hampton. The monthly publication contained accounts of activities at the school and featured stories about the graduates and other matters of interest to the Hampton community. Harold arranged for his father and Bertha to receive copies. He described the work as easy, with his day beginning at 7:45 and ending at 5:00.

Harold taught himself to type and sent several letters on *Southern Workman* letterhead. This talent helped him make a positive impression on his sisters. Helen asked Bertha, "He surprised me wonderfully with such good work. What does pa think of his improvement?" Harriet was proud of her brother's growth and development. "Harold came in to see me . . . He has grown to be such a great big boy that had it not have been for having a place of meeting appointed I would hardly have recognized him elsewhere."

As Harold was making plans for the coming school year, Helen devised an itinerary for him to travel home via Washington, Philadelphia, Jersey City, and New York, visiting her friends along the way. "This trip would not cost much over three or four dollars more than the other way and would pay you well. This is the way that people who have little money see the world." Harold had more grandiose ideas: "Wait until about five years from now," he told Bertha, "and I will be far from the U.S., in another country."

Once the school year started, Harold's schedule changed. He never explained his reasons, but he told Harriet that he intended to stay at Shellbanks for the entire year. "He is not attending even night school as he retires at 7 P.M. and rises at 3. A.M.," Harriet wrote to Bertha. "Were you to see him I think you would quite agree with me in noting his improvement and I don't persuade him to come in to the institute for the reason of believing Shellbanks is an ideal plan for him for a year. He has grown more erect, taller, broader and so manly. His voice is changing. Every body speaks unusually well of him which seems so good hear and know."

He was still thriving in the spring of 1902. "Harold continues to rejoice my heart with his letters," Helen told Bertha. "His last was very expressive of gratitude to you and Peter for your kindnesses to him. I should love to be at home to see him this summer. He must be a fine boy: the reports of him from Hampton are most encouraging."

After Harriet died, however, Harold changed. George Blount told Bertha, "It made me feel so sad to see poor Harold weep as he did before leaving here. I sympathize with you, Mrs. Lane, and all of the friends of Miss James in this bereavement. Hope Harold will soon recover." He did not.

Harold accompanied Harriet's body back to Connecticut and never returned to his studies at Hampton Institute. Mary Galpin told Helen, "Harold came in church with Major Moten [Moton], and he went home last night. He was to have gone the 1st of June but he said he would like to be home and at the home burial, so he went, he has grown to be a strong fellow, his year at the Farm has made him really strong and robust in his looks." Harold stayed in Hartford but did not live at his father's house. Willis told Bertha in June, "Harold was in . . . and stayed quite a while and makes him self quite to home whitch I am very glad to see. I give him my watch that I have carried for some time. I was glad to see him so plased with receiveing it. he was comeing in to take dinner with us yesterday but it rained so all day that he could not ride his wheel in."

For months afterward Harold stopped visiting and writing his family. Helen asked Bertha about him in early August, "Not one word has he written me this summer which makes me rather dubious." Bertha had not heard from him either, and Helen wrote again, "I am rather worried about Harold that he writes to neither of us. If he is not doing well or intends throwing up his schooling do tell me." Mid-September came, and still they had no word. Helen eventually decided he would succeed even if he did not return to Hampton.

As I think of Harold, I feel that we have no need to worry. He has had a glimpse of the right sort of life, had a chance given him, and now is old enough to plan a little for himself. While I regret his decision I shall hope for the best but not worry. Worry is neither healthful nor wholesome and really should never be indulged in. As to this, I am a convert. The little German poem which says:

'Lasz regnen, wem es regnen will, laz allem feinen Lauf!
'Und ween's genug geregnet hat
'So hör's auch wiederauf.'

The sense of which is: let it rain if it will and when it has rained enough it will stop, quite helps me. For if it will rain, how can I help it / So much for my mundane philosophy.

During his silent period, Harold lived on a farm in Bloomfield, just north of Hartford, where he worked for a milk peddler by the name of L. W. Dean. His work consisted of milking six cows, an easy task from his point of view. "I am very well and enjoy life very much & hope you and Pete do the same" he finally told Bertha in January 1903. He reconciled with his family and took a job at Newton and Robertson, a Hartford grocery. After moving back to his father's house, Harold supplemented his income by raising pigeons. Willis had enough faith in his son's project to invest in the business. He told Louise, "Harry has 15 young pigeon and they are doing nicely I think he is going to make a good thing of them." Father and son faithfully reported the progress of the birds in letters to Bertha and Louise.

Harold contemplated becoming a peddler and announced in February 1907, "I am this spring going to start in peddling for myself. I have bought my horse & wagon and will start business next month. I think I will benefit of the open air and sunshine anyway. Of course I have a good job now but I want to be my own boss. If I don't succeed why I will not suffer." Their father said, "He has my best wishes for his success," but when Harold changed his mind and decided to stay at the grocery store, Willis concluded, "I truly think it is the best thing for him." When he wasn't at the store or tending his pigeons, Harold continued to enjoy the countryside around Hartford and gave himself a case of "poison iva," as his father called it, so serious that it required a doctor's visit and kept him home from work for three days.

Not long after Harold returned to his father's house, Helen paid a visit and was not pleased with the state of the housekeeping. Harold particularly disappointed her in this regard, and she told Bertha that while Fritz kept his surroundings fairly neat, Harold's bed could almost "walk alone. . . . Of course if Harry was the kicker that his older brother is his would be cleaner too." Still, there was hope that he might find a way to live a cleaner life, in the literal sense. He had met a young woman and was escorting her to church picnics, concerts, and the theater.

"I was *de*lighted to hear from him," Helen told Bertha. "When he comes down, you must have him tell you about his new girl. Evidently she is a great prize." Her name was Helen Blanche Robinson, and she came from a family of free Negroes who had moved from Virginia after the Civil War. Harold had definite ideas on the need for maturity before one married, as he told twenty-one-year-old Louise in New York: "About that fellow in Hampton, you know you are very young as yet and don't need to worry about any body. If I were you I would not write to him at all. There are lots of men in the world; and you will surely meet up with some that you will like equally as well as Stubbs. I was twenty-one before I even thought of going with a steady girl. Now take my advice and forget all about that kid. He is not worth thought let alone writing to him. . . . You must be very carefull who you take as friends there, especially among the young men. If you write to Stubbs tell him that you are willing to become a friend and will remain so for the present."

Harold soon ran into a snag in his own courtship. "I came near losing the devine friendship of my dear Blanche. Someway or another. I forgot to call on her for over a week. Last Sunday night I agreed to go to her house and I didn't. I went somewhere else. Of course it was all my fault, but you can bet your life I will not let anything happen like that again." He did not, and they continued to court.

By the fall of 1907, Helen concluded that her brother had finally grown up. "Harry is fine. I am head over heels in love with him. He is nearer my ideal than any beau that I have. What do you think? He bought him a flexible file and manicures his nails. More than that, he owns a *dress suit* [underlined three times]. Tonight he took Blanche and me to the theatre. His attire and manners were perfect. I was so proud of him! Pray that he may keep in the right way. I liked Blanche and her people. She is a very pleasing girl. We are fortunate that Harry fell into such good hands."

By the spring of 1908, Harold and Blanche were planning their wedding. "Three cheers for Harry!" Helen wrote. "May he be spared to realize his dreams. When will he marry? I should like to be at home for the wedding. I think that in Blanche he has an ideal wife." He paid a deposit on sixty acres of land and a farmhouse in Beckley, now part of Berlin, Connecticut, but lack of money postponed his plans to marry. "Harold wrote me asking for the loan of $100 until fall," Helen wrote in May. "I have just written to him that I haven't it, so can not let him have it. I fear that the disappointment will be very severe, and I am so sorry. He wants to marry and hasn't the money. I told him he had best postpone the event until fall. Write him a nice letter to cheer him. I imagine that in his loneliness he gets almost desparate." She had sent Louise ten dollars and a dress and concluded that she was "strapped" until Louise no longer needed help with her school expenses.

Harold and Helen spent part of the summer of 1908 in Beckley. "I have promised to make a rasberry shortcake for Harry's supper. His boyish appetite has changed very little." After dinner she reported, "The rasberry short-cake has been made and eaten. The tea things have been put away. Harry is in the front room playing the mandolin, and I at the kitchen table writing. The day has been a delightful one. Like the others it was made up of little things. . . . Harry and I are using a quart of milk a day. They let us have a pint in the morning and a pint in the evening. We usually use it right up. This morning I made griddle cakes for breakfast, using sour milk and soda. Harry ate twenty-three of them."

Shortly after Helen sent that letter, Harold married his beloved Blanche. They rented an apartment at 8 Winter Street, next door to his father. Blanche bore her first child, Harold, in 1909. The family moved to Wethersfield before the birth of their second son, Floyd, in 1916. Harold ran a dairy farm, raised pigs and horses, and bred Airedales for some twenty years. Then they moved to Virginia, where Harold became the manager of the Hanover Industrial School until his death at age sixty-one in February 1945.

Chapter 6

SETTING THE STAGE

Compared to her brothers and sisters, Helen Lou Evelyn James was barely five feet tall. What she lacked in stature, however, she compensated for with an indomitable spirit. Born September 1, 1876, Helen was the most prolific James correspondent and, except for Willis, the best traveled.

She was the first member of the James family to attend Hampton Institute, a tradition that ended when her niece, Anna Houston Lane (Ann Petry), withdrew in the early 1930s. In 1901 Helen left Hampton, where she had been a teacher-trainee, and took work as a maid in a school in Honolulu on the island of Oahu. She met Liliuokalani, the last Hawaiian queen, and Anna Cate Dole, the wife of the first territorial governor, Sanford Dole, and later became a teacher and manager of a school and foster home on Hawaii. After her return to the mainland, she attended Atlanta University, where she studied with W. E. B. Du Bois, then taught at the Penn School on St. Helena, South Carolina, and at Florida Agricultural and Mechanical College. During breaks in her academic schedule, she worked in summer homes owned by Emily Morgan.

Helen wrote to Bertha every two weeks. The best educated of the family, Helen had the most literate, and literary, style. Despite the long narratives, she was reticent about expressing her feelings, even about minor details such as why a particular vista moved her. Nonetheless, Helen's letters were long and filled with graphic images. She enclosed church bulletins, brochures, and sometimes even bits of leaves and pieces of cloth. A letter from Hawaii written in 1902 still smelled of sandalwood a century later. Helen was aware that her experiences were unusual and asked Bertha to preserve her correspondence: "Get a letter file and keep the family letters also any newspaper articles, magazine articles, etc. It will be a most valuable collection of family history to be handed on, if there will be any one to hand it to. From the present outlook papa is the only one who is looking out that the name James be perpetuated."

Helen was "Lou" to everyone in the family, but once she acquired a measure of sophistication, she followed her father's penchant for self-reinvention. At Hampton she began to sign her letters "H. Lou E. James," then "Helen L. James." She explained the change to Peter, "In running through my mail to-day I found a copy of the 'Hartford Courant.' My interest caused me to scan it immediately when lo! my eyes fell on an old letter of mine written to Miss Rathbun. The letter sounded good: I liked it and feel that it may do good; but the introduction nearly made me faint! How *glaring* [triple underline]; I haven't recovered yet. Seeing that 'Lou' in quotation marks made me grateful to Dr. Waldron for her suggestion that Helen was more dignified."

Helen enrolled at Hampton in 1897, but Bertha did not start saving the letters until December 1898. The first was typical:

Sunday afternoons I am usually quite indulgent allowing myself to sleep from dinner until time to dress for church. To-day I have decided to use this time in writing my Xmas letters, and really feel no inclination to sleep. Perhaps this is because I was up late last night. In chapel Mr. Daniel Webster Davis, whose poems Miss Arnold sent me last year, read a paper before the Folk Lore Society. His subject was Echoes From the Plantation. It was very very funny. He dwelt chiefly on the pastimes of the negroes on the plantation, taking up their dances and games. Among the ring games he mentioned "The Ole Lady Turn to See the Ole Man Turn." Do you remember that? Mr. Davis was too comical for anything. He is one of the homeliest black men one would be liable to meet on a long day's journey, and just as his poems are so he is. It is easily seen that he is the embodiment

of them. He recited two: Bacon & Greens and "Those Stolen Breeches."
I am glad that I heard him, although I wanted last evening for sewing: Sat.
is the only free evening that we have. . . .

I noticed by the [New York] Age that Mrs. P.C. Lane had opened
"Parlours." How is business?

How are things at the United Workers? Remember me to the Misses Pratt
and the girls, also to Mrs. Richie, Mrs. Daniels, Mrs. Lane and family and
other friends. . . .

I shall write to Hattie soon. I am so glad that she is able to resume her
studies. Had their been a good chance for me like that two years ago,
I probably would have been back in Hartford now instead of here.

For Xmas we are going to give Miss Galpin a piece of work, what called
I do not know—evidently plaster paris, and is in base relief. Each one
contributes so much towards it. I wish papa would send me some money that
I can bear my part of it. . . .

I am reading "Hon. Peter Stirling," and am so infatuated with Peter
that I can scarce bear him out of my sight. Easily he is my ideal. You would
all enjoy it, and I hope you will get it from the library. In literature we have
been studying Chaucer and Milton. Our lesson yesterday was on the "Hymn
on the Nativity." Read it before Xmas if you have time. It is by Milton. In
"Canterbury Tales" the Clerk tells the story of Patient Griselda, which you
would be rewarded for reading.

Helen's schedule at Hampton was sometimes frenetic. She told
Bertha shortly before graduation, "Lessons are hard, but seem to go
smoothly. I have six recitations a day, which keeps me quite busy." They
were studying Pope's "Essay on Criticism," she said. Her recreation
included playing whist and euchre.

Hampton Institute imposed strict rules, and Helen did not approve of
those who took advantage of the illness of one of their chaperones.
"Some of the girls and boys of the Senior class have been doing what
they should not going off the grounds with out permission, dancing
together, which is a crime. The school is much agitated about it in the
mean time they are more strict with the others."

Illness—her own and other people's—occupied much of Helen's time and energy. "This place like every other has been grippe ridden, nearly every one having at least a touch. I have been fighting it for about a week, and though I succeeded in not being ill have felt wretched and lost a day and half from school. I managed to pass time, though, for the drawn work continues to fascinate me. I have made one very pretty doily, and am at work on another." She told Louise that the Yale choir would not appear at Easter. "Owing to the prevalence of the small-pox around these regions the Yale boys will not sing here this week as is their custom at this season of the year. We are all very sorry indeed." Smallpox was a recurring problem during those years, as she wrote from Honolulu of an outbreak aboard the transport ship carrying the mail from San Francisco. Packages and letters were held for fumigation.

What she termed "the plague" repeatedly invaded Hawaii, and Helen saw the effects first hand. In the spring of 1902, she was invited to speak about Hampton at a girls' school. "The students and teachers were all pretty sad and depressed. Plague had been in their midst and removed two of their girls. . . . The result is a terrible gloom over the school. They were quarantined for weeks against the outside, and daily expected others to sucumb to the dread disease. The nervous strain on all was terrible."

The state of her own health caused Helen almost constant anxiety. She had helped to nurse their mother, and she suffered recurring bouts of illness that she was convinced would kill her as well. After Harriet died, Helen became extremely vigilant and spent years in the South, in part because she felt less at risk for illnesses that she associated with cold urban climates. She managed to avoid tuberculosis but contracted various fevers and other ailments.

Just after she turned twenty-five, Helen wrote from Honolulu, "How rapidly the time does fly! Another birthday has gone into the past. How old I am getting! My, it is alarming to think of when I get back East. I fear that you will not recognize me for the marks of age. Tell Peter that I am putting on old woman's fat as he tells of and that I weigh about 122 lbs. now. I am thankful for every pound of it too, as it never pleased me to be so thin." Despite her reference to "old woman's fat," Helen generally worried about being too thin. Her expenses in Atlanta included fifty cents a month for eggs, which she ate raw, a dozen at a time. This regimen had been standard treatment for consumption since the time of her mother's illness.

The start of 1902 found Helen "tired and lazy. . . . It is just after the holidays, you know, and an annual occurrence with me, for true to my southern instincts, I enjoy all that is to be enjoyed for the entire week. . . . I fear that the tropical climate at times gets the best of me, for I never before did 'nothing' as successfully as I do now." By "southern instincts" Helen meant that she did not feel compelled to fill every hour of the day with work. Those instincts did not have a chance to surface often, but occasionally she stayed in bed all day, reading and dozing: "I fear that the owl and I judging from habits are a bit related. Here it is close on to ten o'clock, the campus wrapped in slumber, and I just beginning to write. The strange part of is that this entire day I have been free of responsibility and might have written many of the letters, which should have been written."

The move to Hawaii and a new job helped her through the early stages of mourning Harriet's death. Kona Orphanage "came into my life at the right moment, for with out it I fear the effects of this sad blow. You do not know what it means to bear a thing of this sort away from home and friends." The "sad blow" also freed Helen to talk about fears that she had never revealed before: "I am enjoying my work more and more and am just as well as can be. I think that this sojourn in the islands may make me a strong woman. I had rather expected to go as our dear Harriet did."

Helen stayed healthy during this period of heightened anxiety by keeping busy. "With the mental scientists I am beginning to feel there is no time, for the days seem like hours." The "mental scientists" believed that the mind had power to heal the body. In some respects Helen and William James were years before their time. Helen's mental powers had her at work by 5 a.m. and "pau" (done) by 7:30 p.m.

Despite a good work environment and healthy schedule, fear of going "as our dear Harriet did" returned when her charges became ill. "I have a fine Puerto Rican boy about fourteen years old, who is suffering from swollen glands. The trouble is [of] a scrofulous nature. I recognized it immediatley for his neck was as full as mine has often been. The tendency to this trouble (in my own system) has been one of the chief motives that has pushed me so far from home into warmer climes. I was not surprised at the turn Harriet's trouble took for it was [the] end that I expected for myself." Helen concluded, "'Life is sweet' as the bird sings and worth even great sacrifice. For this I labor in foreign climes and while doing it shudder at the thought of those bleak New England winds that have taken away so many of our colored people. Life there is rigid for the strongest found among us, because we have to toil and stand so much. We are not able to earn to live above sordid cares which undermine the health."

Helen's physical health mirrored her mental health—bouts of depression alternating with periods of mania:

This is a lovely bright morning [February 19, 1903], the waters leaping for joy and the winds blowing glad and free. It makes me feel better, removing some of the terrible unrest that seized me during the past week. I have been getting tired for a long time: the first of this week feelings reached their climax and I just wished with all my heart that I might "run away." I can assure you that the only thing that detered me was the thought of Miss Beard being left alone with no available person on whom to call.

I am alive however, even though I didn't run and shall probably work on for many weeks. Yesterday I rode for five or six miles, my horse galloping to my heart's content. At the end, I dismounted, lay on the ground, rested while the horse walked about me nibbling the fresh green grass. It was a beautiful place where I stopped under a wide spreading mangoe tree where to the one side I could see the clouds enveloping the tall mt. peaks and to the other the broad blue Pacific's stretching unruffulled to the horizon. A few moments rest in this land does as much good as might hours in another.

She grew to understand more about her manic phases. "Do not worry about me," she wrote from Florida, "the most that ever ails me is that terrible superabundance of energy which keeps me driving like a steam engine." That energy allowed her to teach school from 8:00 a.m. to 5:30 p.m., rehearse students for "rhetoricals" until 8:30 p.m., and fill in idle moments studying German.

When Helen was suffering from real or imagined illnesses, she turned to the family pharmacists, Peter and Louise, for advice and medicine, being the only family member who ingested any quantity of their wares. Peter and Louise did not trust doctors because they saw the mistakes and believed that most drugs lacked efficacy. Louise never deviated her belief that only three types of medicines actually cured disease: digitalis for cardiac ailments; the anti-inflammatory and febrifuge salicylic acid; and later, penicillin and the sulfa drugs for infections. Neither Peter nor Louise let their personal opinions deter them from selling patent medicine, however, or from compounding their own tonics.

Helen became one of their best customers as Peter supplied her requests, among them a cheaper version of Fellow's hypophosphites. "I am suffering for a tonic of that sort, yet am deterred from purchasing because of the price. Write me this *at once* [double underline]," she told Bertha. Fellow & Co. compounded its syrup from quinine, iron, arsenic, hypophosphites, and strychnine. South Carolina's climate caused problems, and she asked Peter to send two-grain quinine pills, calomel (a laxative), and "salts." In October 1906, she told Louise, "My head is tired, being tightly bound with a cold contracted on the boat and feeling queer from a dose of quinine taken to-day. One of the habits which I am to form this year is taking this drug at regular and frequent intervals for malaria which is a foe of the Island. Even now many people are down with 'the fever.'" She asked Louise to send her literature on malaria and quinine and found other customers for Peter's tonics, which she sold to her fellow teachers for fifty cents a bottle.

Sometimes the medicine did more harm than good. "For last week I was almost ill, my stomach refusing to do its work. Black blotches came on my face, my eyes were heavy, causing me to look all that I felt." She apparently did not suspect that she was having an allergic reaction to one or another of the tonics. Soon she was able to give up the quinine.

"The weather is quite cold now. So cold that from the bottom of my trunk I have unearthed my warmest clothes, and find myself in certain garments that I have not had on in five years. This sudden change is good for the island, as it takes the frosts to kill the malaria." She continued to experiment with anti-malarials in Florida but with her limited income mostly took the "cure-alls" hydrogen peroxide and Marburg's tincture tablets, a combination of quinine, alcohol, salicylic acid, and other ingredients.

Boredom often undermined her health, she found. "I am . . . utterly lacking in ambition. This life, with no variations, not even a change of faces, does pall on one sometimes," she wrote from South Carolina. "This week I have felt as if I could 'fly de coop.'" Peter's tonic worked, and within a month she told Bertha she was getting "quite languid" again. Languid probably meant high. The James women never drank alcoholic beverages, but until Congress passed the Harrison Act in 1937 many of the tonics sold at the pharmacy contained opium or alcohol—or both— up to 90 proof. Opium and alcohol relaxed Helen enough to let her body recover from the underlying ailment, and her faith in the efficacy of the potions supplied the rest of the cure.

At the age of thirty-three, Helen suffered a serious illness while she was planning her wedding to Frank Chisholm, an agent for Tuskegee Institute. Instead of going to the altar, she checked in to Hartford Hospital and underwent surgery. Continuing the tradition, she kept her illness a secret from the family until she began to recover. She confided instead in their benefactor Mary Lewis, who paid for a private room at twenty-five dollars per week, plus, "Nurses and doctors in procession. A bath and clean bedding every day. A bed as soft as down. My back rubbed and powdered every night." Helen remained in the hospital for two weeks and then went to Putnam Elms in Brooklyn, Connecticut.

Though it was mid-November, she sat outside "in a sheltered corner" except for meals, "even when the days are coldest. I do not somehow care to stay within though the house is beautiful. Each day I am better and better. If I was beyond a certain stage I should have no fear whatever." Helen never said what was wrong with her, but she slept with the windows open and took cold baths, treatments prescribed for patients with consumption. With no distractions and plenty of opportunity to rest, she began to improve. "I know that you [Bertha] are looking for a letter from me telling where 'I am at' physically. Well, just now I am breathing lightly to see if it will make things any easier for me during this week which is my first milestone. I am really far better than I have been before, and am doing absolutely nothing just now, and hope that I may be spared any anxiety."

More anxiety followed on Christmas Day as she was visiting with her fiancé, Frank Chisholm. "We were to talk over the plans for the wedding, when lo, I collapsed right before him and had to go flat to bed where I have been ever since: same old trouble in the same old way. Don't you worry, I am not going to. I can't understand, only that there is yet some great lesson in patience and submission for me to learn. I feel sure that it is not wise for me to marry until I am stronger. Not just to either of us."

Helen remained seriously ill for three weeks but began to recover in mid-January. Her tonic again was the cold. Her daily routine involved "exercises unhampered by clothing with the window open," followed by a cold bath. When Bertha asked for a complete account of her sister's illness, she received as much of an analysis as Helen ever managed regarding the connection between her physical and mental health. She blamed her respiratory problems on the surgery that "weakened nerves and ligaments" and a shaking she received during drives she took just before Christmas. "This is my first collapse. . . . But oh! how I have paid for it all! Nearly 3 wks. in bed, doctor coming, doing nothing as usual. . . . Well, faith worketh great miracles. The mountains can be removed by it where it is strong enough." She insisted that she did not understand why she had collapsed again. "It makes me feel much like the snail who constantly comes to an obstacle which causes him to go back and start again. However hope comes up whenever there is an opportunity." And she was glad that she had not married earlier. She preferred to be ill at Putnam Elms because she felt men lacked the patience to care for an invalid.

Despite the wrenching isolation of St. Helena, South Carolina, Helen's outlook improved once she discovered she had access "a fine collection of books" in libraries at the school and at the white teachers' residence. Of special interest were "books on social problems and ethics which are tempting me—books by Jane Adams, Jacob Riis, Thomas Nelson Page, Du Bois, B.T. Washington and others whose broad experience has fitted them to write. Then there are sets of Dickens, Thackery, Scott, Dumas, and modern novels, besides poets ancient and modern, histories, etc. I often sigh as I look at them and wish for more time." She found her time could be equally well spent with the library's "fine assortment" of magazines and newspapers, and she was conflicted because she could not decide which to read first.

When a bout of depression threatened to overwhelm her, she overcame it by reading "hundreds of pages" of *Daniel Deronda*. "When strong men take to drink for recreation, I take to a book. Geo. Elliot usually brings me out, too." "Her keen life studies" helped Helen regain some poise and to recover from ennui. She read and wrote about works by and about Negroes with particular interest. While she was in Hawaii one of the Hampton teachers sent her copies of the magazines that featured of Booker T. Washington's *Up from Slavery*. She declared it mandatory reading for Bertha. Also required was Paul Laurence Dunbar's "Xmas poems, so delightfully gotten up under the title of 'Candle-Lightin' Time,'" which Helen borrowed from a colleague. Among other books that held her interest, "I am . . . reading Fannie Kemble's Life or rather Residence on a Georgia Plantation ["Journal of a Residence on a Georgian Plantation"] and Dante's Divine Comedy, from all of which I am enjoying great pleasure." Kemble's 1863 description of her years as the wife of a slave owner on Saint Simons Island in part influenced Helen in her choice of a teaching position on nearby St. Helena.

Periodicals kept Helen supplied with news about Negroes, and she asked Bertha at various times for copies of the *Colored American, the Guardian*, and *Philadelphia Tribune*. "The New York Age, Fortune's Freeman, The Guardian, and Chicago Conservator have given me an insight into the colored world, while the Review of Reviews, Literary Digest, Woman's Daily, etc. have given me the news of the world at large. Just now I feel fairly well informed. I even know something of the policies of [William Jennings] Bryan, [New York governor Charles Evans] Hughes, [President William Howard] Taft, [Roosevelt's labor and commerce secretary George B.] Cortelyou, and [Charles Benson] Foraker, with Hoke Smith's sentiments. The Current Events class in my grades has proved a blessing to both teacher and pupils." The racist Hoke Smith, governor of Georgia, disenfranchised black voters, and his campaign in 1906 sparked the white riot in Atlanta that had so frightened her friend Birdie Ford.

Music gave Helen another form of escape and challenge. As she put it, playing the piano and singing became a source of "deep comfort and help," even though she believed she lacked talent. She played the grand march at a school party in Honolulu. "This meant for several days extra work, as my German and algebra are becoming so absorbing that I am doing little with my music. I am sorry to have to give it up but it is simply a matter of choice." She performed successfully and continued to practice.

Two years later she felt she was gaining both ability and confidence. "My music has been invaluable to me since I came out," she wrote to her father in 1903, "and my experience here has added greatly to it giving me confidence and thus enabling me to in a measure overcome that drawback from which I have suffered so much, timidity and self-consciousness." The piano gave her "a good deal of comfort" after Harriet died, though she found it necessary to "limber up joints now stiffening with years." While she attended Atlanta University, the musical director invited Helen to join the chorus. "I almost tremble over it, knowing the uncertainties of my musical aparatus. However there is no better way to learn to do than by doing, so I shall improve this opportunity to secure both ear and voice training. You know I always loved to sing—regardless."

Helen resumed piano lessons at Atlanta University, practicing the works of Mozart, Heller, Bach, and Loenschörn. She considered it "quite a chance to be able to take music in connection with the other work." As the year progressed, she felt she was not making progress because her fingers and hands were stiff and "the brain is a bit dull." But she continued the lessons because she enjoyed them and wanted to be prepared to "give much to less fortunate ones in days to come." Those days arrived when she taught at the Penn School, where she gave her first piano lesson each day at 7:00 a.m.

Helen also expanded her musical interests at Kona Orphanage. "I play the organ or piano at all of our [church] services. From this you can judge what brilliant musicians the faculty boasts of." On St. Helena she received permission to play the organ at a church near the school. "I played hymn after hymn and got deep comfort and inspiration from the depths of that instrument. We haven't an instrument so I have not been able to play since I came. I am thinking of making some sort of arrangement to get the priviledge practicing in that church. Music and the horse together may keep my soul from starving. In desert places every precaution is necessary."

Religious observance fed Helen's soul as well. Her parents had started her on a lifelong habit of church attendance, which Hampton reinforced with mandatory Sunday school classes and church services. The institute invited a constant stream of religious leaders as guest speakers. "Word was sent around this morning [May 7, 1899] that there would be no Sunday School, as at that hour the delegation of the American Missionary Society Library Association that was at Old Point would be with us. The batallion was inspected after which all assembled in the church. We sang and four of them addressed us. There were the president, Mr. Lane of Cambridge, Miss Hewins of Hartford, Mr. Soul of Boston and Mr. — of New York. Their remarks were excellent, short, full of interest and to the point. When Miss Hewins was speaking, I tell you that I felt proud that I was from Hartford."

Like Harriet, Helen attended as many lectures of the secular variety as her schedule allowed. Two who spoke on the thirty-fourth anniversary of Abraham Lincoln's assassination inspired her. Edwin Mead, editor of *New England Magazine*, addressed the former president's relation to the American poets. "He brought his facts to gether in a smooth pleasing way, but is not himself an easy speaker," Helen said without giving a reason. His wife, Lucia Ames Mead, left a better impression.

Music and lectures formed only a part of Helen's active social life. Shortly before she left Hampton Institute, a young man gave her "as handsome Marcheniel [Maréchal Niel] roses as I ever received. The fun of it is that he is only a *3 Junior* (one of the lowest classes) and I a senior normal. Well it all comes in the course of a school career. . . . Saturday evening we had two young men callers, an unprecedented event in this household."

Most of Hampton's social activities had an educational aspect. The president's reception in June, "one of the finest that we have had," entertained two hundred students, teachers, and graduates. "Dr. [Hollis B.] Frizzell came into the study where I was talking and taking me by the hand, asked for the story of the 'Little Pigs.' As I assented he led me into the Recreation Room where I did it, though without the music" but "to the satisfaction of all, I think." Practical Helen had an ulterior motive. She considered the recitation a warm-up for daily performance in the classroom. To further her aims, she was tutoring some of the younger students in anticipation of her job in the fall. Her pupils had "all done so well that I feel quite encouraged and hope next winter to make my work *pay*," she told Bertha.

The president's reception signaled the end of Helen's education at Hampton Institute, but she remained at school for the summer. She and her friend Helen Virginia were dinner guests of Mary Galpin, the matron of the girls' residence. They dined on broiled chicken and ice cream in a private room at the Holly Tree Inn, then returned to their residence where they entertained "two of the young men that we were allowed to have call on us." They took advantage of the full moon the next day and went rowing "until past eight when we made a call, had a drive around the grounds and returned home."

Later in the summer Helen went for a sail down to Hampton Roads and saw the sunset drill at the infamous Fortress Monroe, where the government imprisoned Jefferson Davis after the Civil War. The occasion of the drill was Helen's second visit to the area called Old Point Comfort: "The hotels are right on the wharf so to speak and in the evening when the boats come in and go out it presents a very gay scene. Being a government wharf the guards are there to meet the boats, their uniforms with those of the sailors adding much to the picturesqueness of the scene. Then there is the freight—great quantities of it being alive and a small army of colored men who handle it. Large crates of geese, hens, ducks, lbs. of crabs and fish, turtles so large that one comfortably fills a truck, sturgeon as large as or larger than a man with farm products form a large part of the freight. The large wharf is filled with it and it takes a long time to load it on."

The three ladies sat on the "promenade" of the Hotel Hygea for more than an hour. "I kept my face seaward, for colored people are not supposed to be there and it is of course for the benefit of the guests." Helen was afraid to show her face, but she was sufficiently curious about the area to violate Jim Crow. While segregation was the rule almost everywhere in the area, the town of Hampton and its environs were not entirely divided. Helen's friend John Deveaux, a student and later bookkeeper at the Hampton Institute, told her, "Mrs. Brunson, the lacemaker is a very pleasant woman and you have no doubt found her so. She is a great friend of Miss Cleaveland's and through them, I was made at home in the white Episcopal Church in Hampton."

While Helen was living in Hawaii, conditions for Negroes on the mainland were deteriorating. The reports she read inspired fear, not anger or horror. "Have been reading ripples of lynchings etc.," she wrote in the summer of 1903. "What horrible phases the negro problem has been assuming of late. It fairly makes one timid, as the thoughts present themselves, where will the next outburst occur?" The Negro press reported eighty-four lynchings that year. Though she was afraid, thoughts of further "outbursts" did not deter Helen from moving South when she returned to the States. Contact with other colored people explained in part why Helen was willing to risk lynch mobs, segregation, oppressive heat and humidity, yellow fever and malaria, and extended periods of cultural isolation to live in the South. What she received in exchange was the comfort of familiar company—Negro men and women whom she regarded as her social equals in numbers that New England could never offer.

No matter where she lived, Helen craved the company of others of her race. At one point she told Bertha she had met a Mr. Banks, "a Hampton graduate. He is not *colored* though so I could not meet on a comfortable basis." She did report meeting Fred Bonner of New Haven, Yale class of 1901, who spent several days in Honolulu en route to a government-funded teaching position in the Philippines. Helen welcomed his company, "for not seeing any colored people here I know very little of them: in fact the only news that I get comes in letters." They visited for an afternoon, "and you can imagine how we spent it, just talking about Conn. and the people. It did seem good to be able to ask questions once again about things of personal interest and to get answers. Letters prove unsatisfactory at such a distance for I find that most people never answer them. They simply write of things of present interest with no regard whatever to the letter in hand."

Before Harriet died Helen decided, "One of my fondest dreams has been of situating myself in some quiet place in the South where I could have her with me and let her take care of herself first, all else being sub-servient." Helen's goals changed after Harriet's death, but the dream of a quiet place continued. She wanted a smaller, more literary version of Miss Morgan's homes:

You know my dream has always been to attain to a position in my proffesion that will warrant my having a pretty house or suite of rooms, according as environment permits, where books, pictures, music and artistic furnishings will both delight the eye and rest the soul. Here, are to be found kindred spirits who will contribute to each other's happiness and discuss the subjects that will help each other. It is to be not only for such as I have mentioned, but a place where boys and girls will love to come and will always find a friend. Do you think it will materialize? I wonder. It is pleasant to dream, however and a high ideal with hope make the ascent both cheerful and easy.

Helen tried to persuade Bertha to her point of view as well. "I hope that you and Peter will go South again. There is so much that is lovely there and so many things of interest touching our own race that one can not help deriving great benefits." Bertha's aversion to heat, humidity, and white southerners, however, outweighed her desire for extensive contact with other Negroes.

Helen wrote about the discrimination she encountered with delicacy and reserve. As a resident of Hartford she had been part of a tiny minority, but her experiences in Virginia, Georgia, Florida, and South Carolina, among white people who made no secret of their bigotry, strengthened her resolve to live and work among her own race. Throughout her years in the South, Helen did not let her separate and unequal status have a significant impact on her life. She solved the problem by living in all-Negro environments after she left Hartford. Thus, only rarely did she experience the truly hideous aspects of southern living, even as the region implemented and solidified the United States Supreme Court ruling in *Plessy vs. Ferguson* that approved the treatment of Negroes as second-class citizens. By the time Helen began living in the South, strict segregation was the reality in law and in practice.

On her first trip from Hampton to Atlanta with two friends, Helen reported, "We couldn't get a sleeper, though I tried several times. Consequently we had to 'Jim Crow' it the best part of the way." Helen had been in the Deep South for five months when she had her one true Jim Crow experience. It occurred on a hundred-mile trip from Atlanta to Tuskegee Institute and to the Calhoun School in Lowndes County, Alabama:

I . . . had a most delightful time of it. It was interesting, too, from the standpoint that I was a "Negro" and was learning for the first time the true significance of the word.

When I went to buy my ticket here I did not dare seek the waiting room, because I did not know where the one was which I should go into, so I remained on the outside. When the train for Tuskeegee was announced I started off with the crowd but was told to go to the next gate, which was for colored people. Reaching the train I was directed which end of the [double underline] car to enter for the one was for white smokers and was petitioned off from the other which was for Negro passengers. It was a way train, and

though there were many local passengers getting on and off, the majority
were people of intelligence bound for the same place that I was. . . . This
part of the country is especially noticably for its dirtiness after a visit to the
capitol in Montgomery, I didn't wonder at all at the idea of the Southerners
thinking the Jim Crow cars clean and good accomodations for Negroes, if
the same people judged of their cleaness that judged of the neatness of that
building. I never saw such a dirty, disgraceful place in my life. I am sure it
has never been cleaned nor renovated since the days of Jefferson Davis and
the Confederacy.

In contrast to her views of whites, Helen thought southern Negroes superior to their northern counterparts. The senior with the highest honors at Atlanta University, for example, was preparing two speeches for graduation, participating in the Fisk-Atlanta debate, writing a fifty-page thesis on "Occupations of Negroes," and completing his regular class work. "When I look at these boys and girls and see what they are capable of doing I think how blest they are to have been born in the South where the atmosphere for the education of Negroes is so stimulating," Helen decided. "From high and preparatory schools to college is but a natural step with them. You know what an unnatural and unusual one it is for those of the North." Laws in the antebellum South prohibiting the education of slaves had made the freed people and their children hungry for education. Men such as Booker T. Washington and W. E. B. Du Bois, though they disagreed on the type of education colored people should receive, stimulated the environment for learning. Southern Negroes had more role models in the world of higher education than their northern counterparts, Helen believed.

Despite the oppressive atmosphere of inequality, justice occasionally prevailed. Theodore Roosevelt won reelection in 1904 without any southern electoral votes. The populist Rough Rider had infuriated segregationists by inviting Booker T. Washington to the White House. "What a victory the election was!" Helen wrote. "I am afraid the South hasn't caught its breath yet." The rest of the country had demonstrated that it still did not need the former rebels to keep the Union together.

Helen discovered, however, that even the heartland of the Confederacy had institutions that did not enforce segregation. "I have done nothing new or exciting, except visit a Sanitarium where one of the teachers is resting. It was quite a novel experience here in this section to enter the front door, sit in the parlor where there were other visitors and go through the house. I wondered if they felt strange: know that I did not." Racism had not destroyed her pride, but her failure to name the institution and oblique reference to the lack of a colored entrance indicated she feared her mail was being censored, a common occurrence in areas where those in charge were paranoid about potential Negro rebellions.

Shortly before she moved back North for good, Tallahassee gave Helen another taste of the horror of southern living. "There was a man lynched here at the jail between midnight Saturday and dawn of the next day. We knew nothing of it, though many on the campus heard the firing. There may be no account of it in the papers since the South is inclined to conceal these things." According to the Negro press, the man was one of sixty-nine lynched in 1909.

While Helen was sensitive to discrimination and stereotyping by white southerners, she was equally a product of her culture and expressed her own biases. Near the end of her first year in Hawaii she went with friends to a "native" Sunday school, where she heard the children sing a Christmas carol: "Their idea of rhythm seems to be inborn, and tiny as they were they did it well." She saw no irony in commenting on another race's sense of rhythm.

When we reached there we found the South Sea Islanders assembled and having a service in their own language. They were a curious looking congregation, I can assure you. Some barefooted and dirty, while others showed that they had gotten as near to modern regulations concerning church attire as was possible. One old man, who sat in the corner, spit on the floor until he was tired of it, then from a little distance sent it through a broken pane of glass in a sash behind the minister. Altogether they conducted themselves very well. After their service the Hawaiian S.S. [Sunday school] assembled. I said Hawaiian: it was made up of Chinese, Hawaiians (in majority) and South Sea Islanders. Altogether a very novel gathering.

Christians among the islanders could strive for civilization, but Helen was initially convinced that Buddhists could not possibly achieve true humanity. She and a teacher visited the mission house of the Japanese Buddhist Association to observe the celebration in honor of the first anniversary of the Young Men's Buddhist Association. "The experience consisted of addresses both in English and Japanese. . . . The Japs are extremely courteous and made us feel quite welcome. The address that pleased me most was the one that told of the aim of and work done by the Association. They have a membership of nearly three hundred. For them there is a library and reading room, a night school, taught by two English and two Japanese teachers and an employment bureau. Isn't it surprising to find this work done by Buddhists who we generally suppose to be heathens?"

Helen also encountered what she called "peculiar conditions" after she moved to Kailua-Kona and started attending the only Christian church in the area. "Some of the people in the settlement are endeavoring to deprive us of the place. Each week they throw stones into the church right through the panes of glass. On the side towards the road, I think we have not a single whole pane of glass. . . . The people say the devil is in our church so want to drive him out, I suppose."

Perhaps Helen worried so little about racism in part because she found daily living a struggle from the time she left home. She wrote from Hampton Institute that Miss Morgan had sent fifteen dollars to pay her final bills. But, "having no facilities for washing makes it a little hard. The weather being warm and our staying in school all day, which of course makes it necessary for us to keep looking clean, compels us to change our clothes often." Her wash bill was fifty cents that week (more than ten dollars today). "These little calculations disturb me for my money is so limited," she told Bertha. "Please see that I have some immediately."

Money continued to be a problem after she became a student teacher at Whittier, Hampton's primary school. Mid-November arrived, and she had not received her first month's salary. The county was responsible for the payments, which went first to Richmond, "then passes through [un]seen hands before being delivered." She anticipated long delays before she received any money.

Bureaucratic delays did not prevent her from buying a piece of land in Hampton. She made a deposit of eleven dollars on December 21, 1900, and signed promissory notes for payments of sixteen dollars every three months. She grew worried as the time for making the final payment approached. "If anything ever happens to me, that lot is to go to you [Bertha] and Peter. I will mark to that effect on the outside of the deed so that it will come to you. Also any money that I have in the bank will be for Louise after my own expenses are met. I feel this way, death is liable to come to any of us. Should I die out here [Hawaii] I want my body left here, as there is no need of any transportation there after expenses are met. What I have can be sent home. I hope that no such arrangements will have to be made as I want to come home myself well and strong someday."

While she worked as a student teacher, the pace of her life was "such a whirl that it is almost impossible for me to get two minutes to myself. From early morning until late night, soul, mind, and body are drawn on continually." The day she wrote to Bertha she had left for school at 8:30. She taught until noon, then had "Christmas exercises," at which she read for the children. Then she attended a County Teachers Association meeting that lasted until 4:00 p.m., after which she conducted business for the choir and "looked after little affairs in town," including the purchase of the land, until 8:00 p.m. Choir practice followed until 9:45, then she attended a party until midnight. "So goes my time and nothing is accomplished except contracting and paying bills."

Helen maintained her frantic pace through the fall, as she contemplated her options for the following year. Hawaii was beckoning, and in mid-November she wrote that she was "much tempted to go if only for the trip." She made a decision three weeks later:

I have thought and thought over this Honolulu matter and after most careful consideration have to-day decided to go. . . . Yes, it will be possible for me to come east within two years if everything is not going well and it is best that I should feel positively that I shall be much better able to cope with my work when I do return for I shall be so much better prepared in every way. . . . I do worry though about leaving you all so much. Yet I can not see where I can get ahead by staying here. When I return I may be able to accept a position in the Institute proper which will mean a salary that will enable me to help those of our lot who need help. I shall write to Miss Lewis to-night as to my decision. She is so very good that I feel that I shall never be able to thank her for her kindness to us.

Helen was willing to make sacrifices for a better education and was determined that Louise should not drop out of school as Helen had done while their mother was ill. "I hope that she has her mind thoroughly made up to return in the fall. One year will be a little hard for her to lose, but is small compared to five. Tell her to profit by my example. Here I am away from home and friends to acquire knowledge that I lost by being out of school so long and will probably be thirty years old before I am able to accomplish my desire." Helen had just turned thirty when she took the teaching position in South Carolina.

Helen went to Hawaii against the advice of Bertha and Peter. They had offered to support her during the summer of 1901, but independent Helen told Peter, "It was very very kind of you and Bertha to plan so nicely for the summer for me. I appreciate it more than I can say, but could not content my self to taking my living in that way without contributing something and know positively that I could not work through the summer after such a winter as I am putting in." She felt she had not been sufficiently gracious and tried to make amends. "I want to thank you [Peter] for the very kind letter which you wrote me prior to my departure from Hampton. I appreciated it more than I can say even though I went on and carried out my own plans. I feel now as I felt then, since I have gotten so old it is best for me to strike out for myself and make a home for myself. . . . Some day I shall hope to have a home for myself when all will be O.K." It would be nearly ten years, but Helen did achieve her dream.

Chapter 7

WRITING FOR POSTERITY FROM HAWAII

Helen was not the first person to go to Hawaii from Hampton Institute. Samuel Chapman Armstrong grew up in Hawaii as the son of missionaries, and he modeled Hampton on the all-male Hilo Boarding School. Founded in 1836 to train missionaries, Hilo shifted its focus to preparing young Hawaiians to become carpenters, house painters, and shoemakers. Armstrong maintained his ties with the islands during and after his work at Hampton.

Helen left Hampton with mixed feelings. "The people here feel badly at my going away and really make me feel badly by their frequent protestations. I did not know how much my work counted for until now. I am ready to leave it. Yet I feel if I ever get strong enough again to be ambitious it will be worth to me all that I am giving up in leaving all that are dear to me for a time." The thought of leaving her friends and colleagues saddened her more as the time approached. "The people here feel so badly about my going away that I really feel badly myself. I shall stop teaching to-morrow afternoon [January 8, 1901]." She waited until the last minute to complete her arrangements, a habit that continued throughout her life.

Helen started for the West Coast on a night train from Philadelphia. A through sleeper took her from Chicago to San Francisco. She gained "a pretty fair idea" of a western town from spending part of a day in

Kansas City, Missouri. As the train departed Las Vegas, New Mexico, she wrote:

Most of to-day [January 18] we have spent crossing the Rock Mts., where the scenery of course is superb. . . . dining service is splendid and I go out for two or three meals each day. This road supports dining stations where they stop twenty five minutes for meals and does not have on a dining car beyond a certain point.

We have passed many things of interest among them the mining villages, adobe houses, prarie dogs, burrows, coal mines, and have followed the old Santa Fe Stage Road for many miles. The herds of cattle dotted all over the praries have been of course a novely to me. No matter what the outcome of this change the trip has been worth all that I have risked I am sure.

I get healthily tired each day so's that I sleep well at night, and have a good appetite for my meals. . . . As soon as it gets dark the porters begin making up beds for those that desire and that makes us all want to begin preparations.

At the end of the "perfectly ideal" trip, she spent three days in San Francisco. At sea, the ocean threw its worst at the passengers of the newly refitted steamship *Sonoma*. "The sun broke through and cheered us as we sailed out through the Golden Gate. With a brisk breeze blowing we steamed out past the Presidio, the Cliff House and out to sea. We enjoyed the breeze and were accustoming ourselves to the new sensations when the spray began to dash up into our faces and then over the sides of the vessel at such a rate that we were glad to move back. It grew worse and worse and by five o'clock we all realized that we were right in a wind storm and had a bad night before us." Most of the passengers fled to their cabins as the crew raced to lash down the furniture and close the portholes. Intrepid Helen remained on deck:

I have always felt that if you can only keep in the air you will feel much better than by staying in closer, smaller quarters. Knowing from every indication that I myself was getting ready for a "squall" I lunged forward to a seat grasped it and sat down. Then, immediately down came the sickness and I was thankful that it was on the deck where the darkness of night and the storm in a way spared others the sight. So sick, so sick! I thought that nothing worse in this life could be. I could fully appreciate what the whale felt after swallowing Jonah and was glad to have been relieved of my own burden. Over I keeled on the setee with scarce life enough to hold my head up, and the boat rocking and lunging and plunging and I wondered how I ever could reach my room.

As she lay immobilized, an elderly gentleman came and sat by her. They remained silent for some time. At last he spoke: "This little girl is pretty sick, isn't she! The best thing you can do is to get to your room." Helen said she could not move. "Then he fairly carried me, wet and dripping as I was to my room, removed my wraps and shoes, opened my case for me and gave me such things as I needed. Then after administering a dose of medicine left me for the night. I have nothing I can say that would express my appreciation for this kindness, such as I have never known." She never learned the man's name.

Wind and waves battered the *Sonoma* for two days. "That first night and the second day were terrible and even now to think of them makes one feel a little green. Port holes blew open, dishes broke, panes of glass were driven in, trunks (steamer) walked and bumped from one wall of the rooms to another, doors banged and while the passengers held on to their beds with both hands and gasped for breath, pandemonium seemed to reign supreme. This kept up all Friday and well into the night Friday night. It is said that even the captain was sick and he has been following the sea since '48."

As the *Sonoma* neared Hawaii, the sea calmed and the passengers began to enjoy the shipboard amenities. There was a choice of morning baths—hot or cold, fresh or salt—and meals that included "elevenses" and tea at 4:00 p.m. Helen "saw a whale at some little distance from the ship and he threw water into the air a number of times to our great satisfaction." Flying fish inspired her to recite Rudyard Kipling's "Where the Flying Fishes Play." She suggested to Bertha, "When you go to sea be sure that your mind is well stored with poems and songs of the sea and of Nature. You will find great need for them all," especially "Rocked in the Cradle of the Deep."

Her chaperones were Charles Dyke and his wife Estelle, who had been the principal of the Whittier School. Mr. Dyke was to serve as principal of the Kamehameha Schools, where Helen went to work. Named for Kamehameha I, the warrior king who united the Hawaiian Islands, the schools opened after the death of his granddaughter, Bernice Pauahi Bishop. She had inherited an enormous tract of land on Oahu and in her will decreed the establishment of schools for Hawaiian children "to provide instruction . . . in such useful knowledge as may tend to make good and industrious men and women." Just as Samuel Chapman Armstrong had used Hilo Boarding School as a model for Hampton Institute, Kamehameha was modeled on Hampton.

Helen went to work immediately, as she told Harriet, in "the kitchen as well as the parlor" of the boys school for a salary of twenty-five dollars a month. "The last time that I wrote you there had been company; to day [October 20, 1901] it was the same thing. At 5.30 I had to serve a five-course dinner to six people. You know what this meant after preparing it and setting the table. Then came all of those dishes and the putting up and cleaning up. I wade through a great many such times. I can't say that I care particularly about either. I am learning from it all much that I wanted to know though the experience cost dear as to feelings sacrificed etc. You know better than I can explain."

Despite the long hours and arduous work, Helen assumed additional responsibilities by tutoring a student in English and helping the school nurse organize and prepare her lectures. Helen took an interest in all the students and sent home detailed reports. "Here we have two boys under surveillance for leprosy. It is sad, both being very bright. One is a little fellow, part South Sea Islander whose hair and features strongly suggest the negro. He stands before the glass and smoothes and smoothes his hair with an attitudure that says, 'oh, if it was only straight.' He is as cute as can be." The boys were probably consigned to the leper colony on the island of Molokai.

Another student had an accident that caused him terrible pain. The pain subsided, but "he is now suffering agonies while giving up the morphine which has for these six weeks kept him in comparative comfort," a teacher told Helen. A few days later, the boy was "suffering much less, and this morning looks bright and cheery as a well boy." While one person cared for the recovering addict, the rest of the staff was nursing a measles epidemic and administering daily treatments for pink eye.

Helen's duties allowed her ample time for socializing, beginning with a reception the school had arranged for nine hundred people to meet Mr. and Mrs. Dyke. "The entire place, Bishop Hall (one of the school buildings) was festooned with greens. A great many whole banana trees were used to good effect and in that great large place, looked as much in place as hot house palm could in a hall at home. Palms and ferns were used in great profusion and the balaustrades and hallways were a perfect bower." Full dress was the "order of the evening" for the Americans, but it was the exotic clothes of the Asian students that impressed Helen. A Chinese kindergartner "dressed in her long silk pants and jacket, a Japanese woman in her kimona accompanyed by a Japanese man in our approved evening dress, and several Hawaiian women in their Holokoos, which to us are loose mother hubbards."

A whirlwind of activity followed the reception, beginning with a visit from three young Hawaiian women, "Two of whom, ladies, are teachers here on the grounds. It is the first time that I have met them to really become acquainted and am completely charmed. The young ladies that I have just mentioned, Miss Shaw and Miss Bates, are both graduates of a normal school in New York State." The next day, a Friday, she went to tea at "the home of a lady of great wealth. . . . Saturday morning Queen Liluokalani called accompanied by an attendant and her ward Joseph Iia, who is a candidate for West Point. She was very regal, still gracious. The teachers all came in and we were all presented. Just think, I have met a queen and have shaken her hands with her! She is a portly brown skinned woman with a heavy head of straight black hair. She was perfectly gowned in a soft gray, with hat, gloves and veil to match. It was worth a great deal to me to have this opportunity. I am extremely anxious to make some good friends among the Hawaiians as I know they will be delightful and that I shall learn a great deal from them."

Helen never made derogatory comments about the native Hawaiians while she was in the islands, but after she returned she told a reporter that they were "inclined to be lazy" because they could live easily without doing much work. Nevertheless, she enjoyed their food and hospitality, especially a luau in honor of Mrs. Bishop:

The cooking was done out of doors in ovens made in the ground. These were made by lining a large opening in the ground with stones upon which a fire was built. Stones covered the wood, and upon these the cooking was done. The meat, pork and beef together, and fish were wrapped in ti (pro. tea) leaves and placed on these heated stones. Hemp sacks were covered over the huge mound, which contained packages of the meat sufficient for three hundred, then the whole was covered with earth, and cooked all night. The fish, sweet potatoes and a taro and cocanut pudding were cooked in the morning after a similar fashion. The "luau" was at one oclock. The table cloth was of ferns and ti leaves on which was placed the dishes. By each plate was an orange a bottle of soda, a fish in its wrappings of leaves and a bundle of meat, a sweet potatoe and a bowl of poi. Ice cream and cake followed. It was all very good, the taro and ti leaves used in the preparation, giving the food a most delicious flavor.

She next "made an excursion into 'swelldom,' " attending a reception given by Anna Cate Dole and Governor Sanford Dole. Helen found the surroundings and the company entrancing. The house was "filled with statuary, painting, tapestries, furniture of costly woods and curios from many climes. The first floor had but two rooms, excepting kitchen etc. at the back, as far as I could see beside the immense verandah, called here lanai. These were the parlor and dining room both being the size of several good sized living rooms." The dining room table was so big Helen wondered how people could converse with each other. "Mrs. Dole is a remarkable woman, remembering the names and faces of her hundreds of callers and having something real personal to say to each, making her feel comfortable. I did not want to go, feeling that my clothes and position were not in keeping. But my common sense told me that if I was so honored as to be invited I had better go, and that people would be paying so great attention to the appearance of those of high degree, that I could easily pass unobserved. I hope I did. At least I was very comfortable and had a nice time among pleasant friends who were there." The polite reaction of Mrs. Dole and her guests was typical of Helen's treatment by Hawaii's white ruling class. Everyone was "so extremely kind to me that I simply marvel."

Like her brothers and sisters, Helen had coloring and features that people could mistake for any ethnicity except white. Mrs. Dyke, who of course knew Helen was colored, "is lovely to me. She tells every one that I am here preparing for college and they treat me accordingly in spite of the fact that my work is in the kitchen as well as the parlor and that I am a Negro as well as an American." But most casual observers did not know Helen had African blood. Local residents spoke to her in Hawaiian, "discomfiting me a little," she told Louise. She learned a few words of the language and used it to make an excellent impression on a Japanese man: "As I said 'thank you' for the water, I added I will give Kura [his daughter] your 'Aloha nui nui,' and how pleased it made him. His hearty laugh and profuse bows were a pleasure. The Hawaiian language is the medium of speech among this varied population and with it one can always get on. Even a few words and phrases are exceedingly helpful, for they bring light and pleasure to many a face that is utterly blank at the sound of English."

Helen gained the respect of the staff at Kamehameha and continued to receive praise after she left. "Success seems to attend my efforts. Letters come from Honolulu and the other islands saying that I am spoken highly of in educational circles for my work . . . This, in a strange land, among strange peoples, and for one of supposed inferior race, really seems incredible. It is simply a realization of the truth, that 'God helps those who help themselves.' "

Some people continued to patronize, however, even if it was with the best of intentions. Allie Felker, the principal of a school in Honolulu, wrote, "The boy who lifts [Mrs. Heapy] about is a Negro. His name is Grace and he is a regular 'Uncle Tom' for kindness and faithfulness. I did not see him when I was there the last time, but I told Mrs. Heapy to tell him that I loved him and all of his people. Dear old Grace!" On another occasion she told Helen, "I had fried chicken and hot biscuits for breakfast. I thought of you." Such comments made Helen's encounters with other colored people all the more precious.

When Helen did meet Negroes, they did not always meet her expectations. "Lawyer Stewart and his wife called last week [November 25, 1901]; I felt that they did not call on me, although Mrs. Dyke invited me in to meet. I fear that I shall never know them well as I smell *patronage* in the air. This never agrees with me so I expect I shall not often get near enough to scent it." The American-born Thomas McCants Stewart, whom Helen called "one of the brightest men on the islands," practiced law in Hawaii for seven years between stays in Liberia. His wife, who remained nameless in Helen's letters, displayed rudeness, but Helen demonstrated that she was more than capable of deflecting bad manners:

I got nicely snubbed a few evenings ago at a musicale. This was the first time I have been so treated so hardly know how to take it. I felt that I had been "crushed" . . . Who do you think treated me to this new experience? Mrs. Stewart, wife of T. McCant. I wrote you that she was a bit supercilious and feeling this, was not surprised. It so happened that I sat in front of them . . . after the affair turned to speak and wanted to introduce a friend, one of the teachers who was with me. The latter priviledge was not given me for in answer to my "A delightful evening Mrs. St." I received so cold a response that I beat a retreat. I fear I shall not be so bold again. On the whole, I think it quite amusing since we are the only colored people about here.

Helen learned subsequently that the Negro population in Honolulu was larger than she thought. A missionary "who works in the slums of Honolulu . . . gave me the surprising information that in his district reside many negroes. They came out with the Puerto Ricans, having first gone from the Southern States to Puerto Rico to work in the cane.

They are a low ignorant class and have given up plantation work to enjoy life in the Hawaiian metropolis." Samuel Armstrong had tried and failed to help the Hawaiian planters recruit Negroes to work in the islands. A subsequent drive to import labor brought plantation labor from Puerto Rico just before Helen arrived.

There were others of her race that Helen shunned. "On the car yesterday [November 24, 1901] were two colored men dressed to kill, patent leather shoes, fancy socks, etc. One of them, of a very, very dark complexion, was dressed in white according to custom here. He even had on a white silk shirt. This being so airy in its nature, fanned in the breeze, displayed a vast expanse of ebony, for he had no undershirt on. They probably belonged to Hogan's troupe which is playing at the Orpheum. . . . I often wish that there were some nice colored people here to know. I get lonesome for them."

Other Negroes whom she encountered received Helen's stamp of approval. "While in town the other day I saw a colored letter carrier in uniform," she told Harold. "He seems a very young man and appears quite bright. Then too, I saw a colored painter at work on a new building. I thought perhaps these facts would be of interest to you since they prove Dr. Frissel's doctrine that the man who is ready will find work any where." She was pleased to report later that "T. McCant Stuart's daughter is teaching in the Honolulu Normal School. How's that? This place is all right for prepared colored people, I think."

She found the behavior of other cultures both uplifting and barbaric:

Yesterday I saw the loveliest thing which brought the Hampton spirit to me most forcibly. On Saturdays the museum is opened and is greatly frequented by Chinese and Japanese. Seeing two Chinese women battling with the wind, I took special care to observe. One was leading a tiny child by the hand while the other had a still smaller one in her arms. The former was being blown about so recklessly by the wind, that I wondered at it, and looking yet more closely discovered that she had small feet. Her feet looked about three inches long making her practically a cripple. In the midst of her difficulty, a young Chinaman employed here on the grounds came along, and beholding her dilemma, took the child from her, carrying it to the electric car, a walk of about seven minutes. Being thus relieved, she was able to take her companion's arm, and the last I saw of her was walking slowly and painfully towards the car. I felt personally grateful to "Marn" for that is the young man's name, for his timely assistance. The Chinese of Honolulu are getting too enlightened to bind their girl's feet which is a real blessing, as the deformity of the women who were so treated in infancy plainly shows.

Racial tolerance for Helen was a lesson easier taught than learned. From her post at Kona Orphanage, "I am convincing people in this part of the world that colored people are really good for something. I can see that some of the people of the community are unbending necks, which they tried to hold stiff. I had some 'pilikia' [trouble] with my Japanese boys over their singing coon songs. Before I got through with them they were so ashamed of themselves that I hardly expect another outbreak of that sort."

Despite the dearth of "nice colored people" Helen led an active social life. To entertain an acquaintance from New Haven, she organized a mountain-climbing expedition to a 1400-foot peak, "enjoying the magnificent views of sea and valleys below us and the very imposing and lofty ones of mountains around us." They ate wild guavas and had a "very satisfactory jaunt," she reported. A climb up Tantalus featured a "very very steep" three-hour ride in a horse-drawn bus into the rain forest, where it was pouring as they looked down on the sun shining on the beach and the ocean below.

Vacations and holidays offered Helen an opportunity to explore her surroundings, and she took full advantage of every occasion. In the fall of 1901 she experienced one of nature's exquisite displays. "It does seem as though the wonders of this place are inexhaustable. To-night we saw for the first time a Luna rainbow. The mist was falling fine and fast and the sky pretty well o'erspread with dark clouds. In the East they were somewhat broken, and the moon, which was trying to appear could be seen at intervals. During one of these we observed this magnificent large bow towards the West. It was almost perfect. It seemed to be almost white. At one end we thought we detected some coloring, green and pink, but it may have been wholly imaginative. The bow, though, we are sure of."

Travel allowed Helen to enjoy other aspects of her surroundings, beginning with a twenty-five mile, three-hour train ride to Waialua on the northwest coast of Oahu. As they passed "acres and acres of sugarcane, rice, taro, bananas and cocanut palms," Helen befriended a half-Chinese student who invited Helen to visit her family's plantation on Maui. "Miss Akana . . . gave a good deal of valuable information about the different fibres from which they weave. Thursday I went to see her and she gave me my first lesson in weaving, the result being a small mat. The Hawaiian mats are beautiful, some of them being large enough to cover an entire room."

Helen's next trip was closer to home. "The party consisted of three doctors, a surveyor and several young ladies. One of the gentlemen had a large demijohn suspended between his shoulders filled with drinking water and had a pocket cup both of which proved a blessing to us as we climbed." The young men had brought four one-pound boxes of candy, which the group devoured after they had climbed eight hundred feet up Diamond Head. "We sat there long enough to see the sunset and the moon rise. Between the afterglow on the one hand and the reflection of the moon on the blue of the ocean on the other we reached bottom. In the several conveyances on horses, and on wheels we left this point and went on two miles in the direction of home to Waikiki beach. We stopped here and all had a lovely salt bath. The surf was beautiful and under the light of the full moon nothing more beautiful could be imagined." And just so Bertha and family wouldn't think she was swimming nude, she added, "The Kamehameha teachers are all furnished with suits gratis here the grounds being leased by the hotel from the Bishop estate. You are given garters, stockings, a suit that fits, and two large bath towels and a room to use."

On the return trip, "We were driving through a gate way when the horses bolted throwing the bus with great force into the fence. The young lady on the seat with the driver was thrown headlong in one direction, the driver landed between the hind feet of the mules, and the horses took flight." No one was hurt, and everyone returned to the school safely.

Helen enjoyed Hawaii's fauna, too, though she did not want quite such intimate acquaintance with the many-legged variety: "Were you [Bertha] to come into my room and see the large red ants walking about, I know that you would be horrified. . . . An ant is parading before me now. I doubt not that it knows that I am writing, and do not care to stop to kill it. It seems real cruel to kill them but what is one to do? One was walking up the sleeve to my dressing sacque a minute ago."

Far more intimidating were the tropical storms that battered the islands. As she told Peter, "Were you by any means to descend upon Honolulu to-night and experience the terrible wind storm which is raging, I doubt your realizing that you had entered the tropics. We have the windows and doors closed, which enables us to be comfortable within while without the wind is raging most terribly. The windows and doors are rattling while the trees and shrubs are making a noise like unto the beating of the surf on the shore. They are quite accustomed to such storms, lending themselves, bending and swaying and tossing without ever breaking."

Helen took a break from her active social life in the fall of 1901 because "in the midst of all came the news of the president's death and the great strain on everyone which followed. Large memorial services were held and sadness held sway for some time." Helen's letter to Harold about President McKinley's assassination turned into a slight complaint about her family. "My kind regards to Mr. Deveaux. He was the only one thoughtful enough to send me papers from the States at the time our great National Calamity. He sent me two New York and two Savannah papers which I appreciate very much. The president had been dead ten days before we had any word of it. Not having a cable we are much behind in our knowledge of the world's events." Those sentences constituted Helen's only mention of the event and one of only a handful of references to national politics in her ten years of correspondence.

Because they felt isolated and homesick, the Americans on the islands made every effort to replicate life in the States. Helen's first island

Christmas was as traditional as Mr. and Mrs. Dyke could make it. "Mr. Dyke insisted that we hang up our stockings, so we did. In the morning we made haste to see what was in them. To our surprise they were filled to the brim. On inspection, it proved all a joke. Mr. D. had put in bars of kitchen soap, potatoes, boxes and any thing which he found handy after first wrapping them up most carefully." An exchange of real presents followed, and Helen received German editions of Andersen's and Grimms' fairy tales and a lauhala pillow. A Chinese friend gave her a fan made of the same materials. On Christmas afternoon she went with the teachers to an entertainment at the girls school, and Mr. and Mrs. Dyke played host at a dinner party in the evening. "One of the features was a Christmas Pie, on the Jack Horner order. 'We stuck in a thumb and pulled out a plumb.' This we did twice, drawing first a favor, a toy, then a souvenier; all were different."

To celebrate the New Year, she attended a party that featured pulling candy, popping corn and hunting for peanuts. The guests played Forty-two, a game combining elements of dominoes and bridge. "Then it was twelve o'clock. We went on to the lanai (verandah) and as the bells began to ring, the whistles to blow, cannons, guns, fire crackers etc., to raise their voices, we wished each other a happy new year. Being on an elevation, we were able to enjoy the fire works which were set off in town. So lively a New Years morn I have never welcomed." She was so thrilled she stayed awake to watch the sun come up.

Helen had two opportunities to visit the beach at Waikiki. During an overnight stay in February 1902, she discovered that "The people of wealth keep up three or four houses, as a rule. One in the city, at the shore, in the mountains and some times on the peninsula besides. When they are away, the frequently let people who are not so fortunate take possession. Having such an invitation, all a person has to do is to take bedding, i.e. linen, table linen and food. Every thing is in running order. It was at one of these cottages right on the ocean that I went. In the morning we dressed in bathing suits and took a plunge before breakfast. Then we gathered pebbles, shells and coral on the beach. It was glorious. You may be assured I didn't want to return when the time came."

She took a vacation at Waikiki two years later, renting a room from Miss Allie Felker. She told her father that "the whole place seems to breathe of rest." Miss Felker's house "is almost hidden by gigantic date and cocoanut palms, while the yard is a perfect bower of tropical foliage oleaner hala trees, algerobas, ferns, crotans and plants too numerous to mention growing in profusion." The property extended three hundred feet to the sea, and midway was a "dear little summer house where one may rest undisturbed and enjoy the peace that pervades the atmosphe[re]." This vacation was one of the few times Helen spent money almost solely on leisure. She told her father, "Living is very, very high here, board being Ten and Twelve Dollars per week. I think my vacation expenses will come to about One Hundred Seventy-five or Two Hundred Dollars. I shall record it as the most expensive one I ever took." Her expenses included a dozen photographs at a cost of eight dollars and a dress at fifteen dollars—for a total of more than four thousand dollars today.

Part of her expenses were for academic pursuits, and she described her studies in detail as part of her campaign to have her father contribute toward college tuition when she returned to the States. "My subjects are quite foreign to any that I had under consideration, but have been chosen because my work for the next term seems to require them: short hand, type-writing and music are the three, the latter being the 'tonic sol-fa' system which is used entirely in the schools of the territory. My aim is to take a . . . course with the hopes of securing a primary certificate at the end of that time. It is an expensive course, the teacher charging two dollars per hour for lessons and I shall have two lessons a week."

Much of her education came from the people she met, she told Peter. "As one travels about the world the more is he impressed with its advantages in the way of contact with people." While she was meditating on the beauty of her environment "the sea, the mountains, cloud effects, rainbows, mist, sunshine, rain, varieties in foliage, boatmen, children in the water," she encountered an English nurse who had just returned from a trip home that included study at a London hospital. She spent seven years worth of savings in thirteen months but considered the investment worth it "because of the added strength she gained by its expenditure.

She talks volubly of home industries, protection. . . . Many a good story I hear and many a glimpse obtain of the inner life of people who have mounted the rungs of the ladder by labor and sacrifice."

Continued church attendance reinforced Helen's devotion to the work ethic and motivated her to succeed. By the time she arrived in Hawaii, she had acquired definite ideas about the practice and did not entirely approve of the order of worship at Kamehameha. She called the new Irish chaplain "a curiously interesting man." A graduate of Cornell and former Columbia professor, the Reverend William B. Elkin inspired her the first time she heard him preach. She declared his sermon based on Revelations 21:1 ("And I saw a new heaven and a new earth: for the first heaven and the first earth were passed away; and there was no more sea") "extremely interesting as well as scholarly." Soon, however, she found it "strange, withal, he is little adapted for his position. While his talks Sunday mornings to the students are very helpful being masterful, they are quite like lectures on sociological questions. There is nothing whatever spiritual about them so one wonders how he has the courage to enter the pulpit Sunday to deliver them." She confessed to Peter that she had gained part of her knowledge in an unorthodox manner:

He writes his prayers, then reads them, holding the paper in his hand, with utmost unconcern. How do I know? O, I have peeked and seen him. Once, on a very auspicious occasion, the exercises commerative of the birth and death of Mrs. Bishop, the founder of these schools, he started to pray from memory and then forgot about in the middle. There was a most embarassing pause, during which nearly every one looked up to see what the trouble was. There he stood face and head as red as a beet, trying to think. Finally he got in and finished, thus relieving us all. This lack of the spiritual in him seems to be felt throughout the school. My idea is that Mr. and Mrs. Dyke are much like Mr. Elkin on religious matters: from this you can see that the atmosphere of the place is not at all like Hampton.

Helen attended Central Union Church in Honolulu when she had the opportunity. She sent Bertha the program from the March 10, 1901, service and wrote on top, "The church is attended mostly by Americans. It seems to be a home church for foreigners. They are very fashionable. The pastor [the Reverend William Morris Kincaid] is one of the finest that I have ever heard."

Once Helen had settled in Honolulu, she began to formulate plans to further her education, writing to Peter in the summer of 1901 that she planned to attend Columbia University. "They have established several scholarships for colored students there and Mrs. Dyke feels that when I am ready that there will be little doubt of my being able to obtain one. Mr. is from Columbia and has a good bit of influence with the heads of the various departments. Isn't it lovely to think of. I am studying very, very hard, putting in seven hours a day all as a result of this new inspiration. Keep this bit of talk in the family, please for the time is yet long and there is many 'a slip twix the cup and the lip.'" She was studying algebra and German and planned to take up geometry and Latin. She decided to stay in Hawaii until the spring of 1903, "then for home, friends and associations so dear to me once more," she told Bertha. "It seems long to say it yet at the rate time flies I can almost see it now."

Those plans to attend Columbia never materialized "because of certain conditions regarding the scholarships," and Helen set her sights on the University of California at Berkeley. Bertha did not approve, and Helen replied, "Your letter of Nov. 25, so full of earnest consideration for your *tramp* sister, arrived in due season. . . . While I appreciate your thought more than I can say, still I do not want you to worry over me. I have started out to accomplish a *hard hard* task. . . . I shall not leave a stone unturned, the turning of which might help me towards getting into school in September. There is this though, if I do not succeed, I can remain here another year and work on, as I have done through the past. May this relieve you of any anxiety for me, for succeed or fail, yet will I be safely housed and in good hands."

Helen had saved seventy-five dollars plus the cost of her return ticket and had the offer of another one hundred from a friend. It was not enough for her to return to school, and she asked her father for a loan. "I feel that I want papa's backing if I can have it so if I need more, will know where to turn. Of course he knows best what he wants to do in the matter, and I simply wait his decision. I thought perhaps, since I had gone so far, he might like to help me." He did not.

Helen pursued the idea of attending Berkeley through the early part of 1902, but lack of money brought another change of plans. Instead, her pioneering spirit took her to Kona Orphanage in the tiny village of Kailua-Kona on the west coast of Hawaii. She worked as a teacher and administrator for six hundred dollars a year, twice what she had earned at Kamehameha. With few places to spend money on the island, she was able to save more.

Alice Beard, a devout and wealthy Californian, founded Kona Orphanage in 1899 at her home on the slope of Mount Hualalai. Despite its name, the institution served primarily as a foster home for "needy children" whose parents were still living. Illness, alcoholism, or desertion afflicted both parents of twenty-two children, while "eight have mothers who are immoral and fathers who are opium habitués," Miss Beard wrote in an annual report. Parents had to relinquish their parental rights before the children could enroll. Miss Beard financed the entire operation from her own income for the first two years, supplemented by small tuition payments from parents who could afford it. When Helen arrived, Miss Beard was soliciting funds from wealthy patrons.

Like Hampton Institute, Kona Orphanage stressed manual labor over academic subjects. The children learned farming and housekeeping by picking and processing the coffee beans Miss Beard grew. The harvest reached two thousand dollars the year Helen arrived. The sale of honey, eggs, and a variety of fruits and vegetables brought in about three thousand dollars annually.

Like everyone who worked there, Helen developed an interest in all aspects of school life. "It is raining very hard to day, for which we are extremely grateful. We depend wholly on the rain for all of our water. Every one has one or more immense tanks in which to husband the water. One of our tanks was nearly empty which as you can easily imagine, caused us no small amount of uneasiness with a family of forty nine to wash for and to supply with water for bathing etc. We are in the midst of the coffee season which means that a very large supply of water is required for the washing of the coffee."

The children, age two to seventeen, were a diverse group. They "are lovely: Japanese, Chinese, Norwegians, Americans, Porto Ricans, Portugese and Hawaiians, they form a happy medley." The Japanese comprised the largest group and came from families who supplied the labor on the coffee and sugar plantations around Kona. "We have a dear little Porto Rican here about five years old whose name is Carl. I asked him Carl what and he did not know, so I asked him if he would like to be called Carl James. He said yes, so now when he is asked his name he says Carl James. I am sure you would love him."

Helen felt her arrival at the orphanage was inauspicious for a variety of reasons. She had a rough eighteen-hour ride on the steamer that went out from Honolulu every ten days. She had missed three meals, which reduced her seasickness but weakened her for the main task—caring for a little girl who was traveling with her. Once they disembarked, she and the child waited two and half hours for the "school team" to take them on the four-mile, uphill journey. It took three hours to go the first three miles. "Every once in a while the horses would buck. I frequently expected that we would land in a ditch. As it was, they absolutely refused to stir after making about three quarters of the trip. Mary, my little charge and I then started to climb up." They had walked about a half-mile when

we were met by a Japanese who was bringing a horse for us. I was a little timid about taking it, but finally mounted. Mary didn't have courage to get on behind me and I hadn't confidence in myself to encourage her. A man came along at this point who I asked to help us out. He took the little girl on with him and took the reins of my horse, by which he lead me. I had taken off my collar and neck ribbon which I tied to the handle of my umbrella and put a handkerchief around my neck. With the umbrella across the saddle, and me astride of the horse in a walking skirt I made my entrance to Kona Orphanage. The children were all standing about to meet their new teacher, who really felt a little ashamed to be seen by them.

At the end of her long journey, Helen learned that Harriet had died. Despite her grief and embarrassment, Helen warmed immediately to the orphanage and decided that she could make a significant contribution. "I feel that I shall be happy in my new life, even far happier than when in Honolulu at Kamehameha. . . . I seem to be with nice people here and am in a position of responsibility." A few weeks on the job confirmed her good opinion: "I knew you [Bertha] would be anxiously waiting to hear how I liked my new home. I am really happier in it than I have been in any other position that I have occupied. . . . [The children] all like Miss James and vote her a very good teacher. . . . These long busy hours have been my salvation in this our late grief. At the table my eyes frequently fill and a lump comes to my throat because my mind is then again my own."

Miss Beard was long on Christian charity but short on administrative skills. "I have really got to get this institution in running order as it has been run without system," Helen observed. Her organizational abilities soon made her indispensable. "I know Miss Beard will not want me to think of leaving for already she considers me one of the most valuable assistant she has been able to secure. I enjoy working with her very much," Helen wrote after she had been at Kona for a month.

Helen defied theories of proper teaching but achieved satisfactory results. "I have three new boys in school, one of whom felt he knew more than the class to which I assigned him. However, I think he is now convinced that he yet has something to learn. My boys and I are very good friends which fact adds much to my happiness." She enjoyed the recreation as much as the children did. "Had you have come in accidently to-night I am sure you would have voted us a happy party. After supper we all assembled in the children's sitting room to eat sugar can[e]. It was quite a treat. I did not like [the cane] at first but now enjoy it with the children. It pleases them to have me one of them as I always try to be."

Even Helen could not cope with delinquency, however. "To-day [January 29, 1903] I was obliged to punish my large Puerto Rican boy. I wish you might have seen him; such an exhibition of temper I never beheld and hope never to again. He tore his hair, bit his hands, clenched his teeth and wailed aloud. I have been rather afraid of him for a long time and thought the best thing to do was to come to terms with him. We have had our reckoning, and I shall pray hard that he will be better." He was not, and six weeks later he left Kona Orphanage, "after a sad scene . . . [H]e has been sentenced to the reform school after a trial in Kailua this past week." The boy had run away and "was caught and returned which made him very ugly. He threatened to do all sorts of ugly things to those who were doing for him, so an officer was sent for immediately to take him in charge." The staff had "hopes that he would come out a strong helpful boy" and everyone regretted the outcome.

Helen's success with the children did not extend to infants. After Bertha's first child arrived, Helen wrote, "If you are as awkard with an infant as I am I fear you do not fully appreciate our priviledge in caring for her. We have two babies, and if I tell the truth, I think I must say that I go from them rather than towards them when I have an alternative. Fortunately they are not in the same building with me." Bertha thought Helen was indifferent toward babies, and she became indignant. "You spoke of [my] not caring for little ones. What do you think? I have a family of *52* [double underline] children on my hands for *6 months* [triple underline]." Several weeks later she admitted that a two-month-old baby was too young to appeal to her.

Miss Beard became ill in the spring of 1903 and went to California to convalesce. Helen felt overwhelmed. "Miss Beard . . . has left me 'in charge.' Can you imagine such a thing?" Miss Beard had prepared Helen by reviewing the school's correspondence, finances, and building plans, but Helen found herself surprised and overwhelmed by the financial aspects of the operation. "Even the business of the place passes through my hands. I have always despised moneyed transactions and even the keeping of my little monthly accounts has been a perfect abomination. They rarely ever balanced unless I made them by accounting for the deficit under the head of incidentals; and here I am juggling with large amts. paying bills making out receipts, writing monthly reports etc. It is like a nightmare. This I do in connection with teaching directing the kitchen and dining room and *running* [double underline] the place. I pray daily that I may not run it on a stone; the place here is covered with enormous ones."

Helen received donations of two hundred to three hundred dollars in a single day and had to oversee minutiae such as ordering talcum powder, pins, and the like from Honolulu, where Allie Felker filled the orders. Helen had given someone one hundred dollars to buy a money order, but it never arrived. Miss Felker planned for money from California and ended her letter to Helen, "assuring you *that better times are in store for the institution.*"

A staff member contracted dengue fever while Helen was in charge. "This ailment has been raising havoc with the people on the islands. Honolulu was under its powerful sway for many weeks," and travelers had brought it to Kona. Dengue, a viral infection, causes a rash, fever, and severe joint pain. It is generally not fatal but "very uncomfortable causing from one to two weeks of intense suffering," Helen said. After "many days and weeks of hard work," she, too, caught it. She complained that it "left me pretty weak and ambitionless, far more so than I can afford." As she convalesced, she again began making plans to leave Hawaii. She eagerly awaited the arrival of Hampton graduates John and Estelle Evans, who would assume her responsibilities.

In the meantime, personnel problems and complaints about the school from well-meaning neighbors needed resolving. Helen fired a staff member, and Miss Felker praised her. "'Revenge is mine' saith the Lord. Long ago I learned that the Creator was able to deal out his own punishment. Mr. H. was not there long enough to do any great harm. You dealt with him too quickly. The girls you have are not angels. They all know how to defend themselves. I don't feel at all worried."

Next, a woman who lived near the school complained to Miss Felker that the children were not eating enough. The grounds supplied sufficient food, Helen responded. The acreage around the orphanage produced bananas, pineapples, sweet potatoes, and taro; cows provided milk from which they made butter and cheese. Miss Felker used her diplomatic skills to diffuse the situation. "I advised [Mrs. C.] to call on the ladies and said some nice things about them, and some nicer ones about you. Then

I complimented her on the many good things she has done for the orphanage. She was highly pleased." Miss Felker was giving lessons in diplo-
macy. She had provided the flattery and relied on Helen to placate the
critic. "Now don't get '*mad*,' Miss James. Just use tact. Get up a good
dinner some day and invite Mrs. C. up to see the animals feed, or something of that sort. The orphanage has its enemies. The people who were
dismissed from there in the past have spread reports. However, right
will prevail, and I believe Miss Beard is on the right track and means
well." In Miss Felker's view, good intentions more than compensated for
limited rations or dietary imbalance.

With Miss Beard's return, Helen's duties changed, but she was still
"so busy that I scarce no my own name . . . with an amount of work that
you never even dreameded of." Staff turnover continued, and she had
three new teachers to supervise. Some days she worked from 4:30 a.m.
to 11 p.m., and she began to find the lack of variety exhausting.

Her enthusiasm for her work waned because of the new teachers who
criticized all the aspects of the operation, "the whole institution is wrong;
the children a worthless pack; Miss Beard a tyrant, work hard, etc. etc.
on to infinity. You can imagine the atmosphere created by all this talk. It
nauseates me to the extent that I regret a timely exit as a relief. One can't
help in any work by standing off and criticising: finding a cure for the
evil then administering it is what tells. . . . Doubtless it will be good for
me to live in an unpleasant atmosphere, as it is something I seldom do.
The world is so large, that I have always considered it folly to so harass
my soul and have acted in accordance with my theory."

To combat the negativity, Helen devoted more time and energy to
her pet project, the school library. She demonstrated the James family
resourcefulness by soliciting donations from Bertha's wealthy clientele.
"I am trying to get books sufficient to start a library for my children who
are almost bookless. We are 72 miles from Honolulu where is the near-
est library. Among your patrons do solicit a 'good child's book,' from
each. I want Young People's Cyclopedia of Persons and Places, very
badly, a good United States History and subscriptions to St. Nicholas
Youth's Companion, Success and Harper's monthly. Do help me." Her

requests began to pay off, and in a year's time she had accumulated more than two hundred volumes. Former colleagues at Kamehameha sent copies of magazines; *Living Truths: From the Writings of Charles Kingsley*; and Marcius Willson's *The Wonderful Story of Old*, a collection of illustrated Bible stories.

Among cash donations, the school received twenty-five dollars from Asylum Hill Congregational Church in Hartford, arranged by Miss Lewis. Books came from the *Connecticut School Journal*, which reprinted a letter that Helen had written to the *Hartford Courant* about her project. She continued to write to the *Journal* after her return to the States, and in 1907 received a check for $2.50. "Just think! Really my first literary money! I shall doubtless begin something else on the first full tide of inspiration. I feel like framing my check." The following year she earned a dollar's worth of books for an article in the *Educational Journey*. Helen continued writing to raise money for the orphanage, sending monthly reports to the *Honolulu Advertiser*, but she considered her literary career truly launched with the publication of "In and About Kona Orphanage, Hawaii," in the July 1903 issue of Hampton's *Southern Workman*.

Despite the long days, Helen was able to spend a significant amount of time on horseback. The results were sometimes amusing, sometimes frightening, sometimes both. She recognized that a good gallop, like other exercise, kept her depression at bay. "This morning [June 11, 1902] I rode a horse I hadn't been on before. I had a load of cakes for the girls on behind which displeasing him caused him to dance and buck most beautifully. I was in a narrow path among the coffee trees and the girls behind me. They screamed and ran but I held my own like a major. I am sure you would have been proud of me. I think I told you that we ride cross saddle. I planted me feet firmly in the stirrups and clung to that *animile* like a leach, and really was very little frightened. Still I am riding in my walking skirt the riding one being unfinished." A vacation in early 1904 allowed her to take a three-day trip on horseback to South Kona, about ten miles away, where she saw the monument to Captain Cook, "The City of Refuge," and the battleground where Kamehameha I quelled a rebellion.

Helen enjoyed the mountain air of Kailua-Kona far more than humid, subtropical Honolulu. "My surroundings are more beautiful than I had ever dreamed of living among. Nature is at her grandest at this point. It is glorious moonlight now and my whole nature is craving a draught of it, but I fear I will have to be denied. It is near nine o'clock and we rise at five." The environment made the hard work easier to manage. "The place is conducive to peace and serenity. Thirteen hundred feet elevation enable us to view the sea in all its phases as it lies before us, while behind us the land continues to ascend until at some distance towers a peak 9000 ft high. . . . I really feel in every way that I am a thousand feet above my old self. . . . I feel wise enough to read Emerson now and am simply feasting in his Essays on Nature." Swimming offered a diversion as well, but the orphanage did not supply the necessary accoutrements, so she told Bertha, "Do get me a bathing suit, sensible and servicable, size 34 and send right out. The natives bathe naked, but I do not care to, isn't it strange?"

A year after she arrived at Kona, Helen still found inspiration in her surroundings. When she wrote to Bertha in March 1903 she forgot that the air in Connecticut was more likely to be freezing than balmy. "The view here is magnificent. On the broad verandah on which I am writing one can look for miles across the Pacific the eye travelling down the hillsides covered with sugar cane, coffee and bananas. . . . The air is balmy as it is doubtless with you at present. My new room (temporary) has four doors, all of which are opened always, three opening onto the verandahs in as many directions. At night I have to rouse myself to see where I am as I waken and look down upon the moonlight bathed ocean."

On July 3, 1902, Helen wrote about another of the island's natural wonders. "I am too tired to write a long letter to-night, so send just a short note to assure that the volcanoe has subsided and that I am well and doing well." Mauna Loa blew its top again for a day in September 1903, and on October 6 it began sixty-one days of eruptions. Helen reported on October 18, "The volcanoe is yet flowing. Nearly every night the sky is brilliantly illuminated by the light from it. Many people are visiting it, considering it a great opportunity. No alarm seems to be felt, and I have read that there is nothing dangerous about a lava flow, unless one is directly in its path."

Just before she returned to the States, Helen took a horseback ride up lava beds formed by Mount Hualalai, about six miles from Kona.

Mr. and Mrs. Evans and I, with our lunches and wraps on behind the saddles, started off this a.m. at 6.30 for a trip to the lava beds, twenty one miles north of us. . . . For a distance of four or five miles we were on familiar ground, after which we were in wholly new territory. . . . through a country made beautiful by the variety and density of the foliage and the superb scenery. Never for an instant were we out of sight of ocean and mountains. The kukui and ohia trees were in full blossom and many a plant surprised us by a sudden burst of color that harmonized wonderfully with the greens, grays and browns of the landscape. The higher we went the more beautiful were the ferns and their friends, the ti leaves. A person could easily stand under some of the large tree ferns and find shelter under the tall and wide spreading leaves, yet some distance above them.

Eighteen miles from home they came to a plantation where a butler gave them water. The man's daughter attended Kona Orphanage, and Helen said he was glad to see the visitors. "His 'How's all the childrens?' did my heart good for the underlying strain of tenderness was for his own little girl of whom he is very fond." After they left the plantation the journey produced more surprises—a mountain peak "apparently rising out of the ocean, its whole base being so wholly enveloped in clouds that its existence seemed a myth, the visible point appearing as the continuation of the clouds." They rode over contorted hills of lava and got a view of a bay "nesting in the arms of the lava covered coast which stretched into the deep blue ocean, lying apparently at rest." The greatest surprise was "Mauna Kea one of the highest peaks on the Island (13,805 ft.) whose top was so covered with snow that we had a very plain view of it, though the mountain was many miles beyond. Here we had reached an altitude of 2100 ft. and were cooled by a breeze that suggested the heights from which it was blown."

They donned jackets and rode across the lava flow that spread for miles from the crater of Hualalai. Before heading home, they stopped to explore caves and a natural bridge formed by the lava. "It was more beautiful than I can tell you, suggesting the nave in some mammoth cathedral with its ceiling decorated with the artists' cleverest devices. The lava, in beautiful colors hangs in points and jutties and in intricate forms as though it had dripped down hardening as it fell. We climbed down into the place with some difficulty, the lava being very sharp and breaking easily." She called the place a "perfect waste" with no human inhabitants, estimating that they rode for five miles without encountering another human being. They stopped on the way home to water the horses and visit a German man and his Hawaiian wife. Mr. Müller had just conducted a government auction of seven hundred eighty-eight acres. Appraised at a dollar an acre, the parcel sold for twenty-one hundred dollars.

They galloped home by moonlight, finding themselves "refreshed mentally and physically after a ride of forty-two miles and a whole day spent under the canopy of heaven. It is such days as these that make one feel that Hawaii nei shall ever reign without a rival in ones affections."

After several false starts between March 1903 and April 1904, Helen gave notice at the orphanage and made plans to leave once a replacement arrived. She planned stops in San Francisco and St. Louis en route to the East Coast. In St. Louis she visited the physicist Edward Bouchet, a native of New Haven who was the first Negro to receive undergraduate and Ph.D. degrees from Yale University. He had recently left his teaching position at the only high school for colored students west of the Mississippi and was serving as customs inspector at the Louisiana Purchase Exposition. Helen recognized the value of accepting his offer to visit. "I am not oblivious to the many advantages that this kind act of his will bring to me. His friendship will mean an open sesame to the circles that it will be agreeable and beneficial to be in, both educational and social."

Leaving St. Louis, Helen wrote from Chicago on July 4. "By degrees I am drawing nearer home. To this point my trip has been safe and pleasurable. I had five most interesting and helpful days in St. Louis, attending the meetings of the N.E.A. [National Education Association], as well as visiting in a small way the fair, the proportions of which are great beyond conception." She was about to observe classes at the University of Chicago summer school and visited Hull House.

Helen remained active once she arrived in Connecticut, despite her complaints of fatigue. She wrote in mid-August that she had attended a reception at a social club in Hartford and left the next day for the Women's Northeast Federation meeting in Worcester, Massachusetts, at which Mrs. Booker T. Washington was among "*the* [double underline] distinguished guests." Helen arrived in New Haven at the end of August. "By easy stages I am drawing gradually nearer. I am on my last relay now, looking on towards Saybrook, which place I hope to reach Sept. first. My head aches quite a little. Accordingly I feel that perhaps I have over done some what. I shall be glad to be back in dear old Saybrook where I won't have to hold forth on 'Hawaii nei.'" Part of her "holding forth" was voluntary, as she had arranged to make speeches about her experiences, including one at the Asylum Hill Church.

She returned to her father's house after a short visit in Saybrook and told Bertha, "I am taking Hartford easy: not *playing* society at all." Her lack of activity included meeting a Hampton professor and his wife, a visit to their minister and his wife, a formal call on another group of friends, and a trip with her brother Fritz to Parson's Theatre to see "Mr. Wix of Wickham," "a pretty production of light opera." Once Helen returned to her "beloved" Connecticut, she stayed only until September and then headed to Atlanta University.

Chapter 8

CHALLENGES AT ATLANTA UNIVERSITY

Helen neglected her correspondence for several weeks upon her arrival in Atlanta in September 1904. "You know me well enough to know that I can not accomplish much when unsettled. For this reason I have not written ere this. The days have been a series of packings and unpackings. To-night I feel fairly comfortable as bureau, washstand, closet and desk are in fair working order." On her way to Georgia, she broke up her journey with a visit to Uncle Charley and his family in New York before arriving at "glorious" Hampton. "The lightly flecked blue sky blossoming golden rod and asters and inches of Phoebus dust made it seem like the old days when I returned to school." She surprised her friend Helen Virginia and caught a boat for Norfolk the next day.

Traveling through the South intimidated Helen, as evidenced by her purchase of a three thousand dollar insurance policy, in the event of death by "external, violent and accidental means." She paid twenty-five cents for seven days coverage to cover her trip from Virginia to Georgia.

Atlanta University was a Freedman's Bureau school on one side of the debate about education for colored people. Booker T. Washington, who had graduated from and taught at Hampton Institute, copied its emphasis on manual training when he established Tuskegee Normal and Industrial Institute for the Training of Colored Young Men and Women in Alabama. In contrast, Edmund Asa Ware, a Freedman's Bureau representative, founded Atlanta University to train teachers and set high academic standards for its students. The star of the faculty when Helen arrived was the Harvard-educated W. E. B. Du Bois, who gained fame as an author and cofounder of the National Association for the Advancement of Colored People. He had published his seminal work, *Souls of Black Folks*, the year before Helen enrolled. Washington wanted members of his race to be educated but not so much that they became a threat to the white establishment whose donations kept Tuskegee running, whereas Du Bois believed Negroes should devote their time and energy to achieving total equality. The best and the brightest of the race, the "Talented Tenth," needed as much education as possible to lead their fellows out of poverty and oppression.

Helen's loyalties remained with Hampton. "To me the Univ. pales before Hampton grounds, buildings, students. None seem to come up to those of my beloved alma mater." She reserved judgment on the quality of education. She faced challenges in her classes in history, freshman English, sociology, and Latin, where she was the lone woman in a class of thirty-five boys age thirteen to twenty. The professor became ill and called on her to teach "that mighty class of boys." She and the boys survived.

Du Bois's reputation preceded his appearance in his history and sociology classes. "The students say he is very severe and merciless in the assigning of lessons." Helen had considered history her "Jonah," but she had more trouble digesting sociology. Du Bois required a twenty-five-page paper on ancient and modern slavery. "This scares me out," she wrote.

Helen soon ran up against Du Bois's strict attention to detail. He instructed her to draw a map of the "western continent," and she failed so miserably that he required her to draw five more to bring to class the following Monday. "Can you guess how I spent a large part of my Saturday?" she asked. She decided not to attend a social event to finish the work and concluded that she would never forget that lesson. Du Bois's assignments continued to intimidate her as the semester progressed. When he traveled on school business, he left the class to write "a veritable mountain" of fifty pages on the "Occupations of Negroes," including "conjugal conditions," along with an analysis of the raw numbers and proportions of males and females in each age group.

Outside the classroom, Helen found her professor less intimidating. They were guests at a dinner party at the home of another faculty member. "I came back with Dr. Du Bois at ten, enjoying his company for the first time informally," she told Bertha. "He spoke of positions for the fall, saying I might be interested in the applications which they have on hand. I hope he will not forget me."

Helen gave other faculty members favorable reviews. "My first impression was that the institution needed an infusion of fresh blood. . . . My teachers are good. The instructor in English knows his ground, yet will improve with age and experience." Helen soon acknowledged that young George Alexander Towns possessed far greater knowledge of his subject than she had first believed:

At present I am finding out how little I know about English under a most excellent instructor Prof. Towne. He is a young colored man, graduate from this institution and Harvard. When I found myself under him, I wasn't especially pleased as he didn't impress me as a man of years or experience enough to be looked to as authority. It was but a case of "appearances being deceiving" though for as I follow him in the development of lessons I look at him with the feeling of awe somewhat akin to that [Oliver] Goldsmith must have felt as he gazed on the village school master. "And still he gazed, and still the wonder grew, How one small head could carry all he knew" [from The Deserted Village, 1770].

Helen battled an inferiority complex throughout her first year at Atlanta University. She was ashamed because she could not match the achievements of the students with class honors, and her insecurity carried over into extracurricular activities. J. Max Barber asked her to write about her experiences in Hawaii for his publication *The Voice of the Negro*, which included articles by university professors and "others of lesser fame." She declined. "I hope some day to have ability enough to do a thing of this sort well." Barber and *The Voice* did not survive that long in Atlanta. Racists destroyed the magazine's offices during the 1906 riot and forced him to relocate.

Among the people Helen met at the university was her future husband, Frank Pierce Chisholm. A native of Allendale, South Carolina, he enrolled at Tuskegee to study printing, intending to use the trade to finance a law-school education. He also attended Atlanta University and went on to become the northern agent for Tuskegee, traveling all over the East Coast to raise money and recruit students.

Helen continued to make contact with "brilliant people," as she called them, teachers and others interested in the education of colored people. She was a regular guest of Professor John Hope and his wife. A graduate of Brown University, Hope became the first Negro president of Baptist (now Morehouse) College and then the first president of the Atlanta University System. His biographer, Leroy Davis, portrayed Hope as bridging the gap between Du Bois's insistence on equal treatment and Washington's acceptance of second-class status for Negroes. At the Hope home and at other school functions she met the educator Mary Church Terrell, the wealthy socialist J. G. Phelps Stokes "and his wife (the Jewess)," and a grandson of William Lloyd Garrison. She attended receptions with the president of Spelman College, and with professors from Brown and the University of Chicago.

The academic challenges and social contacts did not compensate for the university's deficiencies, however. She soon complained about the monotony, made worse by the lack of exercise. The school had no gym facilities for women, and she could not freely leave the campus. The school experienced a "wave of excitement" during the winter when two students left the campus without permission. "Then such another search and vigilance was inaugurated that made it impossible for them to get to their rooms without being found out. The result is that both were indefinitely suspended, which is a mild way of stating expulsion. Their friends are extremely sad to-day, and the foremost topic of discussion is whether the decision of the faculty was just."

Like Hampton, Atlanta University imposed a work requirement on its students, an hour a day and two hours on Saturday. Helen's job was to clean the office of the "preceptress." "You could laugh at me now I am sure," she told Bertha. "I have that room to sweep and dust thoroughly each morning and the border to wipe up every other morning. I really do it though it seems strange after so many years away from housekeeping."

Helen was soon wearing herself out with extracurricular activities and social events. "Somehow in the busy years just passed I looked forward to this year off as a year of recreation, a year in which to accomplish things that had been waiting long. I fear it will not accomplish for me what I had dreamed, for I think I was never more busy."

She had saved considerable money in Hawaii, but eight dollars a month for room and board and fifty cents a month for laundry soon ate up her savings. "I am so poor that I am deprived of the pleasure of giving Xmas gifts this year. I trust that the years ahead will be rich enough to repay the vital sacrifices that I am making now." Despite the lack of money, Helen enjoyed the holidays. On Christmas she went caroling, ate dinner, played whist, and "attended a swell reception and met many pleasant young people" at Birdie Ford's house.

Helen was in one of her most euphoric periods. "There is something about my state or condition that is blissful, almost beyond comprehension. There is no care worry nor anxiety, any more than if I was the scion of a millionare with nothing to think of, knowing instinctively that all things would come to me. It must be my trust in God's providence that keeps me thus, for how else could it be with the responsibility of a college course on my shoulders, and a long expensive journey ahead with three or four months vacation following delightful uncertainty. What a future! What a future! I am glad to say with Pope, O! Blindness to the future kindly given that each may fill his circle marked by heaven!"

Her schedule began to take its toll after the holidays. "My body is numb and irresponsive," she wrote in February. "In order to accomplish the many duties of each day I sit up until past midnight almost every night and rise between 5.30 and six. still I am very well and happy in that I am accomplishing." Her schedule, "two hours work for the school each day, and an hour's work for one of the professors, besides twenty recitations a week, keeps me on the gridiron, you can imagine."

In her spare time Helen was "deep into" the debating society and the Athens Society, for which she prepared a eulogy on Lincoln. She also remained active in Christian Endeavor, a nondenominational Protestant organization, but she encountered obstacles to practicing her faith. "Our services, church and chapel, are held in the 'chapel', a large assembly hall which corresponds to the chapel at Hampton. There is no special building for the religious services. Because of this, it requires greater effort to take on that religious frame of mind which slips over one unconsciously as he enters a place of worship."

The religious life of the school was not a total wasteland, however, and Helen found inspiration from the sermons and prayers of the chaplain, the Reverend Edward Twichell Ware. The son of the university's first president, Ware began his career at Atlanta as a fund-raiser and continued his efforts after he became chaplain. According to Helen, he preached "magnificent sermons: so deep, so full of experiences that go to the making of a rich life. I always feel better after the Sabbath, the day's services are so helpful." Following a Sunday school class that he taught, she wrote, "He is a most genuine, intense man; as I look at him and listen to him, I think how near the ideal he is, a man way above the petty and small things of life." Soon, though, she grew to feel sorry for him. "When I realize the great sacrifice he and his sister are making for this work, I wonder if I can appreciate them enough. In this work they get a liberal share of the bitter with the sweet, and have many a trial and disappointment." The bitterness and disappointments came chiefly from the lack of money. Like Du Bois, Ware traveled frequently to raise funds for the university. Though it was a struggle, they were successful enough to create a substantial building fund.

The university held a dedication of the Oglethorpe Building and broke ground for Carnegie Library and Ware Memorial Chapel in the spring of 1905. Helen sent Bertha the program and wrote on the back:

I never saw any one look more wretched. I fear he isn't very happy.
I think he wants to cry.
She speaks as if she was addressing an assembly of "school marms."

I know he's relieved though he doesn't look it.
He sounds like he is translating Latin.
Ideas are the only things that come South by slow freight.
I wish the students would be more quiet, i.e., about talking.
It doesn't sound respectful for the occasion. That's right.
I am wondering what Dr. Sayles [Baptist College president] thinks of it.
That's the colored part.

Monthly rhetoricals also broke the monotony. Part education, part entertainment, each honored famous people. In February the students described Washington's inauguration, delivered the Gettysburg Address and the Emancipation Proclamation, and recited Paul Laurence Dunbar's poem "Frederick Douglass." March's session featured speeches about Milton's travels in Italy, his views on theology and public affairs, and Wordsworth's poem in the form of a plea to Milton to return from the dead and restore England to her former glory. Helen looked forward also to the "sociables" that followed and particularly enjoyed the gathering in January 1905 that included three grand marches.

Helen was finally able to leave the campus in the spring when she took her Jim Crow train ride to Tuskegee. She spent two days there, then traveled via Montgomery to Calhoun, Alabama, "one of the loveliest spots in all the Southland." The little town in the heart of Alabama's Black Belt was the site of the Calhoun Colored School, founded by a woman from New Haven who accepted Samuel Chapman Armstrong's challenge to educate freed slaves.

As the end of the school year approached she accepted an invitation from Hampton Institute to read a paper on her experiences in Hawaii. She wanted her family to attend for moral support and for a cure to her homesickness. "Can't one of you three, Peter, Louise or yourself plan to come down, or Harold or Fritz? I should be so happy and I am sure it would be an event for any of you." She asked Professor Du Bois if she could skip the last month of school and go directly to Connecticut, but he refused. She dreaded the "ordeal" of the return train trip to Atlanta.

Her speech, preserved by Hampton Institute, described her stay in Kailua-Kona and the creative ways a Hampton-trained worker taught and cared for classrooms of thirty children in the absence of books, paper, blackboards, desks, and chairs. Helen made an excellent impression and received an invitation to return the following year, which she accepted with some reluctance. "I am planning once more to go to Hampton to read a paper at the Anniversary exercises. I have sent it on for them to read and critize, so shall not know definitely for a few days. I regret going very much, as it calls for considerable outlay of both energy and money on my part: energy in the rush of school work which must be planned for closing and money to make myself appear half way decent, to say the least. However, it must be for the best, as it comes without any seeking." Helen turned her experiences in Hawaii into a small cottage industry, as she delivered another talk at Hampton in 1909.

Halfway through her first year at Atlanta University, Helen was planning her next move. "I am always in a quandry, though I work so hard to reach a resting place," she told Bertha in January 1905. She wanted to stay at the university through the fall semester and then find a teaching job. "I think that two years here will give me all that I want of this course: then, after another struggle, I shall try to enter another school, I hope nearer home. Already I dream of Columbia."

She considered teaching at a summer school in the South and wanted Bertha's opinion. "I sometimes think how much easier my life would have been if I had not attempted an educational career. Papa's saying 'A little learning is a dangerous thing,' often comes to me with redoubled force. A little will surely cause one to struggle mightily else fall out of the track." Helen was determined to have more than a little education. "I am looking forward to the day when I shall have that independent position, so long dreamed of, when the living and the salary will be so certain that I can cast my fortune in with you and Peter and help with the home beautiful. Perhaps Louise, too, will throw in her aid, and then how easily will the wheels turn. I am sure God will permit us to enjoy being together again and enjoying that peace which is the emblem of the true home life."

For the immediate future she wanted to earn enough money to return to Atlanta University in the fall. Summer jobs in the North would not pay her school expenses and would force her back into teaching before she was ready. "I hate to begin to teach until I have really advanced into the realm of a higher grade teacher. One year is but a foot hold to the beyond." Helen had written to the women's principal at Hampton Institute about a position but otherwise did not pursue options in the South, and she turned down Mary Lewis's offer to work as a "second girl." "I have tried 'serveting' even under most favorable conditions *can* not." Instead she arranged for work at Miss Morgan's house in Blandford, Massachusetts.

En route, she planned to spend two weeks in Saybrook. "They will be happy weeks for me which I am eagerly anticipating. A good laugh with you and Peter and Louise will take off a good deal of the dignity which I have been wearing for the last eight months." Her one concern was to arrive in Saybrook in time to watch Louise graduate from high school.

Helen's schedule of work and study during her second year shortened her letters and reduced their frequency to once a month. The letters were filled with descriptions of the weather and questions about Fritz and about Louise, who had entered pharmacy school. It is possible that Bertha destroyed some of them as well.

After a summer in the North, Helen returned to Atlanta University and immediately began to make plans to return to teaching. "I am thinking now that I will take out an insurance policy in the fall, then sail in recklessly to do as I please with my money. My only fear now is that my health might break while I am financially embarassed; that would indeed be hard after independence." She kept illness at bay and returned North for the summer of 1906, where she spent part of the time in South Byfield, Massachusetts, then went to her father's house. "In spite of the fact that it is hot enough to frizzle beef without the means of artificial heat I have been expecting to see you and Louise walk in at any time. When are you coming? I am crazy to see you both and hear of all those wonderful plans for college." Louise was entering Brooklyn College of Pharmacy as Helen prepared to teach in a remote corner of South Carolina.

Chapter 9

A LARK A FLYIN'

The Penn School began at the Oaks Plantation on the island of
St. Helena in 1862, shortly after the Union Army landed on Hilton
Head and swept north on its way to Beaufort, South Carolina. With the
arrival of the federal troops, the plantation owners fled, torching their
houses. They left behind the descendants of Africans who had lived
in an isolation unknown elsewhere in the United States. They preserved
many traditions from their native land that slave owners elsewhere had
successfully suppressed.

St. Helena and the other Sea Islands form a barrier reef from South
Carolina to northern Florida. The climate resembles that of the Mano
River region of western Africa. Captains of the slavers prized captives
from that region because they knew how to cultivate rice and indigo and
could command top prices in the slave markets. Thousands of men,
women, and children were kidnapped and arrived in chains to populate
the Sea Islands and the mainland area around Beaufort.

The Negroes of the island developed their own language, called
Gullah, a word itself most likely derived from "Angolan." The language
included vocabulary and syntax from Ewe, Mandinka, Igbo, Twi, and
Yoruba. Helen said the local people asked her, "Is you a dove a-settin' or
a lark a-flyin'?" meaning "Are you married or single?" Helen's letters
arrived postmarked from Frogmore, South Carolina, where school

buildings had been erected on a fifty-acre parcel. The school moved there after it outgrew its home at the Brick Baptist Church. The Frogmore name came from a spicy gumbo (a Gullah word) of shrimp, crab, sausage, potatoes and corn-on-the-cob—but no frogs.

When she arrived in the fall of 1906, between six thousand and seven thousand Negroes shared the island with fifty whites. The mainland was only five miles away, but the former slaves had virtually no contact with the outside world until the construction of the first bridge in 1927. As Helen told Louise, "Life here and isolation are synonymous terms. You can not imagine it. In some of my letters I will try to make you realize what it is like." She soon discovered that island life in South Carolina could be more primitive, and more of a threat to health, than island life in Hawaii. Yellow fever raged, and the Penn School's board of trustees delayed opening the school for a week to quell the epidemic. She did find much to admire. "St. Helena is a beautiful wilderness, with many interesting paths leading all over the Island. These I love to follow, wandering on into the unknown. Much of the weather, too, is ideal."

Culture shock, particularly in religious matters, upset Helen as well. The "shout," or ring shout, epitomized the problems of the island, Helen believed. Residents gathered on Saturday evenings in prayer houses that dotted the island. With hands clapping and feet stomping, they sang spirituals. The shouters—men, women and children—circled the crowd until many achieved a trance state. People stopped occasionally to eat and drink, but the singing and shouting continued until dawn. Helen found the practice barbaric and cited it as an example of the urgent need for the civilizing influence of the Penn School in a report she wrote for Hampton's *Southern Workman.*

Other aspects of island life thrilled her, however. "They do make the most beautiful baskets here that I ever saw. The school ships a hamper for Three Dollars, the purchaser paying the express. I never in my life so such beautiful ones. The order has to be in weeks or better months before hand. The waste baskets too, are lovely. They sell for a dollar and a half." Weavers constructed the baskets from marsh grass or rush and used saw palmetto to bind the tops and sides.

Helen may have attended and taught at schools that stressed manual labor, but she preferred to live the Atlanta University ideal. "My writing materials are on the front verandah, where I am employing them talking to you, while a girl is cleaning up my room," she wrote to Louise. "Sometimes I fear that the independence of my life makes me lazy. Perhaps it would be good for me to have to do what she is doing, instead of reading and studying so much."

Laziness did not describe her condition except in the strict physical sense. The seventh-grade teacher never arrived, so Helen took over that class in addition to her eighth-grade and post-graduate assignments. She also taught in the night school for adults once a week, led prayers another night, and on a third attended a Bible-study class. She also went to meetings of Kings Daughters, a civic organization inspired by Edward Everett Hale that promoted religion, education, and philanthropy. Rounding out the week was the Armstrong League, named for Samuel Chapman Armstrong, which served as the local branch of the American Missionary Association. On the seventh night she rested.

In the spring of her second year on the island, Helen started teaching a Sunday school class in a community five miles from the school. Plus "I am crocheting, sewing, reading and studying for recreation. Life does not seem monotonous, although I imagine I will be pretty well run down when May 30 comes." Among her sewing projects, "Last week, I tried to make me a dress. To-night I had hoped to finish it, but alas, and alack haven't even touched it though I am well nigh disgraceful. It is only made of denim, and is to tide me over this tight place I am in. If I do not go to Summer School or do any thing desperate this summer, next year I can breathe free financially. Just know I am enjoying the exquisite agony of being literally broke."

Occasional breaks in routine proved unsatisfactory. "Dr. Bayley, a young physician here, has been entertaining one of his own profession for some days. This means that we have seen something of them too. It was rather tiresome, as the visiting phys. was quite insipid. Chewing (chitlets) [chiclets] as one of our teachers says, all the time, and so meek he could scarcely talk."

Part of her discontent arose from conditions at the school, as she arrived during a period of upheaval. Laura M. Towne and Ellen Murray, the school's founders, had applied the same rigorous academic standards used by the elite northern preparatory schools. For nearly forty years they ran the school with the help of funding from the Society of Friends in Philadelphia and other organizations, but in 1900 they approached the Hampton Institute board of trustees about assuming administrative responsibilities. Hampton's principal, Hollis B. Frissell, became the chairman of the board of the Penn School. Laura Towne died in 1901, and two years later Hampton sent Rossa Cooley and Grace House to run the school. They did not assume full control until Miss Murray died in 1908, but with their arrival the curriculum began to resemble the Hampton-Tuskegee model. The school's name changed to the Penn Normal Industrial and Agriculture School to reflect its new mission.

During the transition, Ellen Murray remained as titular head while Miss Cooley and Miss House became the managers. The board disciplined two staff members for having an affair, and faculty members loyal to Murray felt that Cooley and House were trying to oust the founder and her supporters. Helen arrived in the middle of this conflict and heard numerous complaints about the new regime. She believed they would be able to gain the confidence of the teachers and staff, but the conflict added to her poor impression of the school. Among her personal disappointments, she waited four months to be paid.

Cooley and House also practiced a form of segregation that Helen found distasteful. "The principal and her assistant have their meals alone in the pretty home: the colored teachers in a dining room to themselves, then the students alone, one table, set with an oil cloth and stone china dishes." Helen told Peter, "The teachers dishes are terrible. I never ate from such coarse ones in my life. We have no butter knife and the tea spoons are put in tumblers on the table. The table cloths are the thinnest cheapest things that could be bought. I think that the furnishing of this room alone reflects great discredit on Miss Cooley and Hampton Institute. Label this first impressions. You know I love to spout." The separation represented tangible evidence of the philosophical difference between the old administration and the new. Worse, the colored teachers were treated as second-class citizens, a legacy of Hampton, whose alumni complained that the institute welcomed whites and virtually ignored Negro visitors.

Frissell, whom Helen called "the serious saintly man," paid a visit to the school during Helen's second year and used his diplomatic skills to overcome objections to the new regime. He delivered the Founder's Day sermon and presided over the unveiling of a tablet dedicated to Miss Murray and Miss Towne in Founder's Hall. The festivities included a dinner and the performance of college songs, a whist party, and the launching of a boat built by three male members of the faculty. Frissell's appearance served a far more important purpose. "I think his visiting us has done a great deal of good. He appreciated that we had difficulties and want to reach them. He invited me to walk with him, and asked me to talk it over with him. He went deeply into the policy of the school etc. and I told him that I should think it wise for him to tell all what he had told me. So he called a meeting and talked it over generally. I think that, as a result, we shall all understand Miss Cooley better. He made a brave plea for her."

Helen's opinion of the school improved as her mood brightened. She made a trunk cover, found a box for wood for the fireplace, rearranged the furniture, and hung pictures in her room. She told Louise, "A bare room and I have so little in common that I usually flee from it [until it] takes on a homelike appearance. Having been fully employed with school work I have had little time to devote to home making ere this." She called the wood stove "the joy of my life. I can get out of bed, make the fire and the room warm in five minutes." She was comfortable until the coldest days of winter arrived, as the three-room cottage had no foundation and no rugs.

Once her mental state improved Helen began to feel guilty about ignoring the serious illness that Louise suffered shortly after she entered pharmacy school. Helen gave herself a metaphorical "good thrashing" for her neglect. Her excuse, perversely enough, was boredom and lack of intellectual stimulation:

Somehow, I thought of you as so happy in your pursuit of that elusive possession—education—that you did not need pokey me and my accounts of days that are all the same; of weeks of seeing no one but my children and the resident teachers, with whom current history stopped when they left Hampton, a dear dull set, and of my friendship with the one available man, who flirts with three or four of the teachers and believes that each one "thinks him deeply in love with her and loves him in return."

Provincial! Funny! How you could laugh at it all, and how you could swear too, when over tired, mentally and physically, as you sat down to a dinner identical with the six others you had eaten that week and those charming teachers with their baby prattle.

Isn't it an interesting chapter! Not interesting I am sure to make me negligent of you, but energy sapping enough to prostrate one.

Yet I love it, and already dream of what I can accomplish with children in the next three years.

Soon she was able to take joy in her surroundings. Spring came early to the island, and in February she reported that "the jonquils, narcissus, snow drops, yellow jassimine and some of the wild fruit trees are in blossom, and a few of the birds are here on their way North, yet the weather is not hot." Corn planting started during March. "The ground in all directions has been plowed and is lying fallow, a pretty sight. Yesterday I drove several miles to see one of my boys, and oh! how lovely it was to inhale the deep draughts of spring. So enchanted am I with the spirit of the season that when I am on horseback I do not want to return. I feel as if I could go to the horizon." The island was experiencing a period of temperature extremes—ninety two degrees one day, sixty two the next, but Helen fulfilled her constant need for exercise with weekly horseback rides that cost twenty-five cents.

A trip to Beaufort helped improve her spirits as well. She visited Elizabeth Bampfield and her father, Robert O. Smalls. Helen called Smalls a fascinating man who made a valuable contribution to history, but the description fails to do justice to the drama of his life as a slave who, on a night in 1862 outwitted the captain and other white officers on a Confederate supply boat, sailed past the sentries in Charleston Harbor, and led his family and the rest of the slave crew to freedom. "The Gullah Statesman" later became a member of the South Carolina state house and served in the U.S. Congress. When Helen met him, Smalls was the port collector for Beaufort. Elizabeth was married to Samuel Bampfield, editor of the *Beaufort Free South*. After her father's death, Elizabeth became the postmistress for Beaufort and later worked at the Penn School. The Bampfields and Smalls were among the colored elite of the area, and Helen sought out their company.

Her account of her visit the man called the Gullah Statesman did not survive. In fact more than half of her letters from the period are missing, and gaps in the ones that did survive hint at family problems that Bertha wanted to keep secret. The letters that remain are full of requests for advice about plans for the summer and for the future. Helen planned to work in Saybrook when school closed. She asked Bertha to find a room for her: "Of course the expense will be mine." She left two days after school closed, making stops in New Jersey and in New York to see Aunt Tillie and to shop.

Instead of sticking to those plans, Helen spent most of the summer of 1907 at Yale University, where she studied theme writing with "special instruction in writing the short story." She also took a survey course in American literature that emphasized religious themes, beginning with Increase Mather and ending with the Transcendentalists, with a detour through the works of Edgar Allan Poe. She visited her father at the end of the summer and then returned to South Carolina.

That year Helen spent nearly as much time planning Louise's future as she did her own, sending instructions via Bertha:

If you are thinking of her doing any institutional work now [February 1908] is the time to apply. Most teachers are engaged during February and March. This of course would apply to a pharmacist. I am in hopes that Louise will be able to get remunerative employment at once. It will mean so much to family finances.

Have you thought of applying to those women's drug stores in Hartford? I am not much for her going in with men clerks. There are drawbacks. The colored druggist of Beaufort and his clerk, a Miss Mack were brought into newspaper notorierty through their personal affairs.

Helen was weighing her options as well. She was inclined to spend July and August working for Mary Lewis at a hospital in Winsted, a small town in northwestern Connecticut, or returning to one of Miss Morgan's houses. Still, she was not satisfied. "I dread to think out plans. All of the teachers are the same, dreading the long vacation. A number of them work North all summer. It is very hard indeed." During June and September she wanted a vacation or time to perform "social settlement" work that she would arrange through Dr. Du Bois, probably at the YWCA in New York. She had an easier time deciding on her next full-time job—teaching at Florida State Normal School in Tallahassee.

Chapter 10

ACHIEVING A DREAM

In early October 1906, Helen arrived at the Florida Agricultural and Mechanical College in Tallahassee, where she taught school Tuesday through Saturday. Mondays she filled with sweeping, dusting, and scrubbing her residence, going into town, playing tennis, entertaining students, and preparing the next day's lessons. She told Bertha that she found her fellow teachers "most congenial" and said she wished she had gone there three years before when the president, Nathan B. Young, first made the offer.

She was assigned to teach Latin but substituted a class in first-year German, which "gives me some concern." Her class in first-year technical grammar, "which I thought would be my Jonah, is one of my chief delights," while the fourth-year English class was a source of genuine pleasure, much to her surprise. She assigned Chaucer and texts on fourteenth-century life, including "Chivalry" and "Sir Galahad." Each student was required to read one additional book a month for each class. "Keeping up with them quite refreshes my acquaintance with characters familiar but neglected. In connection with this work, I am perusing Conan Doyle's 'The White Company' to see whether I shall add it to the list of assigned books. It is a tale of 14th century England and very illuminating. Conan Doyle has brought out the minor points with as much care as he does in his detective stories."

As the semester progressed, even the German lessons began to go "fairly well. Once in a while some one runs me up a tree in grammar, but on the whole I hold my own." While enjoying her success, she was anticipating greater challenges. "I believe I am to teach physical geography and that Ancient History which I dread so much. The benefit to me will be great, I know, but oh! the work it requires! Studying ahead of a class is hard work!"

She found her schedule overwhelming by the second semester. "I am in my schoolroom now from 8 A.M. until 5.30 P.M. To morrow though I shall be out at 12.30. It is getting too strenuous. I am preparing a very long program for the Public Rhetorical the 22nd inst. [February] Rehearsing students takes every moment from 12 N. until 8.30 P.M. However, each program has been a great success, and there are to be only two more, March and April. May is given over to commencement doings, so I am relieved and mighty glad too." She added a Sunday school class "of twelve or fifteen boys which I think I shall enjoy. So far, however, it has seemed like experimenting. They are large boys, who are in the lowest grades. Having upper class students, all the week, makes it seem like a transition to come to these on Sunday."

For recreation, Helen visited her new friends. Mr. and Mrs. Cardoza "are dear people, quite after my own heart. Mr. Cardoza is a Tuskeegee-Cornell graduate. His wife is a pretty South Carolina girl, a friend of the Bampfields. I feel perfectly at home with them." She had been invited to join the weekly sessions of the whist club. "I notice that colored society has taken up bridge almost wholly so of course I must learn it too." She eventually joined the club and played once a week. "I . . . hope soon to be able to play a good game. It requires all of one's mental faculties, I can assure you."

As at Whittier and at the Penn School, Helen confronted the problem of delayed pay. She had hoped to write to Louise before she went to Brooklyn but "financially was unable" because October's salary did not arrive until the first of December, and as of December 8 she had not been paid her salary for November. When the money started to flow, she paid a number of bills and had to "replenish from the bottom" her wardrobe with undervests, long-sleeved corset covers, stockings and a Ferris waist. "Some how expenses keep abreast of one's salary." Helen was spending money on clothing but not on Christmas gifts for her family because "This seems to be an off year to me." Presents would arrive, she promised, but not in time for the holiday.

She decided not to spend much money decorating her surroundings because it meant discarding items at the end of the school year. She could not live without some beauty, though, and had sash curtains and a portière made for the closet. The foundation color was "blue—almost a Yale blue. Bedspread, rug, screen, trunk cover and portiere, blend with the paint." Her paintings, collected over four or five years, she called "really worth while. Each one is an old friend and very dear." They consisted of the modern Madonna and Hoffman's Christ in "the temple over the bookcase." Her favorite motto, "Dum Vivimus Vivamus" ("While we live, let us enjoy life"), hung above her writing table. Nearby she had a picture of Frank Chisholm, and the daguerreotype of their mother sat on her desk. A "perfect picture" of Miss Morgan adorned her dresser. By December Helen was able to tell Bertha and Louise, "I am so comfortably and cozily situated that the glow reflects in my heart. Its warmth to night causes me to overflow in your direction. Electric light, lamp light and fire light cast roseate hues over the whole room, softening and toning until the harmony is most pleasing."

Helen decided that she could gain some amusement watching football games, but she became a fan for reasons having nothing to do with the actual contest. "Our foot ball team goes to Tuskeegee Friday. We are quite sure that they will be defeated, but are equally as sure that the experience will be good for them." The team may not have been Big Ten material, but the games built character, a far more important quality in Helen's view.

Holidays found her happier than she had been in South Carolina. Thanksgiving Day began with a football game, followed by dinner with President Young and his family, where they ate "every thing to eat that could be imagined," turkey with oyster stuffing, pumpkin pie, fruit and nuts, and black coffee. The day concluded with bridge and whist. Like her other schools, Florida A and M did not have a Christmas vacation. It closed for a half-day on Christmas Eve and reopened December 26. "Thursday night was the Christmas tree for teachers and students: Friday night there was nothing," but during the day she and another teacher visited the students, who gave them endless gifts of fruit. Helen shared a fruitcake with another of the teachers and decided her share "will keep a long time, so I will have something to nibble on."

Helen had no need to plan for the summer as she had a job offer by the time the holidays arrived. "Mr. Young spoke to-day [December 28, 1908] of my remaining this summer to teach in the Summer School. The fact that he desires it shows an appreciation of the work that I have done." She accepted the offer for the session, which ran from mid-June to the beginning of August and paid twenty five dollars a week.

Her pay was delayed again at the end of the school year. She could not "even buy one postage stamp," she told Bertha. "Will you send me 50c worth of stamps at once? 10—1c stamps and 20—2c stamps—I will return as soon as I get some money. I hate to draw a few dollars if I am not absolutely forced to." When she did receive her salary, "The money is going like water. Every time I turn around there is a new demand. I feel like blindfolding myself and just doling it out. I do so hate to see it go." She planned to supplement her income from summer school with work at another of Miss Morgan's conferences at Adelynrood at the end of August.

In the fall Helen planned to marry Frank Pierce Chisholm, whom she had met in Atlanta. Mr. Chisholm, as she always called him, was not her first serious "beau." She had entertained admirers from the time she lived in Hartford. Like Harriet, Helen confided little to Bertha and nothing to others about the men in her life but made it clear that she expected to spend her early years as a single woman, teaching to support herself and her brothers and sisters.

John Deveaux of Savannah, Georgia, was her most persistent admirer. The son of a free colored man who became a customs inspector and editor of the *Savannah Tribune*, Deveaux Jr. met Helen at Hampton. At graduation Helen told Bertha, "Mr. J.H. Deveaux left for Savannah to-day leaving many friends behind regretting his departure. We went down on the school wharf to see him off. He felt as bad as we did too. He is very handsome and most becomingly arranged. Wish you could have seen him." The gorgeous Mr. Deveaux had made a name for himself at Hampton Institute by getting into a fight with Allen Sawyer, a member of the Cherokee Nation. Deveaux's record was otherwise outstanding enough that he returned to work there as the bookkeeper. Whether it was from him or someone else, Helen had received at least one marriage proposal by the time she left for Hawaii. She rejected it and had no regrets about remaining single. She told Bertha, "I really feel that this is my streak of luck and that nothing better could have happened even to my marrying the professor."

Helen and Deveaux exchanged letters while she was in Hawaii. It was obvious that he still loved her, though he knew Helen did not return his affection with the same intensity. She sent him a picture of herself at Christmas 1903, and he replied,

How good you are to remember me at this Christmas time. How glad I am to get this beautiful picture of you today. I have been longing for one of this size for quite awhile. I shall have it framed to take the place on my dresser that the little one has held so long. You are certainly looking well and your dear face makes me long for you more that ever.

Thank you for the letter that comes with the picture. While I appreciate and enjoy reading it yet it lacks that spirit of warm friendship that former ones have had. Well, I suppose I am to blame as I have been so negligent in writing. You do not know how much I think of you and wish that I might be with you. I know it will be a happy day for me when I do see you. I wonder how it will be with you? . . .

I am kept very busy these days and I am glad of it without plenty of work at Hampton it is very lonesome and dead.

Helen and Deveaux spent a good deal of time together during her visit to Hampton Institute in 1904. "Mr. Deveaux called for me and took me to the Bay Shore at Buckroe, where an informal dance was held.

I had a glorious time as hosts of old friends were there. . . . Mr. Deveaux and I went to Newport News with Helen [Virginia] after the service." When she left, "Mr. Deveaux went over with me so that it was not as great a trial as if I had started alone. Being [a] Southerner, he knows the ways of this part of the world." Helen was tempted to marry him but decided she needed to devote her energy to her studies. In April 1908, Helen told Bertha that John Deveaux's father had died. With that, Mr. Deveaux disappeared from Helen's correspondence.

Helen had another opportunity to marry in the spring of 1905. Without mentioning him by name, Helen made her first reference to Mr. Chisholm. In contrast to Deveaux, her description of Frank Chisholm was singularly unflattering. "Deveaux was over last night, and I think will come again to-night. I expect to put him aside for a less handsome, less cultured fellow, but one whose worth I consider to be many times greater than this beau of earlier school days. If I do, it will be the turning point in my life and a very serious move, because it will mean no more flitting, in the sense that I have flitted, for the life of a butterfly suits me beyond what I know of the life with one person. Still, I don't want to be a burden to you folks in my 'maiden' days, so while I have a choice must make it."

Love was secondary, though she certainly expressed enough affection for Deveaux for him to persist in courting her, and she did not "throw him over" right away. When she headed back to Atlanta University that fall, she stopped at Hampton, and he again came calling. As soon as she arrived in Atlanta, she received a visit from her other suitor. "Mr. Chisholm called the first night I was in the city, and before that bright fire we had our first visit together. Since, we have scarcely seen each other, so close is school life."

Like Deveaux, Chisholm offered Helen a link to the colored elite. He was related to Mrs. B. K. Bruce, though Helen acknowledged, "It may be to the 40th remove." With his election in 1875, Blanche Kelso "B. K." Bruce of Mississippi became the last Negro to serve in the U.S. Senate until Massachusetts sent Edward Brooke there in 1966. Aside from a superior intellect, Chisholm's other saving grace in Helen's view was that he looked white—so white he was repeatedly thrown out of Jim Crow cars. His sense of racial solidarity would not let him sit in the white part of the train. Ann Petry used him as the model for Uncle Johno in her short story "Miss Muriel," and explained his feelings as a "cultivated and developed and carefully nourished hatred of white men."

After a while, Helen grew less reticent in discussing her feelings about Chisholm with Bertha but still demurred. "I trust that the years ahead will be rich enough to repay the vital sacrifices that I am making now. Mr. Chisholm yet persists that he is to help determine those years. He had some pictures taken recently and submitted the proofs to me. I will send you one, asking you to return it at once lest he may ask for it. This shows him at his best, I think. He is very good and tries every imaginable way to be kind to me. I quite appreciate him." A friend helped to clarify Helen's feelings by adding to Helen's letter. "She likes him heap much *almost* as much as you do Mr. Lane." Helen resumed, "May just came in from prayer meeting to see why I was not there. She inscribed the preceding sentence."

Helen did not deny her feelings but remained critical of his appearance, though she demonstrated that she was not utterly shallow. "Yesterday I spent with Miss Birdie Ford in her pretty spacious home. I wish you could see it. She entertained informally at whist, several friends being present. Among them was Mr. Chisholm. I have always considered him about the homeliest man I ever knew, but am modifying this statement as I become better acquainted with him. I am sure that you will like him."

Although she complained about the isolation on St. Helena, Helen flirted there as well. "It will be my good fortune to be in Beaufort Friday night for the dance and if there's no objection I would be *dee*-lighted to be your escort should you so desire? I am sending this to Beaufort for fear of it not reaching Frogmore in time. With best wishes and many kind thots, believe me Sincerely, Prof. S. Bampfield." Helen forwarded the note to Bertha adding, "I hope you may meet this nice fellow some day. About 21 yrs. old. I went."

During the end of her stay in Florida, Helen's time and energy were consumed with discussions about where she and Mr. Chisholm would live after they married. He thought they should rent for a year so they had time to examine options in Boston. "In point of dollars and cents, we would lose little, if we lose anything at all, as I would continue to draw interest on money now in bank every cent of which I would have to withdraw as a deposit on house in case we buy now. Besides, I don't think it altogether wise to invest all your cash money in any one proposition. We must guard against any contingency that may arise." Options included a $5400 bungalow or a "two tenement" for $4900, "i.e. land and all, with every modern convenience. The price of either is to me appalling," Helen said, though they were about average for the area. She was inclined to choose the tenement, because they could collect twenty-four dollars a month in rent. "I am positive we couldn't thinking of starting in so expensive a one family house," she concluded.

Their negotiations continued when Helen went to teach in Florida. Helen told Bertha she had received a delightful letter from "the trump" soon after she arrived, but by December her feelings appeared to be cooling. She made Mr. Chisholm sound as though he were motivated not by love, but by the need to maintain appearances. "I should enjoy the prospect of staying amid these surroundings for several years. Yet it looks dubious. Mr. Chisholm wrote that he was going to see papa at an early date. He says Hartford people are inquiring whether we are engaged. I rather admire their courage." Mr. Chisholm wanted to marry during the summer, but "I do not seem to realize it nor want to because I am so happy in my work here." She was earning sixty-two dollars and fifty cents a month for "congenial work" and had the chance to study and exercise. She resolved to resign her job if Mr. Chisholm built the house, "However I know it will cause an explosion here. Mr. Young is not pleased to have teachers come for only one year. He considers it a sort of imposition."

By March 1909 Helen had resolved to marry in the fall:

I have been fighting a stiff battle with myself on the marriage proposition, which if carried out, will necessitate an immediate resignation on my part.

My battle has been one for health. Before thoughts of the cold east winds of Boston my courage has almost failed. My never over robust physique

I fear has not been prepared for so great a change by the ten years residence in warm climates. Through all these years I have purposely pushed marrying from me because of fears, now I feel as if I am taking my life in my own hands when I make this change.

So much have I thought of it that I have been silent toward both you and Mr. Chisholm, the two people dearest to me in life. My silence so worried him that he telegraphed me from Boston Saturday to see what the trouble was.

I am going to write to him to-night and say yes *for September, so will resign here next week with deepest regret. I do pray over it constantly and want you to pray for me for I fear greatly the wisdom of change of residence. His work I think is permanently in Boston.*

When we first talked of marrying he expected to locate in the South, which was more to my notion. Of this I have said nothing to him and probably shall not, as I see no wisdom in the discussion. A good letter from you, though, will be greatly appreciated.

Frank and Helen became engaged officially in April. "Everything goes well. We are planning in reality for the wedding the engagement gift is on the way. It is to be a surprise, so of course I am eager to see what it is." She was disappointed because the house would not be built during the summer. "We are to live in a very beautiful house, however, in a most desirable locality in Boston rather than Cambridge. Of course this doesn't *set so well* with me but I am just trusting the *best* which will probably happen. Perhaps a rent with more surplus will be better than the house at a sacrifice."

Instead of an engagement ring, Mr. Chisholm gave her "a dear gold watch of marvelous workmanship with the initial J in old English script on the front cover and her name and the date of March 1909 on the inside back cover. The chain looked like "threads of spun gold," and the slide had a "nugett" of gold surrounded by a band of twelve pearls. "The selection was wholy his. Whether it should be the regulation diamond or a watch I left to him, and have nothing to regret in the matter." Helen saved and forwarded the letter that he wrote after she thanked him.

My Own Beloved Helen—

I am glad, I am happy, I am inspired to know that you are so thoroughly and ecstatically pleased with the gift I have sent you. In it, I tried to combine the sentimental with the practical. Mrs. Casman was partial to a ring. She argued that a ring was more customary and with it attaches so much sentiment. I leaned more to that which original plan which I broached to you last summer—that of buying a building a six room home. I am now working to that. In brief, my idea contemplates getting the house first of all, then put the barest necessities to start with and after you come and we move in to purchase things as we need them and only *[double underline] as we need them. In fact so far as furnishing is concerned I shall do practically nothing until you get here as we can better and more agree-ably decide then when we get together. Shall write as present plans unfold themselves.*

One other thing. Who is to make your wedding gown? You know I have said the wedding was to be simple home one. You have said nothing on that point. I should like to have you let my mother make your gowns or some of them. She is one of the best dressmakers in Sav'h. I want you to meet her anyhow before you come North. She could take your measure and perhaps fit you before you come North. Please let me know. I write this early because Com. [commencement] will soon be here for us all. Then you will begin to move northward, no doubt.

The couple continued their discussions about where and how to live, "talking up the 'home,'" as Helen put it. "The practicality of it all I fear I do not enjoy. It seems like getting *down* [underlined three times] to stern realities all ready." Her main concern was money. "For myself, I am only thinking how I can stretch my feeble pittance to the uttermost. He says he prefers a small wedding. Of course that is most harmonious to my surroundings & pocket book. You and Louise can put your minds on that proposition. I have enough to think of the Boston end, a few clothes and my summer vacation."

Helen decided she wanted to stay in Florida and teach summer school and asked Bertha's advice about postponing the wedding until late

September or early October "in order that I could get well rested. This would seem to me wise. The six weeks would surely net me $125.00 and this at a time when it would mean everything to me. Doubtless Mr. Chisholm can arrange his vacation later. He usually has the month of August." She made these assumptions without asking him.

Her desire for extra income arose in part because she was paying to have her summer hats done over in the school's millinery department, though she saved some money by not buying new ones. "One advantage of a late fall wedding would be that I wouldn't have to buy any between season clothes. You see I own no winter clothing at all, so should get in some of the heavier ones." She trusted the school with her hats but wanted a more experienced hand with the rest of her wardrobe. "With my plans everything seems to be working well. It will mean much if Mrs. C_ [Mr. Chisholm's mother] of Savannah helps me with my *gowns* [double underline]. I told him that she would have to write making the proposition herself, before I could consider it. He said that he had just written to you. He is full of joy in the plans for the home." Helen shipped her wedding gown, "made by Mrs. C.," to Bertha in August with the advice "before accepting it, be sure to look in the box to see if it is there."

Helen returned to Connecticut in the fall but fell ill and landed in Hartford Hospital, where she underwent surgery. Her convalescence gave her time for reflection. "The thoughts of marrying as sick as I am were repulsive to me. When I am better and can look forward to it with pleasure then it will be time. Miss Morgan said Miss Lewis affirmed that I must give up the idea for a time. Miss Lewis is coming to see me to-morrow morning [October 18, 1909]. I have not written to Mr. Chisholm yet regarding this *change* but shall when I am more equal to it. To-morrow I will probably be allowed to sit up for the first time, and shall perhaps leave here the latter part of the week."

She was at Putnam Elms in early November. "I think if I make another break at marrying it will be quietly done, for I cannot stand the strain of writing invitations, planning reception, etc. I am in no condition to do it and was not at first. I am sure if I hadn't had that on my mind, I would not have had this 2nd break down." Though Helen hesitated to set a wedding date, she continued to work on her trousseau, hemming a half-dozen napkins and finishing a table cloth. She planned to add to her wardrobe by making a flannel skirt and two calico aprons. She had samples of linen dish towels and hand towels, "which I may invest in later. This done I am through with the things that I had planned, except buying the sheets and pillow cases."

Helen had intended to spend Christmas with her family but changed her mind. "A letter from Miss Morgan this morning invites me to stay on here over Christmas. I think I shall accept." She told Bertha in mid-December, "Everything goes well, and I am looking forward to a happy Christmas. Mr. Chisholm will be down. His letter this morning asks what I want for a gift." He also told her that he would arrange to get her a piano. Helen had entered a contest and won seventy dollars credit. She was skeptical, however: "If it is quite bona fide he will negotiate!"

Helen revealed more of her feelings about the marriage to Bertha on New Year's Day of 1910. "You will be glad to know that Mr. Chisholm came for Christmas—and that we had a happy visit together. He is dearer and dearer to me lavishing on me all that love and tenderness which my long separation from home and family has deprived me of. Now that it has it seems so hard that I can not accept it in full." Helen collapsed again while he was visiting but began to recover slowly.

In February Helen told Bertha that she was feeling "a bit depressed." Among the reasons, "Miss Morgan wrote me that I wasn't in fit condition to marry yet, and that I should yet be patient. She had talked my case over with her night nurse and with Miss Lewis. The worst of that was that I knew it to be true, and I was trying to ignore it, for I do get tired of this do nothing existence. Some times I feel that it gets on my nerves and keeps me back. However, I *hope* [triple underline]. Don't get discouraged. I try not to."

Helen was ready to get married when spring arrived and wanted to plan the wedding for April 20. "I can not but feel that it will go this time, for I am postively better and much like my old self." After another short delay, the wedding finally occurred, as documented in this undated newspaper clipping:

Chisholm-James

At the historic home of Col. Daniel Putnam, now owned by Miss Emily Malbone Morgan of Hartford, on Wednesday, June 1st, occurred the marriage of Mr. Frank Pierce Chisholm, of Cambridge, Mass., and Miss Helen Lou Evelyn James, of Saybrook, Conn.

The ceremony was performed by the Rev. Isaac Peck, in the beautiful little chapel, which had been tastefully decorated with ferns, yellow lillie, and matrimony vine, which was in blossom for the occasion.

The bride wore a quaint gown of delicate yellow liberty satin, trimmed with old lace that her mother had at her wedding. She received the good wishes of her friends standing in the yellow room, making a picture of cheer which the passing showers were unable to dim.

A bountiful wedding breakfast was served to about twenty-four friends of the bride and groom. The bride is a graduate of Hampton Institute and has devoted her life to teaching in Honolulu, Hawaii and the South. She can therefor enter thoroughly into her husband's work. Mr. Chisholm is the Northern representative of Mr. Booker T. Washington. They will reside in Cambridge, Mass.

While Mr. Chisholm worked for Tuskegee Institute, Helen operated a correspondence course on reading and literature. They had two children. Their daughter, Helen Emily, born December 25, 1911, became a teacher. Their son, Frank Jr., was born in 1913 and died two years later. By 1920 the family had moved to Saybrook, where they bought a house next door to Bertha and Peter. Frank and Helen were active in the Episcopal Church. Frank continued his work for Tuskegee well into his nineties, while Helen volunteered for the Red Cross and collected information on her family history. He died in 1977 at age ninety-eight, she in 1971 at ninety-four. Some of their papers are collected at Emory University in Atlanta.

POSTSCRIPT

D ear Family,

By the time you wrote your letters, slave owners had obliterated traditions we brought from Africa, except for one. Through the ages we retained a love for each other that expressed itself by honoring the memory of those who had gone before. For us, ancestor veneration meant not blind worship but a living interaction, a conversation in which we question, challenge, and look for answers to questions that we feel are important to us.

This work continues that tradition. In some ways you are as close to me as living relatives—in some ways closer. This book is my veneration of you, an extraordinary group of people.

To Willis S. James,

I honor you for your courage in escaping from slavery. If you had not, Grammy, Mother, and I would have lacked many opportunities.

I honor you for moving to Connecticut and for your courage in living in an all-white neighborhood. Without that experience Bertha would not have learned the benefits of working for and around white people.

I question your feeling that Negroes should stay as near white people as possible since the advantage was frequently all on their side.

I honor, and deplore, your thrift. You taught your children the value of saving, but you caused them untold pain by abdicating to others your responsibility for supporting them.

I honor your sense of pride in your work, for which the governor of Connecticut praised you. I honor the impression you made on the residents of Hartford. You started a tradition that continued through three generations with the recognition of the James name as a respected one in Hartford.

I deplore your failure to defend your children from harsh treatment by their stepmother.

I question your silence about your early years, for your reticence deprived your descendants of part of our heritage.

I honor, and deplore, your treatment of your son Willis. I honor you for coming to his aid when he was in jail. I deplore your refusal of other aid.

I honor the persistence that compelled you to learn to read and write as an adult.

I deplore your failure to recognize Louise's great achievement in graduating from pharmacy school by refusing to acknowledge it or to attend the ceremony.

I honor your religious faith and your dedication to Hartford's colored churches.

To Anna Houston James,

I honor you for passing on a capacity for boundless love to Grammy, who passed it on to Mother, who loved me with all her heart.

I honor your sense of racial pride that would not let you pass for white.

I honor your courage in taking care of your brother after your mother died.

I honor you for the way you tried to protect your children even when you were ill and away from home.

I honor you for your great beauty, which you passed on to Bertha and to Ann.

I honor the exquisite aesthetic sense that allowed you to surround yourself and your family with elegance.

I honor you for raising your stepson Charles as if he were your own.

I honor you for your bravery in the face of debilitating illness and for
   your steadfast belief that you would recover.
I honor you your religious faith.

To Uncle Charley Hudson,
I honor your bravery in joining the Army.
I honor your ingenuity in escaping from your apprenticeship.
I deplore your need to change your name.
I question your trips across the color line, although I understand that it
   may have been necessary to make money.
I honor you for caring for your sister while she was ill.
I honor you for watching out for Helen and Louise after their mother died.
I honor your continued support for Willis even after he rejected your
   overtures.
I honor your patriotism.
I honor you for the skills that allowed you to find work even in difficult
   times.

To Bertha James Lane,
I honor you for passing a mother's love on to your daughters, especially
   to Ann.
I honor you for your aesthetic sense, which has given me beautiful lace and
   linens, exquisite china and silver, and a memory of a beautiful woman.
I honor you for your many talents: baking, hairdressing, linen-making,
   business ownership and management.
I honor you for your religious faith.
I honor you for your lifelong care of your brothers and sisters, especially
   in the early years after your mother died.
I honor you for standing up to your father's cruelty to Louise.
I regret that you did not keep more information about Willis and Anna.
I honor you for keeping this collection of letters.

To Helen James Chisholm,
I honor your religious faith.

I honor your bravery in traveling halfway around the world, for you inspired Ann to do the same.

I honor your determination to obtain an education, for you became a role model for Ann and her sister Helen.

I deplore your early criticism of Frank Chisholm's appearance and demeanor.

I honor your hard work and dedication to everything you undertook.

I honor you for setting up the library at Kona Orphanage.

I question your hypochondria.

I honor you for your care of Harriet while you were at Hampton.

I honor you for supporting Harold while he was a student.

I deplore the way you ordered Bertha, Peter, and Louise to run your errands.

To Willis H. James,

I honor your bravery in the war.

I honor your battlefield promotion.

I honor your eloquence in your letters, especially the graphic descriptions you sent to your brother Charles.

I deplore the way you manipulated Bertha's emotions: "For dear mother's sake," indeed!

I deplore your repeated pleas for money.

I honor your willingness to stand up to white people.

I deplore your stupidity at shooting someone, especially a white man in Jim Crow Georgia.

I honor your faithfulness to Bertha.

I despise the way you treated Mamie and your children.

I deplore your inability to get along with your father. It wasn't all his fault.

To Harriet G. James,

I honor your bravery in the face of illness.

I honor your sense of fun.

I honor your ability to make friends.

I honor your modesty. You and Harold were the only family members who had it!

I honor your religious faith.

I honor your intention to dedicate your life to improving the race.

I honor your love for George Blount.

I honor you for taking care of your father and the household after Bertha and Helen left.

I deplore the fact that your life ended before you could write more letters.

To Harold E. James,

I honor your humor.

I honor your energy.

I honor your hard work at school.

I honor your intelligence.

I honor your early decision to be self-supporting.

I honor your bravery after you cut off your thumb, and I understand why you waited to tell the family about it. I question your belief that they would not find out.

I honor your love for Blanche.

I honor your lifelong dedication to farming.

I deplore your lack of respect for Anna Phillips, but I honor your ability to remain civil to her.

To Everyone, I honor you for these letters and the feelings they express. Thank you!

Love,

Liz